Old Times on the Upper Mississippi

The Fesler-Lampert *Minnesota Heritage* Book Series

This series is published with the generous assistance of the John K. and Elsie Lampert Fesler Fund and David R. and Elizabeth P. Fesler. Its mission is to republish significant out-of-print books that contribute to our understanding and appreciation of Minnesota and the Upper Midwest.

The series features works by the following authors:

Clifford and Isabel Ahlgren

J. Arnold Bolz

Helen Hoover

Florence Page Jaques

Evan Jones

Meridel Le Sueur

George Byron Merrick

Grace Lee Nute

Sigurd F. Olson

Charles Edward Russell

Calvin Rutstrum

Robert Treuer

GEORGE BYRON MERRICK

Old Times on the Upper Mississippi

Recollections of a Steamboat Pilot
from 1854 to 1863

University of Minnesota Press
MINNEAPOLIS • LONDON

First University of Minnesota Press edition, 2001

First published in 1909 by The Arthur H. Clark Company

Published by the University of Minnesota Press
111 Third Avenue South, Suite 290
Minneapolis, MN 55401-2520
http://www.upress.umn.edu

A Cataloging-in-Publication record for this book is available from the Library of Congress.

Printed in the United States of America on acid-free paper

The University of Minnesota is an equal-opportunity educator and employer.

11 10 09 08 07 06 05 04 03 02 01   10 9 8 7 6 5 4 3 2 1

Dedicated to the Memory of My Chiefs

William H. Hamilton, Engineer, Charles G. Margus, Clerk, Thomas Burns, Pilot, masters in their several professions. From each of them I learned something that has made life better worth living, the sum of which makes possible these reminiscences of a "cub" pilot.

MOUTH OF THE WISCONSIN RIVER.   The ancient highway between the Great Lakes and the Mississippi.   This scene gives some idea of the multitude of islands which diversify both the Wisconsin and the Mississippi Rivers.

Contents

Illustrations

Publisher's Note

Old Times on the
Upper Mississippi

Prelude

The majesty and glory of the Great River have departed; its glamour remains, fresh and undying, in the memories of those who, with mind's eye, still can see it as it was a half-century ago. Its majesty was apparent in the mighty flood which then flowed throughout the season, scarcely diminished by the summer heat; its glory, in the great commerce which floated upon its bosom, the beginnings of mighty commonwealths yet to be. Its glamour is that indefinable witchery with which memory clothes the commonplace of long ago, transfiguring the labors, cares, responsibilities, and dangers of steamboat life as it really was, into a Midsummer Night's Dream of care-free, exhilarating experiences, and glorified achievement.

Of the river itself it may be said, that like the wild tribes which peopled its banks sixty years ago, civilization has been its undoing. The primeval forests which spread for hundreds of miles on either side, then caught and held the melting snows and falling rains of spring within spongy mosses which carpeted the earth; slowly, throughout the summer, were distilled the waters from myriad springs, and these, filling brooks and smaller rivers, feeders of the Great River, maintained a mighty volume of water the season through. Upon the disappearance of the forests, the melting snows and early rains having no holding grounds, are carried quickly to the river, which as quickly rises to an abnormal stage in the early part of the season, to be followed by a dearth which later reduces the Mississippi to the dimensions of a second-rate stream, whereon navigation is impossible for great steamers, and arduous, disheartening and unprofitable for boats of any class.

To most men of our day, the life of those who manned the steamers of that once mighty fleet is legendary, almost mythical.

Its story is unwritten. To the few participants who yet remain, it is but a memory. The boats themselves have disappeared, leaving no token. The masters and the mates, the pilots and the clerks, the engineers and the men of humbler station have likewise gone. Of the thousands who contributed to give life and direction to the vessels themselves, a meager score of short biographies is all that history vouchsafes.

The aim of the present volume is to tell something of these men, and of the boats that they made sentient by their knowledge and power; to relate something of the incidents of river life as seen by a boy during eight years of residence by the riverside, or in active service on the river itself. While it may not literally be claimed, "All of which I saw," it is with satisfaction, not unmixed with pride, that the writer can truthfully assert, "A part of which I was."

G. B. M.

The several quotations from "Mark Twain" which herein appear are from *Life on the Mississippi* (copyright, 1903), by Samuel L. Clemens, permission for the use of which is kindly granted for the present purpose by the publishers, Messrs. Harper & Brothers, New York.

Chapter I

Early Impressions

Descent from an ancestry whose members built and sailed ships from Salem, Newburyport, and Nantucket two hundred years ago, and even down to the early days of the nineteenth century, ought to give an hereditary bias toward a sailor's life, on waters either salt or fresh. A score-and-a-half of men of my name have "died with their boots on" at sea, from the port of Nantucket alone. They went for whales, and the whales got them. Perhaps their fate should have discouraged the sea-going instinct, but perversely it had the opposite effect. A hundred men are lost out of Gloucester every year, yet their boys are on the "Banks" before they are fairly weaned.

I was born at Niles, Michigan, on the historic St. Joseph River, which in those days was of considerable importance commercially. Scores of keel boats plied between South Bend and the mouth of the river at St. Joseph, on Lake Michigan. Keel boats drifted down the river, and after unloading were towed back by little steamboats, about eighty feet long by eighteen feet beam. These were propelled by side wheels attached to a single shaft, driven by a horizontal engine of indifferent power. These steamers towed four "keels" upstream at the rate of five or six miles an hour. The former had no upper cabin answering to the "boiler deck" of the Mississippi River boats — only a roof covering the main deck, with the passenger cabin aft, and the quarters of the crew forward of the boiler and engine.

It was, I suppose, a quarter of a mile from my birthplace to the river bank where we boys of the neighborhood went to see the steamboats pass. In the opposite direction, around a sharp bend and across the low-lying, alluvial land, which comprised the home farm, the river was discernible a mile away. When a boat was seen coming up river, the alarm was given, and we little shavers of the neighborhood raced for the nearest point of view, a high bank of blue clay, rising probably seventy-five feet above the river. We used to think it was as many hundreds of feet; and what I now know as the quarter mile, then stretched away into interminable distances as it was measured by the stubby yet sturdy little legs of six-year-old runners. On the edge of this blue-clay bank, I received my first impressions in river piloting.

My teacher in these matters was a man whom I greatly envied. Kimball Lyon lived in a house three times as large as that in which I was born. His father had left a big farm and a bank account of fabulous dimensions. We knew it was large, because "Kim" never worked as other young men of twenty-five or thirty years did in those days. His mother always kept a "hired man", while Kim toiled not; but he spun.

It was not his riches, however, nor his immunity from toil, that common lot of other men, which excited the envy of the six-year-olds. He could, and did, play on the accordion. Lying on his back in the shade and resting one corner of his instrument upon his bosom, with irresistible power and pathos he sang and played

"A life on the ocean wave,
A home on the rolling deep."

It appealed to all the natural impulses of our being, and the dormant instincts inherited from generations of whale-hunting ancestors were aroused by the power of music, reinforced by the suggestive words of the song itself; and then and there we vowed that when we were men like Kimball Lyon, we too would own and play upon accordions, and do all else that he had done; for marvelous tales he told, of his experiences in great storms at sea and of deeds of aquatic prowess. We learned in after years that "Kim" once sailed from St. Joseph to Chicago in a sawed-off lumber hooker, when the wind was west nor'west, down the lake, and that he did actually lie on the deck, but not on his back, and that it was not music which he emitted, and that the sailors railed at him, and that he came back from Chicago by stage coach to Niles. But we didn't know this when he was awakening our viking instincts, as we lay on the banks of the old St. Joe in the sunny summer days of long ago.

"Kim" Lyon knew all about steamboats, as well as about deep sea ships, and when we asked questions he could answer out of the fullness of his knowledge. We wondered what made the wheels go 'round, and he told us. I have forgotten *what* made them go 'round, but my recollection is that it was a peculiar mechanical process of which I have never seen the like in any other service on river, lake or ocean. His answer to the query as to "what is the man in the little house on top of the boat doing?" I have never forgotten, as it afterward came more in my line of business. The man was twisting the wheel as all pilots before and since that time twist it, a spoke or two to port, a half dozen to starboard, hard up and hard down, there being a shallow piece of river just there, beset with big boulders and reefs of gravel, through which he was cautiously worming his boat and its kite-tail of keels.

"That man", said Kimball, "is drawing water from a well in the bottom of the boat and emptying it into the boiler, just as your father draws water from his well with a rope, a bucket and a crank. If he should stop for a minute the boiler would burst for want of water, the boat would blow up, and we should all be killed by the explosion."

This definition at once gave us a personal interest in the work of the man at the wheel; we all felt that our lives depended upon this man's devotion to his duty. Had he struck a piece of "easy water" at that time, and centred his wheel, there is no doubt that we would have scurried for home before the inevitable explosion should occur. That was my first lesson in piloting. Perhaps this childish concern that the man "drawing water for the boilers" should faithfully perform his duty, was but a prefigurement of the interest with which the writer, and hundreds of others, in later years, have watched the pilot work his boat through a tangled piece of river, knowing that the safety of all depended upon the knowledge and faithfulness of the "man at the wheel."

The steamboats plying on the St. Joe were crude little affairs, and there were but four or five of them, all alike. I remember the name of but one, the "Algoma"; the others are quite forgotten. Doubtless they were commonplace, and did not appeal to the poetic side of the boy. But "Algoma"! The word has a rythmical measure, and conjures up visions of wigwams, council fires, dusky maidens, and painted braves. An Indian name would stick when all the saints in the calendar were forgotten. The "Algoma" and her consorts have gone the way of all steamboats. The railroad came and killed their business, just as a few years later, it did on the Great River.

A few years later I saw the Mississippi River for the first time, at Rock Island, Illinois; and through the kindness of another well-posted bystander to whom the then twelve-year-old boy appealed, I received my first impressions of a stern-wheel boat. There were two steamboats lying at the levee — the "Minnesota Belle", a side-wheeler, upon which we had taken passage, while just above lay the "Luella", a stern-wheeler. I knew about the former variety from observation on the St. Joe, but I had never seen even a picture of one of the latter sort, so it was a novelty. I wasn't certain that it was a steamboat at all, and after referring the matter to my stranger friend, I learned definitely that it wasn't. The "Luella's" wheel was slowly turning over as she lay at the levee, and as I did not comprehend the mechanical details of that kind of craft I began asking questions. My mentor assured me that the "Luella" was not a steamboat at all, but a water power sawmill. The big wheel then moving was driven by the current, and it in turn operated the sawmill machinery on the inside of the boat. As I could not figure any other use for a wheel out in the open, at the end of the boat, instead of on the side where it ought to be, and as I had no reason to doubt the statement of my informant, I readily accepted the sawmill explanation, and hastened to confide my newly-acquired knowledge to my brother and other members of the family. A few hours later both boats pulled out for St. Paul. After she had rounded the first point, ahead of us, we saw nothing more of the "Luella" until we met her coming down the river on her return trip. She was a heavily-powered boat, and showed her heels to the larger and slower "Minnesota Belle". The sight of the "Luella" kicking her way upstream at the rate of two miles to our one, not only dissipated the sawmill impression, but taught me not to accept at face value all information communicated by glib-tongued and plausible strangers.

That steamboat trip from Rock Island to Prescott was one long holiday excursion for us two small and lively boys from Michigan. There was so much to see and in so many different directions at once, that it was impossible to grasp it all, although we scampered over the deck to get differing view points. We met dozens of boats, going back to St. Louis or Galena after further loads of immigrants and freight; and there were other boats which came up behind us, gaining slowly but surely, and finally passing the deeply-laden "Belle". There were landings to be made, and freight and passengers to be disembarked. There were strange Indians to be seen — we were familiar enough with Michigan tribesmen, having been born within a mile or two of old Pokagon's tribal village. There were boys with fish for sale, fish larger than any inhabiting the waters of Michigan streams, sturgeons only excepted, and this promised well for the fun in store when we should reach our journey's end.

Finally, on a bright June day in the year 1854, the writer, then a boy of twelve, with his brother, three years younger, were fully transplanted from their Michigan birthplace to the row of stores and warehouses which fronted on the "levee" at Prescott, Wisconsin, where the waters of St. Croix River and Lake join the Mississippi. The town was then a typical frontier settlement. Two hundred white people were planted among five hundred Chippewa Indians; with as many more Sioux, of the Red Wing band, across the river in Minnesota, a few miles lower down the river. The not infrequent outbreaks of the hereditary enmity existing between these ancient foes, would expend itself on the streets of the town in war whoops, gunpowder, and scalping knives, enlivening the experience of the average citizen as he dodged behind the nearest cover to avoid stray bullets; while the city marshal was given an opportunity to earn his salary, by driving out both bands of hostiles at the point of his revolver.

Chapter II

Indians, Dugouts, and Wolves

In that early day when my acquaintance with the Mississippi began, Indians were numerous. Their dugouts lay at the levee by the dozen, the hunters retailing the ducks and geese, or venison and bear meat, which had fallen to their guns, while the squaws peddled catfish and pickerel that had been ensnared on the hooks and lines of the women and children of the party.

Situated as Prescott was at the junction of the St. Croix with the Mississippi, its citizens were favored with visits both from the Chippewa, who hunted and fished along the former stream and its tributaries in Wisconsin, and the Sioux, who made the bottom lands on the Minnesota side of the river, between Hastings and Red Wing, their home and hunting ground. This was the boundary line which had existed for a hundred years or more; although the Sioux (or Dakota) laid claim to many thousand square miles of hunting grounds in Wisconsin, for which they actually received a million and a half dollars when they quit-claimed it to the United States. Their claim to any lands on the east side of the river had been disputed by the Chippewa from time out of mind; and these rival claims had occasionally been, as we have seen, referred to the only court of arbitration which the Indians recognized — that of the tomahawk and scalping knife.

As a boy I have spent many an hour searching in the sands at the foot of the bluffs below Prescott, for arrowheads, rusted remnants of knives and hatchets, and for the well-preserved brass nails with which the stocks and butts of old-time trade muskets were plentifully ornamented. Just how many years ago that battle had been fought, does not appear to be a matter of historical record. That it was fiercely contested, is abundantly proven by the great amount of wreckage of the fight which the white lads of Prescott recovered to be sold to tourists on the steamboats which touched at our levee. The Indians themselves had a tradition that it was a bloody fight. Taking the word of a Chippewa narrator, one was easily convinced that hundreds of Sioux bit the sand on that eventful day. If the narrator happened to belong across the river, one felt assured, after listening to his version, that the Chippewa met their Marathon on this battle plain. In any case the treasure trove indicated a very pretty fight, whichever party won the field.

Charlevoix, the French historian, relates that in 1689 Le Seuer established a fortified trading post on the west side of the Mississippi, about eight miles below the present site of Hastings. In speaking of this fort, he says:

"The island has a beautiful prairie, and the French of Canada have made it a centre of commerce for the western parts, and many pass the winter here, because it is a good country for hunting."

As a boy I have many a time visited the site of this ancient stronghold, and hobnobbed with the Indians then occupying the ground, descendants of those with whom the French fraternized two hundred years ago. At this point the islands are about four miles across from the main channel of the river; the islands being formed by Vermillion Slough, which heads at Hastings, reëntering the river about two and a half miles above Red Wing. Trudell Slough, which heads in the river about four miles below Prescott, joins Vermillion at the point at which was probably located Le Seuer's post. At the juncture of the two sloughs there was a beautiful little prairie of several acres. On the west, the bluffs rose several hundred feet to the level prairie which constitutes the upper bench. Just at this point there are three mounds rising fifty to seventy-five feet above the level of the prairie, and serving as a landmark for miles around. Whether they are of geological origin or the work of the Indians in their mound-building epoch, had not been determined in my day. There are other prominences of like character everywhere about, and it would seem that they were erected by the hand of man.

On the north, east, and south the islands afforded good hunting grounds for the French and their allies. In 1854 and later (I think even yet), the site of this ancient fort was occupied by a band of Sioux Indians of Red Wing's tribe, under the sub-

chieftaincy of a French half-breed named Antoine Mouseau
(Mo'-sho).   In Neill's history of the settlement of St. Paul he
mentions Louis Mouseau as one of the first settlers occupying, in
1839, a claim lying at the lower end of Dayton Bluff, about two
miles down the river from the levee.   This Antoine Mouseau, a
man about forty in 1854, was probably a son of the St. Paul
pioneer and of a squaw of Red Wing's band.

In the days when the white boys of Prescott made adventurous
trips "down to Mo-sho's", the islands were still remarkably rich
in game — deer, bear, wolves, 'coons, mink, muskrats, and other
fur-bearing animals; and in spring and fall the extensive rice
swamps literally swarmed with wild fowl.   Two or three of the
adventures which served to add spice to such visits as we made
with the little red men of Mouseau's tribe, will serve to illustrate
the sort of life which was led by all Prescott boys in those early
days.   They seemed to be a part of the life of the border, and
were taken as a matter of course.   Looking back from this distance, and from the civilization of to-day, it seems miraculous to
me that all of those boys were not drowned or otherwise sum-
marily disposed of.   As a matter of fact none of them were
drowned, and to the best of my knowledge none of them have
as yet been hanged.   Most of them went into the Union army in
the War of Secession, and some of them are sleeping where the
laurel and magnolia bend over their last resting places.

The water craft with which the white boys and Indian boys
alike traversed the river, rough or smooth, and explored every
creek, bayou, and slough for miles around, were "dug-outs" —
canoes hollowed out of white pine tree trunks.   Some canoes were
large and long, and would carry four or five grown persons.
.Those owned and used by the boys were from six to eight feet
long, and just wide enough to take in a not too-well-developed
lad; but then, all the boys were lean and wiry.   It thus happened
that the Blaisdells, the Boughtons, the Fifields, the Millers, the
Merricks, the Schasers, the Smiths, and the Whipples, and several
other pairs and trios ranging from fourteen years down to seven,
were pretty generally abroad from the opening of the river in
the spring until its closing in the fall, hunting, fishing and
exploring, going miles away, up or down the river or lake, and
camping out at night, often without previous notice to their

mothers. With a "hunk" of bread in their pockets, some matches to kindle a fire, a gun and fishlines, they never were in danger of starvation, although always hungry.

One of the incidents referred to, I accept more on the evidence of my brother than of my own consciousness of the situation when it occurred. He was eleven at the time, and I fourteen. We each had a little pine "dug-out", just large enough to carry one boy sitting in the stern, and a reasonable cargo of ducks, fish or fruit. With such a load the gunwales of the craft were possibly three or four inches above the water line. The canoe itself was round on the bottom, and could be rolled over and over by a boy lying flat along the edges, with his arms around it, as we often did for the amusement of passengers on the boats — rolling down under water and coming up on the other side, all the time holding fast to the little hollowed-out log. Such a craft did not appear to be very seaworthy, nor well calculated to ride over rough water. Indeed, under the management of a novice they would not stay right side up in the calmest water.

For the boys who manned them, however, whether whites or Indians, they were as seaworthy as Noah's ark, and much easier to handle. A show piece much in vogue, was to stand on the edge of one of these little round logs (not over eight feet long), and with a long-handled paddle propel the thing across the river. This was not always, nor usually, accomplished without a ducking; but it often was accomplished by white boys without the ducking, and that even when there was some wind and little waves. The Indian lads would not try it in public. For one thing, it was not consonant with Indian dignity; for another, an Indian, big or little, dislikes being laughed at, and a ducking always brought a laugh when there were any spectators. I cannot, after all these years, get over an itching to try this experiment again. I believe that I could balance myself all right; but the difference between sixty pounds and a hundred and sixty might spoil the game.

Some boys, more fortunate than others, were from time to time possessed of birch-bark canoes — small ones. Of all the craft that ever floated, the birch-bark comes nearer being the ideal boat than any other. So light is it, that it may be carried on the head and shoulders for miles without great fatigue; and it sits on the water like a whiff of foam — a veritable fairy craft. It was the custom of the boys who owned these little "birches" to shove them off the sand with a run, and when they were clear of the land to jump over the end, and standing erect, paddle away like the wind. This was another show piece, and was usually enacted for the benefit of admiring crowds of Eastern passengers on the steamboats.

On one such occasion, a young man from the East who professed to be a canoeist, and who possibly was an expert with an ordinary canoe, came off the boat, and after crossing the palm of the birch-bark's owner with a silver piece, proposed to take a little paddle by himself. The boy was an honest boy, as boys averaged then and there, and although not averse to having a little fun at the expense of the stranger, in his capacity of lessor he deemed it his duty to caution his patron that a birch-bark was about as uncertain and tricky a proposition as any one would wish to tackle — especially such a little one as his own was. He proposed to hold it until his passenger had stepped in and sat down and was ready to be shoved off. This was the usual procedure, and it had its good points for the average tourist. But this one had seen the boys shoving the same canoe off the sand and jumping over the stern, and he proposed to do the same thing, because he was used to canoes himself. Against the cautions of the owner he *did* shove off and jump, but he did not alight in the canoe. That elfish little piece of Indian deviltry was not there when he arrived; it slipped out from under him, sidewise, and with a spring which jumped it almost clear of the water it sailed away before the wind, while the canoeist went head-first into six or eight feet of water, silk hat, good clothes and all, amid the howls of delight from the passengers on the steamer who had been watching him. He was game, however, and admitted that he had never imagined just how light and ticklish a birch-bark was; nor how much science it required to jump *squarely* over the stern of such a fragile creation and maintain one's balance. Woodmen and canoeists familiar with "birches" will understand just how small a deviation is required to bring discomfiture. A little carelessness on the part of an old hand is often just as fatal as a little ignorance on the part of the tenderfoot.

But I digress. On the trip concerning which I started to tell, my brother and I had been down to the Indian village and were on our way home. When we emerged from Trudell Slough we found a gale blowing from the south, against the current of the river, and great combing waves were running, through which it seemed impossible to ride in our little boats. However, we had to cross the river in order to get home, and we did not long debate the question. Being the oldest I took the lead, Sam following. He was but eleven years old, and had a boat all by himself to manage in that sea. But he could paddle a canoe as well as any Indian boy. I also could paddle, and being older, nearly fourteen, was supposed to have the wisdom of the ages in the matter of judgment in meeting and riding combers.

Under these conditions, I started out to make the crossing. My brother has told me since that he never thought of any danger to himself; but he figured, a dozen times, that I was gone — in fact he lost three or four good bets that I would not come up again after going down out of sight. My canoe would go down into the trough of the sea at the same time that his did, thus he would lose track of me. He had to keep his eyes on the "combers" and meet them at just the right angle, or he himself would have been the "goner". Sometimes he would not locate me until he had met three or four big ones. Then he would rise over the tops of the waves at the same time and would be able to reassure himself that I was still right side up and paddling for life, and that he was out another bet. I do not know that I thought of the danger at all, as I simply had my canoe to look out for. Had Sam been in front I would have realized, as he did, that we were taking lots of chances, and would have learned from the diving of his craft just how great the danger really was, as he did. We shipped a good deal of water — that is, a good deal for the amount we could afford to take in and maintain any margin between the gunwales of our canoes and the water outside. Before we got across we were sitting in several inches of water, but a little baling cleared this out as soon as we reached the Wisconsin side, and we proceeded up the river, hugging the shore and keeping in the eddies and under the points, without further adventures. I do not think we mentioned the crossing as anything to brag of, as under the circumstances any of the boys would have done the same thing in the same way.

One other incident in which the little canoe figured, involved the closest call to drowning I ever had as a boy. Again I was out with my brother, some ten miles down the river, near Diamond Bluff, fishing and scouting about in the customary manner. Sam was ahead of me, and had landed on a pile of driftwood lodged against a giant cottonwood which had been undermined by the eating away of the river bank. In falling, one or more of its branches had been so deeply driven into the bottom of the river that it held at right angles with the current, extending out fifty feet or more into the channel. Against this obstruction all sorts of logs, lumber, and other drift had lodged, forming a large raft. My brother had run in under the lower side of this and climbed out, preparatory to dropping his line for fish. I, doubtless carelessly, drifted down toward the upper side. One of the limbs which did not quite reach the surface so as to be seen, caught my little vessel and in an instant I was in the water, and under the raft. I thought I was surely gone, for I supposed that the driftwood was deep enough to catch and hold me. I had presence of mind enough left, however, to do the only thing which was left — dive as deeply as possible, and with open eyes steer clear of the many branches through which I had to find my way toward the open water on the lee side of the raft. Sam ran to the lower side to catch me if I came up — an expectation which he had little hope of realizing, thinking as I did that I would be caught like a rat in a trap, and never come up until dug out. Fortunately the drift was not deep, and the limbs not very close together, and I popped up as I cleared the last log, but with so little breath left that another ten feet would have drowned me. Sam caught me by the hand and "yanked" me out on the drift, where I lay and took in air for some minutes to fill out my collapsed lungs. In another ten minutes we were fishing as if nothing had happened.

In these upsets which we were almost daily experiencing, our costumes played an important though passive part. The entire uniform of the average river lad of those days consisted of a pair of blue jean trousers, a calico shirt, a home-made straw hat, and sometimes a pair of "galluses". The last named item indicated an extravagant expenditure; one "gallus" was ample for all practical purposes; the second represented luxury and wanton extravagance. With such a costume a boy in the water was practically unhampered, and could and did swim with all the freedom of an unclothed cupid. One of the customary relaxations of the Prescott boys was to run down Orange Street when school "let out", in single file, dressed as above described, hats and all, and dive from the ledge of rocks fifteen feet high into water forty feet deep.

It was on one of these excursions that I had the only real scare of my life. This may sound like braggadocio, but it is a fact. I have been in places since that time, where I thought death imminent, and knew that it was possible, if not probable, at any moment; but in such situations I have more or less successfully been able to conceal the fact of fear. In the case in question I did not attempt to conceal from myself the fact that I was sincerely alarmed.

We had, late in the autumn, landed at a desolate *coulee* several miles below Prescott. I had gone back about half a mile from the river, on to the prairie, leaving my brother at the canoe. Suddenly I heard the long-drawn hunting cry of a wolf. Looking in the direction of the sound I saw a big grey timber wolf loping toward me with the speed of a race horse. His cries were answered from a distance, and then I saw six other big wolves bounding over the prairie after me.

I looked around for some place of safety and saw at some distance — a good deal less than a quarter of a mile, as I know it now, but it looked all of that at the time — a small burr oak, the only tree near enough to be available in this crisis. I knew enough about the big timber wolves to know that I would instantly be in ribbons after they were upon me. One alone might be kept off; but seven would have the courage of numbers, and would make short work of a single boy. Then I was scared. I could actually feel every hair upon my head standing straight on end, as stiff as Hamlet's "quills upon the fretful porcupine". It has been worth all that it cost, this hair-raising experience, as an interpretation of the much-quoted expression from the immortal Bard of Avon.

A good runner, I had a full half mile the start of the leading wolf. I did not wait for him greatly to diminish the lead, but "lit out" for the little burr oak. I covered the ground in the shortest time I had ever devoted to a like distance, and although very nearly winded jumped for the lower limbs and pulled myself up just in time to escape the teeth of the forward beast. In another minute there were seven of them, leaping to within a few feet of my legs as I stood on a branch of the small tree, as high up as I dared to go.

My brother had heard the cries of the wolves, and running to the top of the bank had watched the race with great interest. When the tree was safely reached he shouted to me to hold on and he would go for help, and he at once started for Prescott, four miles away, against the current. For some reason which I have never been able to explain, the wolves, after yelping and leaping for an hour or so, suddenly started off across the prairie, and when they had gone a mile away I climbed down and ran for home. In the meantime my hair had resumed its normal position, and never since, under any circumstances, have I experienced a like sensation. I presume that the thought of being torn to pieces by the wolves, a contingency which seemingly was quite probable, added a horror to the imminence of death which was not present at a time when there was an equal chance of being drowned. It was not because I did not know all about wolves, for I did. Their cries were familiar sounds in that wild country, and their ferocity had been proven time and again; but I had never heard nor seen them when it meant quite so much to me, nor when the chances seemed so slim.

Chapter III

On the Levee at Prescott

When we first knew it, Prescott was in many respects a typical river town. But in one, it differed from all others with the possible exception of Wacouta and Reed's Landing. "Towing through" had not then been inaugurated. The great rafts of logs and lumber from Stillwater and the upper St. Croix, were pushed to Prescott by towboats from Stillwater, at the head of the lake. From there to Lake Pepin they drifted. They were again pushed through that lake by other boats, and from Reed's Landing, at the foot of the lake, drifted to their destination at Winona, La Crosse, Clinton, Le Claire, or Hannibal.

The necessary preparation for the trip down river was made at Prescott. Stores of pork, beans, flour, molasses, and whiskey were laid in. The hundreds of rough men who handled the great steering oars on these rafts spent their money in the saloons which lined the river front and adjacent streets, filling themselves with noxious liquors, and often ending their "sprees" with a free fight between rival crews. A hundred men would join in the fray, the city marshal sitting on a "snubbing post", revolver in hand, watching the affair with the enlightened eye of an expert and the enjoyment of a connoisseur.

Prescott was also a transfer point for freight consigned to Afton, Lakeland, Hudson, Stillwater, Osceola, and St. Croix Falls. The large boats, unless they were heavily freighted for Stillwater and Hudson, did not make the run of thirty miles up the lake. The freight was put ashore at Prescott, and reshipped on the smaller boats plying between Prescott and St. Croix River points. This made necessary large warehouses in which to store the transshipped goods. My father, L. H. Merrick, engaged in this business of storing and transshipping, as well as dealing in boat-stores and groceries. Buying one warehouse on the levee, he started a store in the basement, which opened directly on to the levee. Moving his family into the two upper stories, he began at once the erection of a second and larger warehouse. These being insufficient for his business, he bought, in 1855, a third warehouse. These were filled, in summer, with goods in transit, and in winter with wheat awaiting the opening of navigation for shipment to Eastern markets, via Dunleith, Illinois, at that time the nearest railroad connection on the river. The name of this one-time prosperous city has, however, disappeared from the map, to be replaced by East Dubuque.

From 1854 until 1858 the firm of L. H. Merrick & Co. (the company being William R. Gates, my brother-in-law) did all the transfer and storage business for the regular packets belonging to the Galena, Dubuque, Dunleith & St. Paul Packet Company, commonly shortened to Minnesota Packet Company, and also for such "wild" boats as did not make the run up the lake.

The business was very profitable. Much of the freight consisted of pork and beef in barrels, whiskey, sugar in hogsheads (refined sugar was then scarcely known on the upper river), rice, soap, etc., which, if there was no boat ready to receive it, could be covered with tarpaulins on the levee, thus saving the cost of putting it in the warehouses. The perishable freight and household goods were of course stored under cover. A man was always on duty to meet incoming boats at night, and to watch the freight piled on the levee. Sometimes, when there was a large amount of such freight left outside, we boys spent the night skylarking about the piles, keeping our eyes open to see that the ubiquitous raftsmen did not surreptitiously transfer some of the packages to the ever-present rafts. The transfer agents paid the freight on the goods from the lower river points to Prescott, and charged a commission of from five to twenty-five per cent for such advance. In addition, a charge was made for storage, whether the freight was actually placed in the warehouse or simply covered and watched on the levee. If the goods were from Pittsburg or St. Louis, the freight bills were usually large, and a five per cent commission would produce a quite respectable income. If the cargo were divided into small lots, so much the better. No package, however small, escaped for less than a quarter ("two bits", as money was then

PRESCOTT LEVEE IN 1876. Showing Steamer "Centennial" and the little Hastings ferry, "Plough Boy." The double warehouse, showing five windows in the second story and four in the third was the building in which the author lived when a boy.

PRESCOTT LEVEE IN 1908. But one business building — one of the old Merrick warehouses, left intact. Dunbar's Hall gutted by fire recently. The large steamboat warehouse next to it destroyed some years ago. All the shipping business gone to the railroad, which runs just back of the buildings shown.

reckoned) ; and in addition to the commission on the money advanced, there was an additional charge for storage, graduated, as I have before stated, upon the value and perishability of the freight handled. Altogether it was a very profitable occupation until the year 1858, when there appeared a new bidder for the business, knocking down the rates of commission and storage, as well as cutting the business in two by getting the agency of many of the boats, heretofore served by the old firm.

My brother and myself "bunked" in the garret of the warehouse in which we had made our temporary home. There were two windows fronting the river, and I feel sure that at night no steamboat ever landed at the levee without having at least two spectators, carefully noting its distinguishing characteristics. Was she a side-wheel or stern-wheel? Was she large or small? Had she trimmings on her smokestack, or about the pilot house, and if so of what description? Had she a "Texas", or no "Texas"? Were the outside blinds painted white, red, or green? What was the sound of her whistle and bell? All of these points, and many others, were taken in, and indelibly impressed upon our memories, so that if the whistle or bell were again heard, perhaps months afterward, the name of the boat could be given with almost unfailing accuracy. It was a part of the education of the "levee rats", as the boys were called. A boy that could not distinguish by ear alone a majority of the boats landing at the levee from year to year, was considered as deficient in his education. Of course every boy in town could tell what craft was coming as soon as she whistled, if she was one of the regular "packets". Every boat had a whistle toned and tuned so that it might be distinguished from that of any other boat of the same line. The bells, which were always struck as the boat came into the landing, also differed widely in tone. There was one, the music of which will live in my memory so long as life lasts. The tone of the "Ocean Wave's" bell was deep, rich, sonorous, and when heard at a distance on a still, clear night, was concentrated sweetness. Were I rich I would, were it a possibility, find that bell and hang it in some bell-less steeple where I might hear again its splendid tones, calling not alone to worship, but summoning for me from the misty past pictures indelibly printed upon boyish senses.

A picturesque and animated scene, was one of these night landings; the discharge and taking on of freight, the shouting of orders, the escaping of steam, and all the sights and sounds which for the time transformed the levee from its usual quietude and darkness, broken only by the faint glimmer of the watchman's lantern and the ripple of the water upon the beach, into life, light, and activity.

The advent of the electric search-light has driven from the river one of the most picturesque of all the accessories to such scenes as we boys looked down upon, night after night, during the busy times of 1854 and 1855, before I myself became part and parcel of it all. The torch, by the light of which the work went on by night, was within an iron basket, about a foot in diameter and eighteen inches deep, swung loosely between the prongs of a forked iron bar or standard, which could be set in holes in the forward deck, leaning far out over the water, so as to allow live coals from the burning wood to fall into the river, and not upon deck.

When a landing was to be made at a woodyard or a town, the watchman filled one or perhaps two of these torch baskets with split "light-wood", or "fat-wood" — Southern pine full of resinous sap, which would burn fiercely, making a bright light, illuminating the deck of the boat and the levee for hundreds of feet around. As the boat neared the landing the pine splinters were lighted at the furnace door, the torch being carried to place and firmly fixed in its socket. Then came out the attending demon who fed the burning, smoking "jack" with more pine fat-wood, and from time to time with a ladle of pulverized rosin. The rosin would flare up with a fierce flame, followed by thick clouds of black smoke, the melted tar falling in drops upon the water, to float away, burning and smoking until consumed. This addition to the other sights and sounds served more than any other thing to give this night work a wild and weird setting. We boys decided, on many a night, that we would "go on the river" and feed powdered rosin and pine kindlings to torches all night long, as the coal-black and greasy, but greatly envied white lamp-boy did, night after night, in front of our attic windows on the levee at Prescott. The cleaner and brighter, but very common-place electric light has driven the torch from the river; and if one is to be found at all in these degenerate days it will be as a curiosity in some historical museum.

And thus we grew into the very life of the river as we grew in years. I finally attained an age when my services were worth something in the economy of a steamboat's crew. My first venture was made in company with one who afterward attained rank and honor in the civil service of the state — the Honorable Sam. S. Fifield, lieutenant-governor of Wisconsin. I have a letter written by Mr. Fifield since I began writing these sketches, in which he says that he recollects the writer as a "white-haired boy, full of all sorts of pranks". I presume this description of how I looked and what I did is correct; but forty years ago to have applied to him any such personal description of his thatch would have been a *casus belli* for which nothing but blood could atone. It is white, now; at that time it was a subdued brindle, with leanings toward straw, and a subject not lightly to be discussed in the presence of its owner.

The stern-wheel steamer "Kate Cassell" wintered above the lake — that is, above Lake Pepin — I think at Diamond Bluff, where at the close of navigation she was caught in the ice. In the spring her captain appeared, with an engineer, a pilot, a steward, and possibly some other officers, and picked up the remainder of officers and crew 'longshore. I remember that one of my schoolmates, Nat. Blaisdell, went as assistant engineer, Russ. Ruley as mate, and a number of longshoremen from Prescott as deck hands, while Sam Fifield and I were pantry boys. Sam got enough of it in a few trips between St. Paul and Rock Island. I stayed through the season. We both were printers. Sam went back to the case at once; I went to mine again in the fall, after the close of navigation, and stuck type during the winter, as I also did each returning season while on the river.

The next spring I engaged with "Billy" Hamilton, as a "cub" engineer. Prior to starting out on the season's run the machinery of the boat ("Fanny Harris") had to be put in order. There was a regular blacksmith's forge on board. All river engineers were, perforce, good blacksmiths, able to make anything pertaining to the machinery which it was possible to make from wrought iron bars with an ordinary forge and anvil, with a twelve-pound striking hammer and a two-pound shaper. We made scores of extra "stirrups" — the double bolts, with nuts, that clamp the "buckets" to the wheel-arms. We made hog-chains and chimney guys, and, as needed, bent them into place. The boilers, engines, and "Doctor" — the steam pump for feeding water to the boilers, pumping out the steamer, etc. — were all overhauled and put in perfect order. The engines were leveled and "lined up"; the eccentrics were carefully adjusted and securely fastened; the "nigger" hoisting engine, for handling freight and warping the boat over sand-bars was fitted up, and a hundred other minor but important matters were attended to, so that when steam was raised and turned on, the wheel would "turn over", and the boat go. Some wheels did not at first turn over, and it was not to the credit of the man who had lined the engines and set the eccentrics. Billy Hamilton's wheel, however, turned over the first trial.

Had I followed up this line of activity under Billy's tutelage, no doubt I would have become a capable engineer, for I liked the work and took a genuine delight in handling machinery, a liking which I have not yet outgrown. But there were decided drawbacks. The reversing gear of a Mississippi River steamboat, in old times, was like nothing else of its kind, anywhere under the sun. The engines were of the lever and poppet-valve order, and the reversing gear was heavy. The connecting-rod (cam-rod, we called it) weighed at least fifty pounds, even though it was attached to the "rock-shaft" at one end. In reversing, the end of the connecting-rod was lifted off its hook at the bottom, the lever thrown over, in which operation two heavy valve-levers were raised, the rod lifted about three feet, and dropped on to the upper hook. It was all right when you did this once or twice in making a landing; but in a piece of "crooked river", the boat dodging about among reefs and bars, with the bells coming faster than you could answer them, it was another matter, and became pretty trying work for a stripling boy; his arms could not keep the pace.

Another drawback in the life of a "cub" engineer was the fact that when in port there was no let-up to the work. In fact, the worst part of it came then. As soon as the steamer reached her destination at Galena, the pilots were at liberty until the hour of sailing; not so with the engineers. We usually reached

Galena Thursday evening or night, and left for up river Friday evening. As soon as the boat was made fast the "mud-valves" were opened, the fires drawn, the water let out of the boilers, and the process of cleaning began. Being a slim lad, one of my duties was to creep into the boilers through the manhole, which was just large enough to let me through; and with a hammer and a sharp-linked chain I must "scale" the boilers by pounding on the two large flues and the sides with the hammer, and sawing the chain around the flues until all the accumulated mud and sediment was loosened. It was then washed out by streams from the deck-hose, the force-pump being manned by the firemen, of whom there were eight on our four-boiler boat.

Scaling boilers was what decided me not to persevere in the engineering line. To lie flat on one's stomach on the top of a twelve-inch flue, studded with rivet heads, with a space of only fifteen inches above one's head, and in this position haul a chain back and forth without any leverage whatever, simply by the muscles of the arm, with the thermometer 90° in the shade, was a practice well calculated to disillusionize any one not wholly given over to mechanics. While I liked mechanics I knew when I had enough, and therefore reached out for something one deck higher. The unexpected disability of our "mud clerk", as the second clerk is called on the river, opened the way for an ascent, and I promptly availed myself of it.

Chapter IV

In the Engine-room

Before leaving the main deck, with its savory scents of scorching oil, escaping steam, and soft-coal gas, let me describe some of the sights, sounds, and activities which impressed themselves upon the memory of the young "cub" during his brief career as an embryo engineer.

The engine-room crew of a Mississippi steamer varies as the boat is a side-wheeler or a stern-wheeler. In my day, a stern-wheeler carried two engineers, a "first" and a "second". The former was chosen for his age and experience, to him being confided the responsibility of the boat's machinery. His knowledge, care, and oversight were depended upon to keep the engines, boilers, etc., in good repair, and in serviceable condition. The second engineer received less wages, and his responsibility ended in standing his watch, handling the engines, and in keeping enough water in the boilers to prevent the flues from burning, as well as to avoid an explosion. If a rival boat happened to be a little ahead or a little behind, or alongside, and the "second" was on watch, the margin of water between safety and danger in the boilers was usually kept nearer the minimum than it would have been were the "chief" in command. It is very much easier to get hot steam with little water than with much; and hot steam is a prime necessity when another boat is in sight, going the same direction as your own.

On the "Fanny Harris", the pilots always depended upon Billy Hamilton when in a race, as he would put on the "blowers" — the forced draft, as it is called in polite, though less expressive language — and never let the water get above the second gauge, and never below the first, if he could help it. Sometimes it was a matter of doubt where the water really was, the steam coming pretty dry when tried by the "gauge-stick" — a broom handle, which, pushed against the gauges, of which there were three in the end of the boiler (three inches apart, vertically, the lower one situated just above the water-line over the top of the flues), opened the valve and permitted the steam and water to escape into a short tin trough beneath. If a stream of water ran from the first and second gauges when so tried, but not from the third, there was a normal and healthy supply of water in the boilers. If the water came from the first, but not from the second, the "Doctor" was started and the supply increased. When it reached the third gauge the supply was cut off. If, as I have seen it, there was, when tried, none in the first or lower gauge, there followed a guessing match as to just how far below the minimum the water really was, and what would be the result of throwing in a supply of cold water. The supply was always thrown in, and that quickly, as time counts in such cases.

The pilot at the wheel, directly over the boilers, is in blissful ignorance of the vital question agitating the engineer. He may at times have his suspicions, as the escape pipes talk in a language which tells something of the conditions existing below decks; but if the paddle wheels are turning over with speed, he seldom worries over the possibilities which lie beneath him. His answer to the question, whether the water is below the safety point, comes as he feels the deck lifting beneath his feet, and he sails away to leeward amid the debris of a wrecked steamboat.

Probably four-fifths of the boiler explosions which have taken place on the Mississippi River during the last eighty years — and there have been hundreds of such — were the result of these conditions: low water in the boilers, exposing the plates until red-hot, then throwing in water and "jumping" the steam pressure faster than the engines or safety-valve could release it, followed by the inevitable giving away of the whole fabric of the boiler, wrecking the steamer, and usually killing and scalding many of the passengers and crew.

On a side-wheel boat the make-up of the engine crew is different. In addition to the first and second engineers there are two "cubs", or "strikers". The stern-wheeler has two engines, but they are both coupled to the same shaft, by a crank at each end. The throttle wheel is in the centre of the boat. One man operates the two engines, and assists at landings, but in a bad piece of river is helped by one of the firemen, who is called aft by a little bell controlled by a cord from the engine-room. This man "ships up" on the port side, while the engineer "ships up" on the starboard. "Shipping up" was the term used to describe the act of shifting the cam-rod from the lower pin on the reversing lever to the upper, or *vice versa*. If done at a sudden call, the engineer ran to one side and "shipped up", then across the deck to the other, and then back to the centre to "give her steam". That is all changed now by the adoption of an improved reversing gear, similar to that on a railway locomotive, the throwing of a lever at the centre of the boat operating the reversing gears on both engines at once. Instead of the old-time "short-link", or "cut-off hook", the equivalent of the "hooking-back" on a locomotive when under way is performed by the engineer at the centre of the boat by hooking back the reversing lever one, two, or three notches, exactly as on the locomotive. Fifty years ago this simple device had not been adopted on the river.

On the side-wheel boat, to get back to my subject, the engines are independent — one engine to each wheel. One may be coming ahead while the other is backing, or they may both be reversing at the same time. A man is therefore required to operate each engine, hence the necessity for a "striker", or "cub", to take one engine while the engineer on watch takes the other. The engineer on duty, be he chief or assistant, takes the starboard engine and controls the running of the machinery and the feeding of the boilers during his watch; the "cub" takes the port engine and works under the direction of his superior on watch. As I have stated at the beginning of this chapter, the handling of these powerful engines was hard work, even for a grown man, when the river was low and the pilot was feeling his way over a crossing in a dark night, with both leads going, and the wheels doing much of the work of keeping the boat in the intricate channel between the reefs. Then it was that the bells came thick and fast — to stop, to back, to come ahead again, to slow, to come ahead full steam, and again to stop and back and come ahead. Then the cut-off hook was pulled up by a rope attached to the deck beams overhead, and the heavy cam-rod was lifted from the lower hook to the upper by main strength, or dropped from the upper to the lower with scant regard for the finish on the bright work, to be lifted again at the call of the next bell from the pilot, and all this a dozen times, or even more, in making one crossing.

And all the time the "cub" was in deadly fear of getting his engine caught on the centre, a calamity in both material and moral sense, as a "centre" might mean the disablement of an engine at a critical moment, throwing the steamer out of the channel, and hanging her up for hours, or even for days, on a sand-bar. It might even have a more calamitous sequence, by running her on the rocks or snags and sinking her. Hence, for pressing reasons, the most acute alertness was necessary on the part of the "striker". The moral obloquy of "centring" an engine was so great among river men, especially among engineers, that no "cub" ever again held his head high after suffering such a mischance; and it was a proud boast among the embryo engineers if they could honestly claim that they had never "centred" their engine. On general principles they always boasted of it as a fact, until some one appeared who could testify to the contrary. I enter that claim here and now without fear of successful contradiction. All my confederates in that business are now out of commission.

One of the beauties of the puppet-valve engine, with its long stroke [1] and consequent "purchase" on the shaft-crank, was that by the aid of a billet of wood, about two and a half inches square, with a handle whittled off on one end, and with a loop of cord to hang it up by, or to hang it on one's wrist (where it was usually found when the boat was navigating a crooked piece of river), an increase of fifty per cent of steam could be let into the cylinder by the simple device of inserting the club between the rocker-arm and the lever which lifted the inlet valve, as graphically described in the paper by Mr. Holloway, quoted in this chapter. If the valve were normally lifted four inches by the rocker-arm, the

---

[1] The "stroke" of an engine is the distance traveled by the cross-head of the piston in making a complete revolution of the wheel — equal to twice the length of the crank on the water-wheel shaft. If the crank is three feet long, the stroke will be six feet. The stroke of the "Grey Eagle" of the Minnesota Packet Company was seven feet; that of the "J. M. White", lower river boat, was eleven feet. The cylinders of course equaled the full stroke in length. The longer the crank the greater the purchase, but at a consequent loss in the number of revolutions of the wheel per minute.

insertion of the club would increase the lift by its thickness. This additional power fed to the cylinder at the right moment would drive the wheel over the centre when reversed with the boat going upstream at a speed of eight or ten miles an hour, against a four-mile current, with almost absolute certainty. With a ten-foot wheel, and three buckets in the water, one submerged to its full width of three feet, and the other two perhaps two feet, it can readily be understood by an engineer that to turn such a wheel back against the current required a great expenditure of power at just the right time. The "club" of the Western steamboat engineer solved the question of additional power at the critical moment. No short-stroke engine would respond to such a call. While this service tried the cylinders to their utmost — many times a little beyond their utmost, with a consequent loss of a cylinder head, and worse yet, a scalded engineer — the use of the club was justified by experience; and results which, with finer and more perfect machinery would have been impossible, were, day after day, made possible by reason of the crudeness and roughness of this usage.

The great steamers plying on Long Island Sound attain a speed of twenty miles an hour, or even more. It is said that when under full speed it is possible to turn the wheels back over the centre within half a mile after steam has been shut off. Under ordinary conditions it is not necessary that they should be handled any faster. But think of the conditions under which a Mississippi River steamboat must stop and back, or suffer shipwreck. And imagine, if you can, the remarks a river pilot would make if the wheel were not turning back within thirty seconds after the bell was rung. I think five seconds would be nearer the limit for reversing and giving steam. In fact, on all side-wheel boats, the levers controlling the steam valves are attached to small tackles, and these are controlled by one lever, by which the steam levers may be raised in an instant, without closing the throttle at all, and the steam allowed to pass out through the escape pipes while the engine remains passive.

Two ends are attained by this device: steam can instantly be shut off, or as quickly given to the cylinders, thus making a saving in time over the usual opening and closing of the steam ports by the throttle wheel. Another advantage is, that this device acts as a safety-valve; for, were the steam to be entirely shut off, and the safety-valve fail to work, an explosion would certainly follow. By opening all the valves at once, and permitting as much steam to escape through the exhaust pipes as when the engine is in motion, the danger of an explosion is minimized. At the call of the pilot the levers can instantly be dropped and full steam ahead or reversed given at once — of course at the expense of a good deal of a "jolt" to the engines and cylinders. But the river engines were built to be "jolted", hence their practical adaptation to the service in which they were used.

J. F. Holloway, of St. Louis, who, in his own words, "was raised on the river, having filled every position from roustabout to master", in a paper read before the American Society of Mechanical Engineers at St. Louis in May, 1896, contributes the following description of a steamboat race as seen and heard in the engine-room — a point of view somewhat lacking, perhaps, in picturesqueness to the ordinary observer, but nevertheless very essential in winning a race. The writer is evidently as thoroughly at home in the engine-room as he is upon the roof:

"The reason which induced the builders of engines for these Western river boats to adopt such peculiar construction could hardly be made clear without a careful description of the hull of the boats, and of the varying conditions to which both engines and hulls are subjected, and under which they must operate. The steam cylinders are placed on foundations as unstable as would be a raft, and the alignment is varied by the addition or removal of every ton of freight which the boats carry when afloat, and they are further distorted when aground, or when the boats are being dragged over sand bars having several inches less of water on them than is required to float the hull. While the calm study of the machinery of a Western river steamboat while at rest would be an interesting object lesson to any one at all interested in such matters, it can only be seen at its best at a time when some rival boat is striving with it for "the broom," and close behind is slowly gaining, with roaring furnaces, and chimneys belching out vast volumes of thick black smoke; when all on board, from the pilot above to the fireman below are worked up to the highest pitch of enthusiasm, and when engines, boilers, engineers and all concerned in the management of the boat, are called upon to show the stuff which is in them. I know of no more exciting scene than was often to be witnessed in the days of the old famous Ohio River ports, when a "ten-boiler" boat was trying to make a record, or take a wharf-boat landing away from some close-following rival steamer. To stand on the boiler deck at such a time on a big side-wheel boat, when in order to get ahead the pilot had made up his mind to close-shave a "tow-head," or take the dangerous chances of a new channel or a new "cut-off," and when all on board knew the risk he was taking, and standing by to help him through, or help *themselves* if he failed, was exciting to a degree. Then it was that the two most skilful and daring engineers were called on watch, and took their stands alongside their respective engines, stripped like gladiators for the tussle which soon came as the clanging starboard bell rang out to "slow down," and as the hasty ringing of the "jingler" over the port engine meant "crack it to her." Then as the bow of the big boat swung, all too slow to suit the emergency or the impatience of the pilot, a stopping starboard bell would ring, quick followed by a backing one which would set the engineer to wrestling with his "hooks," one of which he hangs up with a cord, and the other he picks up seemingly from somewhere on the platform. As the suddenly stopped and quivering wheel in the swift-flowing current hangs for a moment poised on the centre, the engineer, grasping his ever-at-hand club of wood, quickly thrusts it between the uprising rocker-arm and the lever that lifts the inlet puppet valve, to which widened opening of the steam-valve port the engine responds with a noise of escaping steam not unlike the roar of an enraged elephant when prodded with the iron hook of his keeper. The battle of the bells thus begun, waxes more fierce as the excitement increases. There are bells to the right, and bells to the left, and amid their discordant jangle the engineers are working like mad as they clutch the throttle, open or close "the bleeder," hook her on "ahead," or stop and back, in such rapid succession as that soon neither they, nor any one else, can tell how far behind the bells of the pilot they are. Then soon amid the wild roar of the pent-up steam as it rushes out of the safety-valve pipes, the exploding exhausts of the engines which at the end of each stroke sound as if the cylinder-head had blown off, and to which is added the shrill noise of the warning bell which calls to the firemen to "throw open the furnace doors," there comes from out the huge trumpet shaped pipe above the head of the engineers, and which leads down from the pilot-house, a hoarse shout, heard above all else, partaking alike of command, entreaty, and adjectives, urging something or other to be done, and done quick, else the boat and all on board of her, in a brief time will land in a place which by reason of the reputed entire absence of water could not well be called a "port" (and certainly is no port mentioned in the boat's manifests). This battle of the bells and irons goes on until, if in a race, the rival boat is passed or crowded to the bank, or the narrow channel widens out into the broad river, when the discordant jangle of the bells ceases, the tired engineer drops on the quiet "cut-off hook," lays by his emergency wooden club, and wiping the sweat from his heated brow, comes down from the foot-board to catch a breath of the cool air which sweeps over the guards, and to formulate in his mind the story which he will have to tell of the race just over, or the perils just past.

But the old-time flyers which before the war tore their way up and down through the muddy waters of these Western rivers are all gone, and the marvelously skilled pilots of those days have gone too; the men who, through the darkest hours of the darkest nights, knew to within a few feet just where their boats were, and what was on the right or on the left, or beneath them, which was to be shunned. The engineers too, who with a courage born and nurtured amid the vicissitudes of a backwoods life, and with an experience and skill the outgrowth of trials and dangers gone through, have also passed away, and to the generation of the present are unhonored and unknown, as are the men who designed and built the hulls, and the workmen who, with crude and scant tools, built for them the machinery which they so well planned and handled.

Who they were, and where they lie, is known to but few, if any. Did I but know their final resting-place, I would, like "Old Mortality," wish to carve anew, and deep, the fading records of their life and death, which time has so nearly obliterated, and to herald abroad the praise and honor due them as the designers, builders, and engineers, of the old-time Western river steamboats."

Chapter V

The Engineer

It would be impossible to pick out any one man who handled an engine on the river fifty years ago, and in describing his habits and peculiarities claim him as a type of all river engineers of his time. The legendary engineer, such as Colonel Hay has given us, standing at the throttle of his engine on the ill-fated "Prairie Belle", waiting for signals from the pilot house, his boat a roaring furnace of fire, and whose spirit finally ascended with the smoke of his steamer, was a true type of one class, and possibly a large class, of old-time river engineers. Reckless, profane, combative; yet courageous, proud of their calling, and to be depended upon to do their duty under any and all circumstances; giving, if need be, their lives for the safety of the passengers and crew of the boat — such was one class. Another was composed of men equally courageous, equally to be depended upon in time of danger, but sober, quiet, religious, family men, who never used a profane word, never went on sprees ashore, never supported one wife at home and another at "Natchez under the Hill."

On the boat upon which I gained the greater part of my river experience, we had the two types: George McDonald, chief, and Billy Hamilton, assistant. Either would have died at his post, the one with a prayer upon his lips, and the other with a jest; both alike alert, cool, efficient. McDonald was a Scotch Presbyterian, and might have been an elder in the church at home — perhaps he was. He was a religious man on board his boat, where religion was at a discount. He was a capable engineer; he could make anything that it was possible to make, on the portable forge in the steamer's smithy. He was always cool, deliberate, ready, and as chief was the captain's right-hand man in the engine-room.

Billy Hamilton was his opposite in everything, save in professional qualifications. In these he was the equal of his chief, except in length of service, and consequent experience. The son of a Maryland slave owner, he was a "wild one" on shore, and a terror to the captain when on board and on duty. In a race with a rival boat his recklessness in carrying steam was always counted upon by the pilot on watch, to make up for any inherent difference in speed that might handicap our boat. He would put on the blower (forced draft) until solid chunks of live wood coals would be blown from the smokestacks. He would keep the water at the first gauge, or under it. He had a line rigged from the safety-valve lever, running aft to the engine-room. In times of peace the line was rove over a pulley fixed under the deck, above the safety-valve. A pull on the line in this position would raise the valve and allow the steam to escape. When another boat was in sight, going our way, the slack of the rope was hauled forward and the bight carried under a pulley fixed in a stanchion alongside the boiler, below the safety-valve, running thence up and over the upper pulley as before — but with all the difference in the world, for with the fifty-pound anvil hanging to the end of the line thus reversed in its leverage, the boilers might have blown up a hundred times before the safety-valve would have acted.

I have often heard the signal which Billy had agreed upon with his fireman on the port side, and have seen the darky slip the line under the lower pulley, and then keep one eye on the boiler-deck companionway, watching for the captain. Should he be seen coming below, the line was as quickly slipped off the lower pulley and restored to its normal position; sometimes with a concurrent "blowing off" through the safety-valve, which was evidence enough for the captain, although he might not catch Billy in the act. It is no more than just to say that the visits of the captain below decks were not frequent. He was a New Orleans man, of French extraction, with a fine sense of honor which forbade any espionage of this nature, unless there seemed to be an especially flagrant case of steam-carrying on the part of his junior engineer.

Billy had another device which greatly galled the captain, and later it was the cause of a serious affair. The captain had a private servitor, a colored man who cared for his rooms in the "Texas", served his lunches there, and ran errands about the boat as required. The captain used to send him down to the engine-room when he suspected Hamilton was carrying more steam than was nominated in the license, to look at the gauge and take readings.

It was not long before Hamilton became aware of this surreptitious reading, and set himself to work to defeat it without the necessity of ordering the captain's man out of the engine-room. To this end he made a cap of sheet lead which covered the face of the dial, leaving only about two inches in the centre, showing the pivot and a small portion of the pointer. This balked the colored messenger completely, as he could not see the figures, and he was not well enough acquainted with the instrument to read it from the centre. On his last visit to the engine-room, Hamilton saw him coming. Pretending that he was going forward to try the water, but keeping his eye on the messenger, he saw him reach up and take off the cap. In an instant Hamilton turned and threw his shaping hammer, which he had in his hand, with such true aim that it struck the poor darky in the head and knocked him senseless. As he dropped to the deck Hamilton called one of his firemen, telling him to give his compliments to Captain Faucette and tell him to send some men and take away his (profanely described) nigger, as he had no use for him. The darky pulled through all right, I think. He was put ashore at the first landing and placed under the care of a doctor, and Hamilton paid his bills. His successor never came into the engine-room, and the cap on the steam gauge was laid aside as unnecessary.

Whenever the mate had a "shindy" with the crew, which was composed of forty Irishmen, all the other officers of the boat were bound to "stand by" for trouble. Hamilton was always ready, if not anxious, for such occasions, and he and Billy Wilson, the mate, always supported each other so effectively that many an incipient mutiny was quickly quelled, the two jumping into a crowd and hitting every head in sight with whatever weapon happened to be at hand until order was restored. Usually, however, it was with bare hands, and the show which authority always makes in face of insubordination.

At times, Billy's vagaries were of a grisly and gruesome

character. I recall that at Point Douglass, on one of our trips, we found a "floater" (body of a drowned man) that had been in the water until it was impossible to handle it. To get it on shore it was necessary to slide a board beneath, and draw out board and body together. It was a malodorous and ghastly undertaking. Something said to this effect, Hamilton laughed at as being altogether too finicky for steamboatmen. To demonstrate that it need not affect either one's sensibilities or stomach, he stepped into the cook's galley for a sandwich, and sitting down on the end of the board, alongside the corpse, ate his lunch without a qualm.

Another and rather more amusing incident took place while the "Fanny Harris" was in winter quarters at Prescott. The night before St. Patrick's day, Billy made up an effigy, which he hung between the smokestacks. As the manikin had a clay pipe in its mouth and a string of potatoes about its neck, it might have reference to the patron saint of the Old Sod. The loyal Irishmen of the town so interpreted it at least, and Billy had to stand off the crowd for several hours with a shot gun, and finally get the town marshal to guard the boat while he climbed up and removed the obnoxious image.

He had a little iron cannon which he fired on all holidays, and sometimes when there was no holiday; in the latter case, at about three o'clock in the morning, just to remind people living in the vicinity of the levee that he was still "on watch". In retaliation for the effigy affair, his Irish friends slipped aboard the boat one evening while he was away and spiked his cannon by driving a rat-tail file into the vent; this was after he had carefully loaded it for a demonstration intended to come off the next morning. He discovered the trick when he attempted to fire the gun, and offered pertinent and forcible remarks, but unprintable in this narration. He lost no time in vain regrets, however. Lighting up his forge he made a screw and drew out the load. Then with the help of several chums he moved his forge to the bow of the boat (the foc'sle), rigged a crane so that he could swing his little cannon in a chain sling, from the capstan to the forge, and back again. When the time came for firing the salute he had his gun heated red-hot on the forge; it was then swung back on to the capstan-head, where it was lashed with a chain. A bucket of water was then thrown into the gun, and instantly a hardwood plug, made to fit, was driven home with his heavy striking hammer.   In a minute the steam generated by this process caused an explosion that threw the plug almost across the river, fully a quarter of a mile, with a reasonably fair result in the way of noise.   It was a risky piece of work, but "Billy" was in his element when there was a spice of risk mixed with his sports.

Billy's humor was broad, but never malicious.   He never missed an opportunity to play a practical joke on any one, save, perhaps, the captain himself.   The deck hands who "soldiered" by sitting on the side of their bunks when they ought to be at work toting freight, were sometimes lifted several feet in the air by the insertion of two inches of a darning needle ingeniously attached to the under side of the board bench upon which they took their seat.   It was operated from the engine-room by a fine wire and a stiff spring, the whole boxed in so securely by the carpenter that there was no possibility of its discovery by the enraged victim.

He was one of the most open-handed and liberal of men in his givings, and in spite of his escapades a valuable officer.   In 1862 he left the boat, as did all the crew, to enlist under the call for three hundred thousand troops, made in July of that year.   In all discussions of the war he had asserted his determination to keep away from any place where there was shooting, as he was afraid of bullets of any size from an ounce up.   As he was a Southern man, son of a slaveholder, we thought that this badinage was to cover his determination not to take any part in the war on the Union side; we never questioned his courage.   He went into the navy as an acting assistant engineer, and was assigned to one of the "tin-clads" that Commodore Porter had improvised for service on the Mississippi and tributaries, and that did such heroic service in opening and keeping open the great river.   Within a few months after his entry into the service, his old friends saw with pleasure, but not surprise, his name mentioned in general orders for gallantry in action. He had stood by his engine on the gunboat after a pipe had been cut by a shell from a Confederate shore battery, a number of men being killed and wounded, and the engine-room filled with escaping steam.   Binding his coat over his face and mouth to prevent inhalation of the steam he handled his engines at the risk of his life, in response to the pilot's bells, until his boat was withdrawn from danger. It was in keeping with his known character; and his talk of being "afraid of guns" was only a part of the levity with which he treated all situations, grave or gay.

I do not know Billy's ultimate fate. When he left the "Fanny Harris" for gunboat service, I also left to enlist in the infantry. After three years in the army I was mustered out in Washington, and soon went to New York where I remained for ten years or more. In the interim between 1862 and 1876, when I returned to the West, I completely lost sight of all my old river acquaintances. When, later, I made inquiries of those whom I did find, they either did not enlighten me as to his fate, or, if they did, I made so little note of it that it has escaped my memory.

Chapter VI

The "Mud" Clerk[2] — Comparative Honors

The transition from the "main deck" to the "boiler deck" marked an era in my experience. It opened a new chapter in my river life, and one from which I have greatly profited. When I went upon the river I was about as bashful a boy as could be found; that had been my failing from infancy. As pantry boy I had little intercourse with the passengers, the duties of that department of river industry requiring only the washing, wiping, and general care of dishes and silverware. A "cub" engineer slipped up to his stateroom, and donned presentable clothing in which to eat his meals in the forward cabin, at the officers' table, where all save the captain and chief clerk took their meals. After that, his principal business was to keep out of sight as much as possible until it was time to "turn in". He was not an officer, and passengers were not striving for his acquaintance.

As second clerk all these conditions were changed. In the absence of the chief clerk, his assistant took charge of the office, answered all questions of passengers, issued tickets for passage and staterooms, showed people about the boat, and in a hundred ways made himself agreeable, and so far as possible ministered to their comfort and happiness while on board. The reputation of a passenger boat depended greatly upon the esteem in which the captain, clerks, and pilots were held by the travelling public. The fame of such a crew was passed along from one tourist to another, until the gentle accomplishments of a boat's *personnel* were as well known as their official qualifications.

---

2 "Mud" Clerk: Second clerk, whose duty it was to go out in all weathers, upon the unpaved levees and deliver or receive freight. As the levees were usually muddy in rainy weather, the name became descriptive of the work and condition of the second clerk.

ALMA, WISCONSIN.   A typical river town in the fifties.

Captain William Faucette was, as I have said, of French Creole stock, from New Orleans. In addition to being a good and capable officer on the roof, he was also highly endowed with the graces that commended him to the ladies and gentlemen who took passage with him. Polite in his address, a fine dancer, a good story-teller and conversationist, his personality went far toward attracting the public who travelled for pleasure — and that was the best-paying traffic, for which every first-class packet was bidding.

Charles Hargus, chief clerk, was not far behind his chief in winning qualities. An educated man, he was also possessed of the address and the other personal qualities which were necessary to equip one for becoming a successful officer on a Mississippi passenger steamer.

Such was the atmosphere into which the oily "cub" from the engine-room was ushered, when drafted into this service because of the serious illness of the second clerk. It was too late to get a man from the city, and the necessities of the case required an immediate filling of the vacancy. I was invited, or rather commanded, to go into the office for the trip, and do what I could to help out with the work until the return to Galena, where a man or boy could be found to fill the office until the sick officer returned.

The boat was guard-deep with freight, and at night the cabin was carpeted with passengers sleeping on mattresses spread on the floor. The chief clerk simply had to have somebody to help out. On my part, it was the chance of my life. Without much prior business experience, what little I had was right in line. I had checked freight on the levee for the firm of L. H. Merrick & Co., was a good penman, fairly good at figures, and had made out freight bills in the transfer of freight at Prescott, which fact was known to the chief clerk. It is needless to add that I required no second order. While second clerks were not likely to get any shore leave at either end of the route, nor at any intermediate ports, it required no brilliancy of intellect to see that checking freight was comparatively cleaner than, and superlatively preferable to, boiler-scaling.

Regarding my success in this new field, suffice it to say that the trip to St. Paul and return was made, and the freight checked

out with surprisingly few errors for a beginner. The cargo of
wheat, potatoes, etc., was correctly counted in, properly entered
in the books, and correctly checked out at Prairie du Chien and
Dunleith. The sick clerk did not rejoin the boat. The temporary
appointment by the captain and chief clerk was made permanent
by the secretary of the company at Dunleith, Mr. Blanchard, on
the recommendation of Mr. Hargus, my chief. We ran into
Galena on our regular Thursday afternoon time, and instead of
creeping into a steaming, muddy boiler, I walked out on to the
levee and was introduced to the great wholesalers who at that time
made Galena their headquarters, as "Mr. Merrick, our new second
clerk", and the work of loading for a new trip was taken up.

While the office of second clerk was a decided promotion from
my point of view, it was not so esteemed on the river. Leaving
the engine-room was leaving the opportunity to learn the profession
of engineering. Once learned, it was then assumed that the
person so equipped was guaranteed employment so long as he
willed, with a minimum amount of competition. Later develop-
ments revealed the fallacy of this conception. Within ten years
thereafter, steamboating was practically dead on the upper Mississippi. The completion of one or more railroads into St. Paul,
ended the river monopoly. Thereafter a dozen steamboats did
the business formerly requiring a hundred. The wages of engineers and pilots dropped to a figure undreamed of in the flush
times between 1850 and 1860; there were twenty men competing
for every berth upon the river.

My new berth was not silk-lined, however. There was an
aristocracy in the official family above decks. The captain and
the chief clerk represented the first class, and the mate and the
second clerk the other. The line between these was represented
by the watches into which all officers on the boat were divided for
rounds of duty. The captain and his mate, and the chief clerk
and his second stood watch and watch during the twenty-four hours
(that is, six hours on and six hours off) all the season. The pilots
and engineers interposed a "dog watch", to break the monotony.
The captain and the chief clerk went on watch after breakfast, at
seven in the morning, and stood until noon. At twelve o'clock they
were relieved by the mate and the second clerk, who ran the steamboat and the business until six o'clock in the evening, when they

were relieved. After supper, they turned in until midnight, when they were called and relieved the captain and the chief clerk, who retired and slept until morning. While each class of officers was on duty the same number of hours each day, the difference lay in the fact that the junior officers were compelled by this arrangement to turn out at midnight throughout the season. It was this turning out at midnight that made the mate's watch (the port watch) very undesirable so far as personal ease and comfort was concerned. A man can knock about until midnight very agreeably, after a short nap in the afternoon, provided he can have a sound sleep during the "dead hours" from midnight until six o'clock in the morning. To turn out at midnight every night and work until six is an entirely different matter.

The pilots and engineers on our boat — and so far as my experience went, on all boats — stood a "dog-watch" from four in the morning until seven, thus making five watches during the twenty-four hours, bringing the men of the two watches on duty alternately at midnight, and shortening the "dead hours" from midnight to four o'clock, and from four until seven, so that one did not get so "dead" tired and sleepy as he would in standing a watch beginning every night at midnight.

It was believed on the river that more people die between midnight and morning than during any other six hours in the twenty-four. I think that I have heard physicians confirm this. My own experience in going on watch at midnight continuously during six months is, that there is less vitality and ambition available in that period than in any other. In fact, I have no distinct recollection that there was any ambition at all mixed up in the process of writing up delivery books, checking out freight, measuring wood, and performing the hundred other duties that fell to the lot of the officer on watch, when done in the depressing atmosphere of early morning. It was a matter of duty, unmixed with higher motives.

It was not only the turning out at unholy hours, that differentiated between first and second clerk. The second clerk must have his delivery book written up for all the landings to be made during his off-watch. The chief clerk then made the delivery from the book, upon which the receipts were taken. If, during the second clerk's off-watch, there was a particularly large manifest for any landing, the assistant was called to attend to the delivery, after which he could turn in again, if he chose. Of course it took a river man but a moment to go to sleep after touching his bunk; but his rest was broken, and in the course of the season this began to tell on every one. Under the stress of it, men became hollow-eyed and lost flesh and strength.

When on watch, the second clerk not only attended to his own particular duties, but he also assumed for the time those of the chief clerk. He collected fares from passengers coming aboard during his watch; assigned rooms, provided there were any left to assign, or a mattress on the cabin floor if there chanced to be any space left on the floor, whereon to place another mattress; collected freight bills, paid for wood or coal, and performed any other duties ordinarily performed by the chief clerk when on watch. It was not considered good form to call the chief clerk during his off-watch; in fact, to do so would be a confession of ignorance or inability, which no self-respecting second clerk cared to exhibit, and but rarely did. Many the close conference with the chief mate, his companion as well as superior during the long night watches; and many the smiles evoked in after days when recalling the well-meant but somewhat impracticable advice tendered upon some such occasions by the good-hearted autocrat of the "roof" and fo' castle.

Chapter VII

Wooding Up

As second clerk, I was early taught to hold my own with the pirates who conducted the woodyards scattered along the river, from which the greater part of the fuel used on old-time river boats was purchased. There was a great variety of wood offered for sale, and a greater diversity in the manner of piling it. It was usually ranked eight feet high, with a "cob-house" at each end of the rank. It was the rule on the river to measure but one of the end piles, if the whole rank was taken, or one-half of one end pile if but a part of the rank was bought. For convenience, the wood-men usually put twenty cords in a rank, and allowed enough to cover the shortage caused by cross-piling at the ends. Being piled eight feet high, ten lengths of the measuring stick (eight feet long) equalled twenty cords, if it were fairly piled. Woodmen who cared for their reputation and avoided a "scrap" with the clerks, captains, and mates of steamboats, usually made their twenty-cord ranks eighty-four feet long and eight feet high. Such dealers also piled their sticks parallel to each other in the ranks; they also threw out the rotten and very crooked ones. When the clerk looked over such a tier, after having run his stick over it, he simply invited the owner aboard and paid him his fifty or sixty dollars, according to the quality of the wood, took him across the cabin to the bar, and invited him to "have one on the boat", shook hands, and bade him good night.

It took the "pirates" to start the music, however. When only scant eighty feet were found in the rank, with rotten and green wood sandwiched in, all through the tiers, and crooked limbs and crossed sticks in all directions, it became the duty of the clerk to estimate his discount. After running his rod over it, he would announce, before the first stick was taken off by the deck hands, the amount of wood in the rank — nineteen and a half cords, nineteen cords, eighteen and a half cords, or in extreme cases only eighteen.   When the mate could stand behind the rank and see, through a cross-piled hole, more than half the length of the steamboat, it was deemed a rather acute case, calling for the eighteen-cord decision.   When this decision was made and announced, it was, on our boat at least, always adhered to.   We always took wood some time before our visible supply was exhausted, in order to meet just such emergencies.   The owner might, and usually did, damn everybody and everything connected with the craft in the most lurid terms.   But the one question he had to answer, and answer quickly, was: "Will you take it?"   If "No", the bell was struck and the boat backed off, while the woodman and roustabouts exchanged a blue-streaked volley of vituperation.   If, on the other hand, a sale was made, the owner usually took his money and the inevitable drink at the bar, and then went down to the main deck and had it out with the mate, who was always a match, and more than a match, for any merely local and provincial orator.   His vocabulary was enriched with contributions from all ports between St. Louis and St. Paul, while that of the squatter was lacking in the elements of diversity necessary to give depth and breadth to the discussion.

It would be unjust to class all woodyard men with squatters like the foregoing specimens, of whom there were hundreds scattered along the islands and lowlands bordering the river, cutting wood on government land, and moving along whenever the federal officers got on their trail.   On the mainland were many settlers, opening up farms along the river, and the chance to realize ready money from the sale of wood was not to be neglected.   In many places chutes had been built of heavy planks, descending from the top of the bluff, from one to two hundred feet above the river. The upland oak, cut into four-foot lengths, was shot down to the water's edge, where a level space was found to rank it up.   These men were honest, almost without exception, and their wood always measured true.   The upland wood was vastly superior to the lowland growth; steamboat captains not only paid the highest price for it, but further endeavored to contract for all the wood at certain yards.   I remember one, run by a Mr. Smith, between Prescott and Diamond Bluff, and another near Clayton, Iowa, that always furnished the best dry oak wood, and gave full measure.

It was at the latter place that I nearly lost my berth, through a difference with the "Old Man" — the captain. I had measured the rank and announced the amount of wood as twenty cords. The captain was on deck at the time, and watching the measurement. When the announcement was made he ordered the wood remeasured. I went over it carefully, measuring from the centre of the cross-pile at one end to the centre of the cross-pile at the other end of the rank, and again reported "twenty cords". Captain Faucette called down to "measure it again", with an inflection plainly intimating that I was to discount it, adding, "You measured both ends." The rank was full height, closely piled, and the best of split white oak, and I had already taken out one of the ends; further, I had already twice reported twenty cords in the hearing of all the crew and many passengers, who were now giving their undivided attention to this affair. I therefore did not feel like stultifying myself for the sake of stealing a cord or two of wood, and replied that I had already measured it twice, and that I had not measured both ends of the rank. The "Old Man" flew into a rage and ordered me to go to the office and get my money, and he would find a man who knew how to measure wood. There being nothing for it but to obey an order of this kind, I went aboard, hung up my measuring stick in its beckets, and reported at the office for my money. Mr. Hargus, my chief, was astonished, and asked for an explanation, which I gave him. He rushed out to the woodpile with the rod, ran over it in a flash, and reported to the captain on the roof, "Twenty cords, sir!" and came back to the office. He told me to go on with my work and say nothing, which I was ready enough to do. In the meantime, the crew were toting the wood aboard.

When the boat backed off, the captain sent for Mr. Hargus to meet him in his private room in the "Texas", where they had it out in approved style. Hargus only replied to Captain Faucette that if Merrick was discharged he would also take his pay and go ashore with him. Faucette was a new man in the line, from the far South, and a comparative stranger, while Hargus was a veteran with the company, a stockholder in the line, and backed by all the Dubuque stockholders, as well as by the officers and directors of the company; so the captain thought better of it and dropped the whole matter, never deigning to speak to the second clerk, either in way of apology, which was not expected, or of caution "not to let it occur again", which would have been an insult. The affair was "dropped overboard", as Hargus said, and the wood-measuring was thereafter left to the proper officer, without comment or interference.

With a crew of forty men looking on and hearing the whole colloquy, a change in the amount of wood reported at the suggestion of the captain, would have simply wiped out any respect they may have had for the authority of the boy officer; and his usefulness on that boat, if not on the river, would have ended then and there. It was one of the unwritten rules of the service that the officers were to stand by each other in every way; there was to be no interference while on duty, and each was held responsible for such duty. If there was cause for reprimand it was to be administered in the privacy of the captain's office, and not in the presence of the whole crew. It was not desirable to have either office or officer held in contempt.

As the steamboat business developed, and as immigration into the new Territory of Minnesota increased, there was necessity for getting as many trips into a season as possible. This led to the adoption of every device that might lessen the running time of steamers between the lower ports and St. Paul. Not the least of these innovations was the use of the wood-boat for the more ready transfer of fuel from the bank to the deck of the steamer. Flatboats, or scows, capable of carrying twenty cords of wood, and even forty, were loaded at the woodyards in readiness for the expected steamer. As the wood was worth more loaded in the scow, a higher price was given by steamboatmen, and contracts were made ahead; the date of arrival of the boat was determined, and the wood-boat was in readiness, day or night, with two men on board. It was the work of a few minutes only to run alongside, make fast the towlines, and while the steamer was on her way up river, thirty or forty men pitched or carried the wood aboard.

Ordinarily, the wood-boat was not in tow more than half an hour, which would take her five or six miles up river. When the wood was out, the towlines were cast off, a large sweep or steering oar was shipped up at each end of the scow, and it drifted back to be reloaded for the next customer. The steamboat, meanwhile, had lost practically no time in wooding, as the tow was so light as but slightly to impede her speed. The greatest danger in the transaction was that the great packet might swamp the scow by running at too great speed, towing her under by the head, as sometimes occurred. To avoid this contingency the wood was always taken first from the bow of the flatboat. As it was only the fast packets that patronized the wood-boats, this danger of towing under was always present, and the pilots were always very careful in the handling of their boats at such times. Flats were seldom towed downstream, for the reason that there was no way of getting them back, except to pay for a tow. And again, the packets were not in so much of a hurry when going down river, for then they had but few passengers to feed, and no fast freight.

Chapter VIII

The Mate

In writing of life on the main deck of a Mississippi River steamboat fifty years ago, a prefatory note may be in order. The reader must bear in mind that times have changed; and men, in the mass, have changed, and that for the better, in the years that have elapsed between 1860 and 1908. Slavery then held sway on the west bank of the river, from the Iowa line to the Gulf. On the east side in the State of Illinois even, the slavery idea predominated; and on the river there was no "other side" to the question. Slavery was an "institution", as much to be observed and venerated as any institution of the country. A black man was a "nigger", and nothing more. If he were the personal property of a white man in St. Louis, or below, he was worth from eight hundred to fifteen hundred dollars, and was therefore too valuable to be utilized in the make-up of a boat's crew running north. The inclemency of the weather, or the strenuousness of the mate, might result in serious physical deterioration that would greatly depreciate him as a chattel, to say nothing of the opportunities offered him by the northern trip to escape to Canada, and thus prove a total loss.

Of free negroes there were not enough to man the hundreds of steamboats plying on the upper river. Thus it came about that the cabin crews on some boats, and the firemen on others, were colored, while the deck crews (roustabouts and stevedores) were white. So marked was this division of labor that it came to pass that no "nigger" was permitted by the white rousters to handle any freight, on any boat. The modern unions take no greater exception to a non-union workman than the white deck hands then expressed for a "nigger" as a freight handler.

Another class distinction was, that nine-tenths of the deck

crew were Irishmen. In that day the poorer sort of that nationality were the burden-bearers of this country. They dug the ditches, built the railroad embankments, and toted the freight on the river. Since that time they have wonderfully developed; in the present day, very few even of the emigrants handle pick and shovel, and none handle freight as river deck hands. They are the trainmen and policemen of the country, and their sons are our mayors and aldermen, our judges and law-makers. The dirt-handling on the railroads is passed on to the Italians and the Huns, while the river freight-handling, what little there is of it, is done by the lower class of negroes. The abolition of slavery has prodigiously increased their numbers, as well as amazingly cheapening them in value. All this has relevancy in describing an old-time mate and his work.

There was a fellow feeling between the chief mate and the second clerk. For one thing, they were both in the second rank, officially, although that did not count for a great deal, I think, as neither of them thought of it in just that way. My recollection is, that both of them thought of it from the other point of view — they were over so many men, and in command of so many things and situations, rather than under the captain and the chief clerk. You will observe at once that this put an entirely different construction upon the question; and this was, after all, the only reasonable and practical view to take of it, and the one that came nearest to meeting all the conditions. In fact, no other view of the situation could be taken. When the captain and the chief clerk were off duty and asleep in their staterooms, or even off duty and awake, loitering about the boat, the responsibility was immediately shifted to their subordinates. Even though the captain might be sitting in the door of his room in the forward end of the "Texas", while the mate stood at the bell to make a landing, the amenities and traditions of river life put him out of the game as completely as though he were asleep in his berth. The same also was true of the chief clerk and his subordinate. The chief might be smoking his after-dinner cigar within ten feet of the office, or he might walk out on the levee and talk with the agent; but until asked, he never took any part in the distinctive business transactions of his subordinate, or in any way interfered with his manner of transacting the business. He might, later, if necessary, make suggestions looking to the betterment of the methods of his second; but that would be a purely personal, rather than an official, utterance.

It followed, therefore, that my acquaintance with Billy Wilson was much closer than with the captain; and standing watch with him day after day and night after night during a long season's run, I came to know him intimately. He was born in Pennsylvania, the son of a "Pennsylvania Dutchman." Beginning his professional life on the Allegheny River, he worked down the Ohio, and when the great boom in upper Mississippi traffic began in 1854, engaged in that trade. A smooth-shaven, red-faced man, about five feet eight inches in height, he weighed probably a hundred and sixty pounds. Occasionally he took a drink of whiskey, as did all river men, but it was seldom. He was well read, and ordinarily, a very quiet man, therefore all the more to be feared and respected. He would hardly fill the bill as a traditional Mississippi River steamboat mate; and were his prototype shown on the stage it would be voted slow, uninteresting, and untrue to type.

In the beginning of this chapter I endeavored to indicate what manner of men composed our deck crew. Ours numbered forty men. Almost without exception they were Irishmen of the lowest class, picked up alongshore at St. Louis, Galena, Dubuque, and St. Paul, from the riffraff of the levee. They would get drunk whenever they could get whiskey; and as the boat carried hundreds of barrels of this liquor each trip, it required eternal vigilance on the part of the mates and watchmen to prevent the crew broaching a barrel and getting fighting drunk and mutinous. When this happened, as now and then it did in spite of all precautions, Billy Wilson was turned in an instant from a quiet Pennsylvania Dutchman into a dangerous, if not devilish, driver. He carried, on most occasions, a paddle made from a pork barrel stave. This had a handle at one end, and the other, shaped something like a canoe paddle, was bored full of quarter-inch holes. When the case was one of mere sluggishness on the part of one of the hands, a light tap with the flat part of this instrument was enough to inspire activity. When the case was one of moroseness or incipient mutiny, the same flat side, applied by his powerful muscles, with a quick, sharp stroke, would leave a blood-blister for every hole in the paddle; and when a drunken riot was to be dealt with, the

Above Trempealeau, Wisconsin. In the middle foreground, at the head of the slough, is the site of the winter camp of Nicolas Perrot, in the winter of 1684-5, as identified in 1888 by Hon. B. F. Heuston and Dr. Reuben Gold Thwaites of the Wisconsin State Historical Society.

sharp edge of the paddle on a man's head left nothing more to be done with that man until he "came to." With a revolver in his left hand and his paddle in his right, he would jump into the middle of a gang of drunken, mutinous men, and striking right and left would intimidate or disable the crowd in less time than it takes to tell it. He never used his pistol, and to my knowledge never called for assistance, although that was ready if required, for all officers were usually at hand and ready in case of necessity.

In a row that took place at Prairie du Chien one night, when the men had sent up town and smuggled in a jug of whiskey, one man who was hit on the head by the paddle went overboard on the upstream side of the boat. He was instantly sucked under by the swift current, and was never seen again. The coroner's jury in the case brought in a verdict of "accidental death", and Wilson came back to work after a week's sojourn with the sheriff, having won an added prestige that rendered less necessary the use of the paddle.

Ordinarily his commands were given in a low tone of voice, unaccompanied with the profanity which legend and story considered due from the man and his office. When things went wrong, however, the wide range and profundity of his language was a revelation to the passengers who might chance to be within ear-shot. I recall an outbreak, one April morning at about four o'clock, at a woodyard, between Trempealeau and Winona. He had called, "All hands, wood up!" It was a cold and rainy night, and many of the men had crawled in under the boilers to dry their clothes and seek sleep. After the first round or two, he found that ten or fifteen men were missing — they were "soldiering." He went aft and ransacked the bunks without finding the truants. He then dove under the boilers with his paddle, striking in the dark, and feeling for some one to hit, at the same time pouring out a torrent of profanity that in ordinary walks of life, would be called monumental, but which in the more exacting conditions of river life, probably was not above medium grade. The next count found every man in line, toting his share of the wood.

It may be and was asked by Eastern people, unused to river life, "Why do the men submit to such treatment? Why do they not throw the mate into the river?" The answer is, caste. They were used to being driven, and expected nothing else, and nothing better, and they would not work under any other form of authority. As I stated at the beginning, they were of the very lowest class. No self-respecting man would ship as a deck hand under the then existing conditions. One might now travel long and look in vain for a white crew driven as these men then were. Their places have been taken by the freed negro; he to-day is being driven as his white predecessors were then.

There is this distinction, however; now, most of the drivers are Irishmen — the mates and watchmen on the river steamers. Then an Irishman was of little service as a mate. Those officers were, as a rule, Yankees or Southerners or Pennsylvania Dutchmen. We had for a time a second mate, Con Shovelin, an Irishman, as you might suspect from his name. He was six feet high, and big in every way, including his voice. He roared and swore at the crew all the time, but put very little spirit into them. A look out of the corner of Wilson's eye, and a politely worded request that they "Get a hump, now!" was worth a volume of Shovelin's exordiums. At that time an Irishman could not handle an Irish crew; now, he can handle a crew of free negroes with the expenditure of one-half the wind and oratory. If you wish to see for yourself, take a trip on the river to St. Louis and return, and see the Celt driving the Ethiopian, even as the Saxon drove the Celt, fifty years ago.

Chapter IX

The "Old Man"

It would be interesting to trace the origin of this term, which is universally applied to the captain in nautical circles, either on shipboard, among deep-sea sailors, on the great lakes, or on the inland waters. He may not be half as old as the speaker; still, in speaking of him, not to him, he is the "old man." It is used in no disrespectful sense; indeed, it is rather an endearing term. In speaking to him, however, it is always Captain, or Sir. But in detailing what the Captain has said or done the narrator says that the "old man" says so, or is about to do so, and his auditors, if river men, know of but one "old man" aboard the boat, although the steamer may be freighted with octogenarians.

The captain usually reaches the "roof" from one of two directions, either going up from mate, or coming down from the pilot house. Occasionally he emerges from the clerk's office, or from the engine-room; but the line of promotion is usually drawn from mate or pilot to captain, these being also the normal lines of education for that post. Perhaps the greater number of captains serving on the river in the early days, down to 1860, began their careers on the river as pilots, very often combining the two offices in one person.

The captain's official requirements are not altogether ornate. It is true that he must have sufficient polish to commend himself to his passengers. That is essential in popularizing his boat; but in addition he must thoroughly know a steamboat, from stem to stern, and know what is essential to its safety, the comfort of his passengers, and the financial satisfaction of its owners. Nearly every old-time captain on the river could, in case of necessity, pilot his boat from St. Paul to Galena. Every captain could, and of necessity did, handle the deck crew, with the second mate as go-

between, during the captain's watch on deck. Some few might
have gone into the engine-room and taken charge of the machinery,
but these were exceptional cases. All were supposed to know
enough about the business of the office to enable them to determine
between profit and loss in the running of the steamer.

After leaving port, the captain on the river was as autocratic
as his compeer on the ocean. He might without notice discharge
and order ashore any officer or man on board, and he could fill
vacancies en route to any extent; but these appointments were
subject to the approval of the owner or manager on arrival at the
home port. Many, if not most, of the captains owned interests
in the boats which they commanded. Many were sole owners, in
which case they were amenable to no one for their actions, except
to the civil authorities in case of legal technicalities, or to the
unwritten laws of the service, which custom had made binding
upon all. Such, for instance, was the rule that the captain was
not to interfere with the pilots in the running of his boat, even if
he might know, or think he knew, better than they the proper
course to take in certain cases, or under certain conditions; even
though he might himself have a pilot's license hanging in his
stateroom. Neither was it considered good form to interfere with
the duties of his mate, or the engineers, or the chief clerk, in the
way of countermanding their orders when given in the line of
duty. He might call them to account in his office, and not only
caution, but command them not to repeat the error. Only in cases
where such interference was necessary for the safety of the boat
was it deemed permissible; and a captain who so far forgot himself
as to interfere, lost caste among all classes of rivermen, high and
low. Nevertheless, the "old man" had supreme power, and had
the authority to interpose his veto on any command or any action,
by any of his officers or men. This supremacy threw the burden
of responsibility upon his shoulders, and set him apart as a man
by himself.

The seat of power was in the forward part of the "Texas",
where a commodious and handsomely-furnished cabin served as
office, audience-room, sitting-room, and whenever he so willed, as
dining-room. Connected with it was a sleeping apartment, larger
and better furnished than the ordinary staterooms in the passenger
cabin. From the windows on the front and on two sides of his

sitting-room he could look out ahead, or on either side, and see everything that was going on. It was here that he entertained favored guests when in relaxation, or hetcheled contumacious officers when in tenser moods.

From his berth, directly under the pilot house, he could read the sounds of shuffling feet as the man on watch danced from side to side of his wheel; he could note the sounds of the bell-pulls, as signals were rung in the engine-room; and he could tell very nearly where the boat was at such times, and judge very cleverly as to the luck the pilot was having in running an ugly piece of river, or working out a crooked crossing. He could look out and see if his mate was asleep alongside the big bell, in the drowsy hours of the morning watch, if he cared to confirm a shrewd bet that the mate was asleep. He could tell by the roar of the forced draft in the tall chimneys in front of him, that there was another boat in sight, either ahead or behind, and that Billy Hamilton had the "blowers" on in response to a suggestion from Tommy Cushing, at the wheel, that an excess of steam was desirable, and that at once. This last was a perennial, or nocturnal, source of annoyance to our "Old Man", and one that wrung from him more protests than any other shortcoming under his command. It burned out more wood than was justified by the end attained; but what was of more serious import, it suggested the carrying of a greater head of steam than was consonant with perfect safety. At a time when boiler explosions were not infrequent on the Western rivers, any suggestion of extra steam-carrying was sufficient to put the "old man" on the alert; and this led to more interference with his officers than any other cause that came under my observation during my brief experience on the river. A scantily-clad apparition would appear on deck forward of the "Texas", and a request, "Mr. Cushing, please ask Mr. Hamilton to cut off the blowers", would be passed down the speaking tube to the engine-room. While it always came in the form of request, it carried with it the force of command — until it was concluded that the "old man" was again asleep, when the blowers were cautiously and gradually reopened.

While it was not always expected that the captain should take the place of the engineer or pilot, it was required that he should be thoroughly acquainted with the handling of a steamboat under all circumstances. He must be a man possessed of nerve and courage, quick to see what was required, and as quick to give the necessary commands to his crew. As on deeper water, the code of honor on the river held that the captain must be the last to leave his sinking or burning boat; and many a brave commander has gone down to honorable death while upholding this code. In case of fire he must, with the pilot, instantly decide where lay the greatest chances of safety in beaching his boat. In case of snagging, or being cut down by ice, it is his first duty to save his boat, if possible, by stopping the break, at the same time providing for the safety of his passengers by beaching her on the nearest sand-bar. In case of grounding — "getting stuck on a sand-bar", as it is popularly known — all his knowledge of every expedient to extricate his vessel known to river men is called in play at once. An hour's time, or even a few minutes, lost in trying cheap experiments, is sufficient to pile up the shifting sands about the hull to such an extent as sometimes to consume days, or even weeks, in getting free.

Our own boat, the "Fanny Harris", drifted upon a submerged bank on the lower side of the cut-off between Fevre River and Harris Slough, with a falling river. She did not get off that day, and within three days had less than a foot of water under some parts of her hull. Her freight had to be lightered, and then it took two steamboats, pulling on quadruple tackles, "luffed" together, to pull her into deep water. The power applied would have pulled her in two, had it come from opposite directions.

"Sparring off" was a science in itself. Just how to place your spars; in what direction to shove the bow of the boat; or whether to "walk her over" by setting the spars at a "fore and aft" angle, one on each side, and thus push the boat straight ahead — these were questions to be answered as soon as reports were received from the pilot who was sent out in the yawl to sound the whole bar. To a landsman, the use to which were to be put the great sticks of straight-grained, flawless yellow (or Norway) pine, standing on either side of the gangway, was quite unknown until the boat brought up on the sandy bottom of the river. Then, if it was the first time these timbers had been called into play that season, the lashings were cut away with a sharp axe; the detail from the crew sent to the roof eased away on the falls, until the derricks leaned forward at an angle of forty-five degrees. The crew on the forecastle overhauled the great four-by-five, or five-by-six ply falls, and hooked the lower block into the iron ring under the steamer's quarter, just above the load-line. This ring was attached to the hull by massive bolts, extending through several feet of timbers on the inside of the sheathing — the timbers running back the length of the hull, in well-built boats, so that with sufficiently solid footing for the spars, and with sufficient power, the steamer might be lifted bodily off the bar, without "hogging" the boat — the technical term for bending or breaking the hull out of shape.

When it was decided by a conference of the captain, the pilots, and the mate, or by the captain's judgment alone, in what direction the bow of the boat was to be thrown, the foot of the spar was shoved clear of the guards and lowered away by the derrick-fall until its foot was firmly fixed, and the spar at the proper angle, and in the proper direction. The hauling part of the tackle (or fall, as it is called) was then passed through a snatch-block and carried to the capstan, around the barrel of which six or seven turns were taken, and the best man in the crew given charge of the free end. If the case was a very bad one — if the boat was on hard — the double-purchase gear was put on the capstan, to give additional power, and steam was turned on the hoisting engine, (or "donkey") which also operated the capstan by a clutch gear. Ordinarily the boat quickly responded to all this application of power, was slowly pushed off the reef and headed for the channel, and the wheel was soon able to drive her ahead and away from the bar.

This taking care of the free end of the tackle as it came from the capstan, was a work of more importance than might appear to the novice. The barrel of the capstan is concave; the line feeds on to it at the thickest part, either at the top or the bottom of the capstan. After it reaches a certain point all the turns must slip down to the narrowest part, and the work of winding upward begin over. The man who is handling the free end of the line must often slack a little — just enough to start the slipping — and then hold hard, so that it may go down easily, without giving any further slack. It looks easy, but it isn't. I have seen a careless man give so much slack to his line, when there was a very heavy strain upon it — in fact when the whole weight of the forward end of the steamer was pendant upon the spar — that the recoil of the tackle, though not over an inch or two, would let the hull drop with a force that would almost shake the chimneys out of her, and could be felt the length of the boat. It was also a post of some danger, as I have heard of instances in which the recoil snapped the tackle, and severely injured the men under and about the spar and capstan.

The spars are shod with heavy iron points about a foot in length, which would grip the solid clay or gravel underlying the superficial layers of sand forming the bar. When there was "no bottom" to the sand, and the applied power, instead of lifting the steamer only shoved the spar into the quicksand, another footing was used — a block built of two three-inch sections of oak about eighteen inches in diameter, bound and crossed with iron, and having a hole in the centre through which the iron point of the spar was passed until the shoulder rested on the block. This block could not be driven deeply into the sand, and usually gave a secure footing. A rope attached to a ring in the block served to haul it out of the sand after the spar was hoisted aboard.

The spectacle afforded by the "sparring off" process was always one of great interest to the passengers, and of excitement to the officers and crew. There were drawbacks to this interest, however, when the passengers were in a hurry, and the boat lay for hours, sometimes for days, before being released, the crew working day and night without sleep, and with little time even to eat. We once lay three days on Beef Slough bar; and the "War Eagle" was eight days on the same bar, having been caught on a falling river, being only released after passengers and freight were transferred to other and lighter boats.

For the officers and crew, there was no halo about an incident of this kind. In low water, it was to some boats of almost daily occurrence, somewhere on the river, even with the most skilful pilots. The fact was, that there were places where there was not enough water in the channel for a boat to pass without striking; and if one got out of the channel by ever so little, it was of course still worse. There were several places where it was to be expected that the boat must be hauled over the reef by taking out an anchor ahead, or by hauling on a line attached to a tree on the bank, if the channel ran near enough to render the latter expedient possible.

I have injected this description of sparring off into the chapter devoted to the "Old Man", not because the process necessarily devolved upon him alone; but because as captain his will was law in any disputed point, and because upon him rested the responsibility of navigating his boat. He naturally took an active interest in the work, and was always on hand when it was done. But quite often the mate knew more of the *finesse* of poling a boat off a bar, than did the captain; and some captains were shrewd enough to give the mate practically full control, only standing on the roof for appearance sake, while the latter did the work. It was, however, every man's work, and if any one had a practical idea, or a practical suggestion, whether pilot, engineer, mate, or carpenter, it was quickly put to the test. The main thing was to get off the bar, and to get off "quick."

Chapter X

The Pilots and Their Work

We come now to the consideration of that part of river life of which I was an interested observer, rather than an active participant. Had not the great war burst upon the country, and the fever of railroad construction run so high, it is possible that I might have had my name enrolled in the list containing such masters of the profession as William Fisher, John King, Ed. West, Thomas Burns, Thomas Cushing, and a hundred others whose names were synonyms for courage, precision, coolness in danger, exact knowledge, ready resource, and all else necessary in the man who stood at the wheel and safely guided a great steamer through hundreds of miles of unlighted and uncharted river.

Compared with those days, the piloting of to-day, while still a marvel to the uninitiated, is but a primer compared to the knowledge absolutely necessary to carry a steamboat safely through and around the reefs, bars, snags, and sunken wrecks which in the olden time beset the navigator from New Orleans to St. Paul. The pilot of that day was absolutely dependent upon his knowledge of and familiarity with the natural landmarks on either bank of the river, for guidance in working his way through and over the innumerable sand-bars and crossings. No lights on shore guided him by night, and no "diamond boards" gave him assurance by day. No ready search-light revealed the "marks" along the shore. Only a perspective of bluffs, sometimes miles away, showing dimly outlined against a leaden sky, guided the pilot in picking his way over a dangerous crossing, where there was often less than forty feet to spare on either side of the boat's hull, between safety and destruction.

To "know the river" under those conditions meant to know absolutely the outline of every range of bluffs and hills, as well as every isolated knob or even tree-top. It meant that the man at the wheel must know these outlines absolutely, under the constantly changing point of view of the moving steamer; so that he might confidently point his steamer at a solid wall of blackness, and guided only by the shapes of distant hills, and by the mental picture which he had of them, know the exact moment at which to put his wheel over and sheer his boat away from an impending bank. To-day a thousand beacons are kindled every night to mark the dangerous or intricate crossings; by day, great white "diamond boards" spot the banks. At night the pilot has only to jingle a bell in the engine-room, the dynamo is started, and by pulling a line at either hand the search-light turns night into day, the big white board stands out in high relief against the leafy background, and the pilot heads for it, serene in the confidence that it is placed in line with the best water; for he knows that the government engineers have sounded every foot of the crossing within a date so recent as to make them cognizant of any change in its area or contour. Constantly patrolling the river, a dozen steamboats, fully equipped for sounding, measuring, and marking the channel, are in commission during the months of navigation, each being in charge of officers graduated from the most exacting military and technical school in the world, and having under them crews composed of men educated by practice to meet any emergency likely to arise. If a snag lodges in the channel it is reported at the nearest station, or to the first government steamer met, and within a few hours it is removed. Dams and shear-dykes direct the water in permanent, unshifting channels. Riprap holds dissolving banks, and overhanging trees are cut away. Millions of dollars have been spent in the work, and its preservation costs hundreds of thousands annually. All this outlay is to-day for the benefit of a scant score of steamboats between St. Louis and St. Paul. Forty years ago two hundred men, on a hundred boats, groped their way in darkness, amid known and unknown terrors, up and down the windings of the great river, without having for their guidance a single token of man's helpful invention.

There are men now living who may see all this vast expenditure utilized, as it is not now. The building of the inter-oceanic canal across the isthmus is certain to give new direction to the commerce of the world. It is fair to presume that the Mississippi may again assert itself as one of the greatest arteries of commerce in the world, and that the products of the Minnesota and Dakota farms will find their way down the river to New Orleans, instead of across the continent to New York, Boston, Philadelphia, and Baltimore tidewater. If this effect does follow the building of the canal, as many clear-headed students of economic problems predict, the Mississippi will again assume its old-time standing and influence as a great highway of commerce. The hope is at least father to this thought.

As already stated, my personal experience as a pilot was limited. It was confined to a few seasons' study of the river under one of the best men who ever turned a wheel upon it — Thomas Burns. By an agreement with him, I was to retain my clerkship, but was to spend as much as possible of my time in the pilot house, while on watch or off, either with himself or his partner, Thomas Cushing, steering for them in turn, and receiving instruction from both. Later I was to give all of my time, and after becoming proficient was to receive their recommendation for a license. I was then to pay to Captain Burns five hundred dollars from my first earnings, after getting a berth as a full-fledged pilot. Under these terms I received instruction from both men, and as opportunity offered acted as their wheelsman relieving them of much hard work.

This arrangement was ended by the breaking out of the War of Secession and the enlistment of Captain Burns in the army. He raised a company for the Forty-sixth Illinois Infantry, at Galena, taking about thirty men from the "Fanny Harris" alone. That was in August, 1861. Thomas Cushing then went down the river to try his fortune. Two new pilots came aboard, Jim Black and Harry Tripp, and I was left out of the pilot house. Later in the season the "Fanny Harris" was left so high on the bank of the cut-off between Fevre River and Harris Slough that the whole crew were discharged. It was necessary to build ways under the boat and launch her, in order to get her back into the water — a labor of weeks.

After a short time spent on the "Golden Era" I went up river and engaged with Charley Jewell, on the "H. S. Allen", Captain S. E. Gray, running between Prescott and St. Croix Falls. After a few trips I graduated as a pilot for that run, and conditionally

1   2

3   4

1.   DANIEL SMITH HARRIS.   Steamboat Captain, 1833-1861.

2.   CAPTAIN THOMAS BURNS.   Pilot on the Upper Mississippi River from 1856 to 1889.   Inspector of Steamboats under President Cleveland and President McKinley.

3.   CHARLES G. HARGUS.   Chief Clerk on the "Royal Arch," "Golden State," "Fanny Harris," "Kate Cassell" and many other fine steamers on the Upper Mississippi.

4.   GEORGE B. MERRICK.   "Cub" Pilot, 1862.

for the Galena and St. Paul run.   When the call for three hundred thousand additional troops came in August, 1862, I decided that it was my duty to go to the front and "put down the rebellion", as the "boys" of that time put it.   Acting upon this commendable resolve, I dropped off at Hudson, where I was well acquainted, and where several companies were organizing for the three years' service.   I enlisted in a company intended for the Twenty-fifth Wisconsin Infantry, of which Jeremiah Rusk was lieutenant-colonel; but when we came to be mustered in we were assigned to the Thirtieth Wisconsin Infantry, as Company A.

My idea was, that if I survived I would return and take up my work on the river where I left it.   That was the boy idea. It was not realized.   After three years of service I was mustered out in Washington, D. C.   I married in the East, and entered the employ of a steamship company in New York as agent and superintendent, remaining there until 1876.   Returning to Wisconsin in 1876 I found a half dozen railroads centring in St. Paul, and these were doing the business of the hundred steamboats that I had left running in 1862.   A dozen boats, confined to two lines, were handling all the river business between St. Louis and St. Paul, and the profession of piloting was at an end.   Of the hundred boats that I had known fourteen years before, not one remained.   The average life of a river steamboat was but five years.

Curiously enough, I had by this time lost all interest in river life, except the interest of a trained observer.   I enjoyed watching the few boats that chanced to come under my observation, and could appreciate fully the dexterity of the men who were holding their wheels in the pilot houses; but all my ambitions to again be one of them appeared to have evaporated, for other lines of work had engrossed my attention.   Engaging in the newspaper business, and later on adding the responsibility of the agency of a railroad company, I had enough to think about without pining for lost opportunities on the river.

The work accomplished by the old-time Mississippi pilot while guiding his steamer through hundreds of miles of water beset by snags, wrecks, and reefs, has been so fully described by "Mark Twain" in his *Life on the Mississippi,* that it would be temerity in any one else to attempt to add to what he has so humorously, and yet so graphically delineated.   It rarely occurs that a man combines a perfect knowledge of a profession so far removed from the world of letters as is that of piloting a steamboat with the literary skill to describe its details. It will probably never again happen that a great master in literature and humor will graduate from a pilot house.

The experiences of a pilot were the same, however, whether he turned a wheel on the lower river, as described by "Mark Twain", or on the upper river. It will not be plagiarizing, therefore, to tell something of the acquirements necessary in a pilot, even though the narrative coincides very closely with what he has recorded of similar experiences on the lower reaches.

Thomas Burns [3] had the reputation of being one of the most reliable pilots on the upper waters. He was a Scotchman, in middle life, without vices or failings of any kind, unless smoking may be a vice. It certainly wasn't so considered on the river, and for the sake of this story we will not consider it so here. He was conservative, and would not take any chances, even in a race, preferring to follow the deep water with safety, rather than cut corners involving risk to the boat and its cargo, even though a rival boat did pass him, or he was losing an opportunity to show off some fancy piloting. It was said of him that he was the only man who could and did steer a stern-wheel steamboat of four hundred tons through Coon Slough, downstream, without slowing or stopping the wheel — something requiring nerve and fine judg-

---

[3] Captain Thomas W. Burns was born in Boston, Massachusetts, in 1836. He removed with his parents to Galena, Illinois, in 1842, where he received his education in the public schools. After leaving school he went on the river as a "cub" pilot, and upon reaching the age of 21 years received his certificate as first-class pilot between St. Louis and St. Paul, in which capacity he served on many of the best boats of the Minnesota Packet Company, including the "War Eagle," "Key City," "Itasca," "Fanny Harris," "Kate Cassell," and others. In 1861 he recruited a company of steamboatmen at Galena, and was assigned to the 45th Illinois Infantry. He remained with his company until after the capture of Fort Henry, when he was discharged for disability. Upon his return to Galena he took up the work of piloting again, continuing until 1885, when he was appointed by President Cleveland to the office of United States Local Inspector of Steamboats, with headquarters at Galena. His long years of experience on the river, and his high sense of duty made him an excellent official, and upon the advent of a Republican administration he was re-appointed to the office, in which he was serving at the time of his death, March 4, 1890.

ment. A side-wheel boat usually went around the sharp bend with one paddle wheel backing and the other going ahead. A stern-wheel boat was often compelled to "flank" around the elbow, by backing against the point and letting the current swing the bow around the bend.

By the old reckoning, the distance from St. Louis to St. Paul, was eight hundred miles; from Rock Island to St. Paul, four hundred and fifty. The later survey, after straightening the channel by wing-dams and dikes, makes the distance seven hundred and twenty-nine miles from St. Louis, and three hundred and ninety-eight from Rock Island to St. Paul. It is safe to estimate a "crossing" in each and every mile of that river. Some miles may have missed their share, but others had a dozen, so the average was fully maintained. That was fifty years ago. There are less crossings now, but more dams and dikes — two hundred and fifty-one dams, dikes, and pieces of dikes in the little stretch of river between St. Paul and Prescott, a matter of thirty-six miles. If a pilot attempted to make a crossing now, where he made it fifty years ago, he would in five hundred different places butt his head into a dike instead of a reef.

Tom Burns, and scores of others like him, knew every rod of this river better than the average man knows any one mile of sidewalk between his home and his office. He knew it by day and by night. He knew it upstream and downstream — and this amounted literally to knowing two rivers eight hundred miles long, for the instant you turn your boat's prow down river you have entered an entirely new country. Every mark is different; the bold outlines of bluffs with which you are familiar as you go up the river, are as strangers when viewed from the reverse side. You have to learn the stream over again, and worse yet, you have to learn to handle your boat differently. A novice in the business might take a steamer from St. Louis to St. Paul with very fair success, while the same man would hang his boat up effectually on the first bar he came to, if in going down river he handled his wheel in the same manner. Coming upstream he might feel of a reef with the bow of his boat, and if he did not strike the best water the first time he could back off and try again; but going downstream he must hit the channel the first time or he is gone. The current is all the time irresistibly pushing his boat down the river, and if he strikes he is immediately, with the most disastrous consequences, swung broadside on to the reef. Tom Burns knew his river so well that he could jump from his berth on the darkest night and before he reached the pilot house door could tell what part of the river the boat was in; the instant his eye caught the jack staff he knew to a certainty what crossing the steamer was making, and on what part of the crossing she was at the moment. This was what every first-class pilot must, and did know. I use Burns only as an illustration.

It was courtesy for the relieved pilot to state the position of the boat as he relinquished the wheel to his partner: "Good morning, Mr. Cushing! A nasty night. She drags a little, to-night. Just making the upper Cassville crossing. Should have been farther up. Hope you'll have better luck." This was only a matter of form and politeness, and not at all necessary. Mr. Cushing or Mr. Burns knew at a glance that it was the upper Cassville crossing, and as he took the wheel from the hands of his retiring partner he did, the next instant, just what the other would have done had he continued. He saw the "swing" of the jack staff and met it; he felt the boat edging away from the reef, and coaxed her back, daintily but firmly, a spoke at a time, or possibly half a spoke. The continuity was not broken. The exact knowledge of the retiring pilot was simply carried along by the pilot coming on watch.

In all the hundreds of miles of river traversed by the boat in its voyage up or down, there could be no other combination of marks just like the one which met the pilot's eye as he grasped the wheel. The problem for the "cub" was to learn the combination. In the day time it was not customary for the retiring partner to mention where the boat was at the time. That would have been stretching the point of courtesy too far. All this, however, was between equals. When the wheel was turned over to the "cub", it was generally a prime necessity that he be advised as to the exact position of the boat. Thus primed, if he was reasonably advanced, he could take the wheel and with the clue given the river would shape itself in his mind, and he would pass from one set of marks to the next with some degree of certitude. Without the clue, however, it was possible to imagine one's self in a hundred probable or improbable places. "All bluffs look alike to me", might under such circumstances be set to music and sung with feeling and expression by the learner.

What the pilot must know to enable him to run the river at night, is strikingly suggested in the conversation between young "Mark Twain" and his chief, Mr. Bixby. When the boy had begun to take on airs as a pilot, his chief suddenly fired the question:

"What is the shape of Walnut Bend?"

Of course he did not know, and did not know that he must know.

Mr. Bixby: "My boy, you've got to know the shape of the river, perfectly. It is all there is left to steer by on a very dark night. Everything else is blotted out and gone. But mind you, it hasn't the same shape in the night that it has in the daytime".

"How on earth am I going to learn it, then?"

"How do you follow a hall at home in the dark? Because you know the shape of it. You can't see it."

"Do you mean to say I've got to know all the million trifling variations of the shape of the banks of this interminable river as well as I know the shape of the front hall at home?"

"On my honor you've got to know them *better* than any man ever did know the shapes of the halls in his own house. . . You see, this has got to be learned; there is no getting around it. A clear starlight night throws such heavy shadows that if you didn't know the shape of the shore perfectly, you would claw away from every bunch of timber, because you would take the black shadow of it for a solid cape; and you see you would be getting scared to death every fifteen minutes by the watch. You would be fifty yards from shore all the time when you ought to be within fifty feet of it. You can't see a snag in one of those shadows, but you know exactly where it is, and the shape of the river tells you when you are coming to it. Then there's your pitch-dark night; the river is a very different shape on a pitch-dark night from what it is on a starlight night. All shores seem straight lines then, and mighty dim ones, too; you'd run them for straight lines, only you know better. You boldly drive your boat into what seems to be a solid straight wall (you knowing very well that there is a curve there), and that wall falls back and makes way for you. Then there's your gray mist. You take a night when there's one of those grizzly gray mists, and then there isn't *any* particular shape to a shore. A gray mist would tangle the head of the oldest man that ever lived. Well, then, different kinds of *moonlight* change the shape of the river in different ways. You see —"

But the cub had wilted. When he came to his chief reassured him somewhat by replying to his objections:

"No! you only learn *the* shape of the river; and you learn it with such absolute certainty that you can always steer by the shape. That's in your head, and never mind the one that's before your eyes."

And that was approximately the case. The details of the river, once learned, were so indellibly printed on the mind of the pilot that it seemed as though eyes were almost superfluous. Of course Mr. Bixby stated the extreme case. While the pilot was running a bend "out of his head" in darkness that might be felt, there were always well-known landmarks to be seen — shapes of bluffs so indistinct as to seem but parts of the universal blackness. But these indistinct outlines were enough to confirm the judgment of the man at the wheel in the course he was steering. The man in the hall, in Mr. Bixby's illustration, could not see anything, and didn't know what hall he was in. He might just as well have been blind; and I never heard of a blind man running a steamboat, day or night. In the short experience that I had in the pilot house, I did not reach this perfection; but I have stood on one side of the wheel, mechanically following the orders of my chief, and listening to the churning of the wheel reëchoed from the banks not fifty feet away, when I could scarcely see the jack staff, and could not distinguish between the black of the woods and the all-pervading black of the night.

Mr. Burns or Mr. Cushing would translate the situation, as the boat plowed along under a full head of steam, somewhat like this: "Now we're going down into the bend. Now we're opposite the big cottonwood. Now we must pull out a little, to avoid that nest of snags. Now we will let her begin to come out; the water begins to shoal here; we'll keep away from the point a little, and cross over into the west bend, and follow that down in the opposite direction."

This in the way of instruction; and so far as my observation went he was drawing on his imagination for his facts, as I saw no big cottonwood, nor nest of snags, nor any point. The only thing that I could share with him in common was the fact that we were nearing the point and getting into shoaler water — the boat told me that. The floor under my feet seemed to hang back and drag; the motion of the paddle wheel was perceptibly retarded; the escape was hoarser from the pipes. I knew that there was shoal water on the point at the foot of the bend, and the boat herself told me when we had reached the point; but I had not seen it, either with my eyes, or in my head. Mr. Burns had it all in his head, and did not require to see it with his eyes. He simply ran the bend as he knew it to be; and he ran a hundred others in the same way.

What might happen to any one who ran by sight, and not by faith, was illustrated in the case of a young pilot on the "Key City", of our line. He had his papers, and was standing watch alone in the pilot house. He was going downstream. In going into Lansing, Iowa, one runs a long bend on the left-hand shore. At Lansing the river turns sharply to the south, from a nearly westerly course. Just at the turn, and fronting the river toward the east, is a solid limestone bluff four hundred feet high. On a starlit night the shadow of this bluff is thrown out upon the river so far as totally to obliterate the water, and for several minutes one must point his boat straight into an apparently solid bluff before he "opens out" the turn to the left. On the night in question the young man forgot to run by what he knew to be the shape of the river, and trusted to what his eyes showed him. He lost his head completely, and instead of stopping both wheels and backing away from the impending doom, he put his wheel hard over and plumped the "Key City" into the alluvial bank of the island opposite, with such force as to snatch both chimneys out of her, and very nearly to make a wreck of the steamer.

I have myself been tempted to run away from the same bluff; and but for confidence inspired by the presence of one of the pilots, might have done so. Mr. Burns drilled his "cubs" upon one point, however, which made for the safety of the boat: "When in doubt, ring the stopping bell and set her back." There was no place of safety to run to in a panic on the Mississippi, and a boat standing still was less likely to hurt herself or any one else than one in motion.

In no other particular, perhaps, has the art of piloting been so revolutionized as in the adoption of the electric search-light for night running. Time and again have I heard the question asked by people new to the river: "Why don't you hang up two or three lanterns at the front end of the boat, so that you can see to steer?"

It is easy to answer such a question convincingly. Go out into the woods on a very dark night with an ordinary lantern. How far can you see by such a light? Perhaps thirty feet; twenty feet would probably be nearer the mark. Until a light was discovered that could project its rays a half mile or more, and so concentrated as clearly to reveal landmarks at that distance, the other extreme, no light at all, was not only desirable, but positively necessary if the boat was to be kept going.

After long usage, a pilot's eyes came to possess powers common to the cat family and other night prowlers. He could literally "see in the dark"; but he could not see in any half light, or any light artificial and close at hand. For this reason it was necessary to cover every light on the boat while running on a very dark night, save the red and green side-lights at the chimney-tops. To accomplish this, heavy canvas "shrouds" or "mufflers" were provided, which fitted snugly around the forward part of the boat, in front of the furnaces on the main deck; another set were placed around the boiler deck, in front of the cabin; and still another set to muffle the transom sky-lights on the hurricane deck. When these were properly fitted and triced up, there was not a ray of light projected forward, to break the dead blackness ahead. So delicate was this sense of night sight, that no one was permitted to smoke a pipe or cigar in the pilot house at such times, and even the mate, sitting by the bell down on the roof below, had to forego his midnight pipe. As for the pilot himself, a cigar in front of his nose would have shut off his sight as effectively as though he were blindfolded.

Of course, were the pilot looking only ten feet, or even forty feet, ahead of his boat, the lights on board might not have interfered greatly, although they would not have assisted him in the slightest. You can not steer a boat by landmarks ten feet ahead of her. The pilot searches for landmarks a mile away, and must be able to distinguish between two kinds of blackness — the blackness of the night below, and the blackness of the sky above, and from the dividing line between the two must read his marks and determine his course. He does not see the woods on either side of him, and often close at hand. The least ray of artificial light would blind the pilot to the things which he must see under such conditions, hence the shrouding of the boat was a necessity, were she to be run at all on such a night. The coming of the electric search-light, and the transfer of the marks from distant bluffs to big white diamond boards planted low down on the banks where the light can be flashed upon them from a distance of half a mile or more, has greatly simplified the work of the pilot, and rendered obsolete the curtains which once so completely darkened the Mississippi steamboat on the blackest of nights.

Chapter XI

Knowing the River

To "know the river" fully, the pilot must not only know everything which may be seen by the eye, but he must also feel for a great deal of information of the first importance which is not revealed to the eye alone. Where the water warrants it, he reaches for this information with a lead line; as on the lower river, where the water is deeper, and the draft of boats correspondingly great. On the upper river, a twelve-foot pole answers instead. The performance is always one of great interest to the passengers; the results are often of greater interest to the man at the wheel. The manner in which the reports of the leadsman are received and digested by the pilot, is not usually known to or comprehended by the uninitiated. The proceeding is picturesque, and adds one more "feature" to the novelties of the trip. It is always watched with the greatest interest by the tourist, and is apparently always enjoyed by them, whatever the effect upon the pilot; whether he enjoys it or not depends on the circumstances.

Soundings are not always necessarily for the immediate and present purpose of working the boat over any particular bar, at the particular time at which they are taken, although they may be taken for that purpose and no other. In general, during the season of low water, the leads are kept going in all difficult places as much for the purpose of comparison as for the immediate purpose of feeling one's way over the especial reef or bar where the soundings are taken. If it is suspected that a reef is "making down", the pilot wants to satisfy himself on that point, so that he may readjust his marks to meet the changed outlines. If a reef is "dissolving", he also wants to know that, and readjust his marks accordingly — only in the first place, his marks will be set lower down the river; in case of a dissolving reef, his marks will be set farther upstream, to follow the deep water which is always found close under the reef — that is, on the down-stream side. The shallowest water is always on the crest of the reef, and it "tapers" back, upstream, very gradually, for rods — sometimes for half a mile or even more, until another reef is reached, with deep water under it, and another system of shallows above.

This is where the perfection of the pilot's memory machine is demonstrated along another line. He has acquainted himself with every bluff, hill, rock, tree, stump, house, woodpile, and whatever else is to be noted along the banks of the river. He has further added to this fund of information a photographic negative in his mind, showing the shape of all the curves, bends, capes, and points of the river's banks, so that he may shut his eyes, yet see it all, and with such certainty that he can, on a night so perfectly black that the shore line is blotted out, run his boat within fifty feet of the shore and dodge snags, wrecks, overhanging trees, and all other obstacles by running the shape of the river as he knows it to be — not as he can see it. In sounding, he is mentally charting the bottom of the river as he has already charted the surface and its surroundings.

As he approaches the crossing which he wishes to verify, he pulls the rope attached to the tongue of the big bell on the roof, and sounds one stroke, and an instant later two strokes. The captain or mate on watch sings out: "Starboard lead!" "Larboard lead!" and the men detailed for the duty are at their stations in a minute or less after the order is given. Then the cry, first from starboard and then from port, long-drawn and often musical: "No-o-o bottom; no-o-o bottom!" rises from the fo'c'sle, and is repeated by the captain or mate to the pilot. "Mar-r-k twain, mar-r-r-k twain!" indicates soundings the depth of the sounding pole — twelve feet, or two fathoms. This is of no interest to the pilot, for he knew there was "no bottom" and "two fathoms" before the soundings were taken. It is of the highest interest to the passengers, however, to whom the cry of "no bottom" seems a paradox, when the boat has been rubbing the bottom most of the way from Rock Island up. They have not yet been taught that this simply means no bottom with a twelve-foot pole, and does not indicate that the Mississippi is a bottomless stream at this or any other point.

On the upper river, the cry of "ten feet, eight and a half", or even "six feet", does not strike any sensitive spot in the pilot's mental machinery, for upper river men are used to running "where there is a heavy dew". On such occasions he might listen to the latest story, detailed by a visiting comrade, and even take part in the conversation, apparently indifferent to the monotonous cries from the lower deck. But all the time his brain is fitting the leadsman's cries to the marks in which the cries have found his boat — not consciously, perhaps, but nevertheless surely. He has not only fitted the cry into the marks, but has mentally compared the present with the depth of water cried at the same spot last trip, and the trip before that, and noted the change, if any has taken place. Say the leadsman has sung "six feet", "six feet", "six feet", six feet", "six feet", until you would think there was no other depth but six feet in the river; then in the same tone he sings "five and a half", "six feet", "six feet", "six feet". The pilot is still talking with his visitor, watching his marks and turning his wheel; but he has picked out that "five-and-a-half" and stored it away for future reference, together with all the surroundings of his boat at the instant the call reached his ear — the marks ahead, astern, and on either side. The next trip, as the leadsman sings "six feet", "six feet", "six feet", he will be shocked and grievously disappointed if he does not find his "five-and-a-half" at just that point. And he will not be counting the "six feet" cries, nor, possibly, will he be aware that he is looking for the "five-and-a-half". When he drops into the marks where the "five-and-a-half" found him last week, if he hears only the "six feet", he will be in a similar frame of mind to the man who, coming into town, misses a prominent tree or house, and asks: "Where is that big tree that stood on the corner, when I was here last time"?

The pilot does all this without realizing that he is making any mental effort. When he begins this sort of drill as a "cub", he realizes it fully; and if he is half sharp he will open an account with every shoal place between Rock Island and St. Paul, and set down in writing the soundings on the lowest place on each reef, and try to supply the marks in which his steamer lay when the cry was heard. As he grows in his studies he will rely less on his notebook and more upon his memory, until the mental picture of the bottom of the river becomes as vivid as that of the surface.

Then, when his chief asks suddenly: "How much water was there on the middle crossing at Beef Slough last trip"? he can answer promptly: "Four feet on starboard, four feet scant on port".

"How much trip before last?"

"Four feet large, both sides."

"Right, my boy; you're doing well."

If that "cub" doesn't grow an inch in a minute, under these circumstances, he isn't the right kind of boy to have around.

Naturally the boys studied the "nightmares", first of all. If they could get over Cassville, Brownsville, Trempealeau, Rollingstone, Beef Slough, Prescott, Grey Cloud, and Pig's Eye, they could manage all the rest of the river. But the leads were kept going in fifty other places which, while not so bad, had enough possibilities to warrant the closest watching. The chiefs were making mental notes of all these places, and could tell you the soundings on every crossing where a lead had been cast, as readily as the "cubs" could recite the capital letter readings of Beef Slough and Pig's Eye. The miracle of it was, how they could do this without giving any apparent attention to the matter at the time. They struck the bell, the leadsman sang, the mate or captain repeated the cries mechanically, while the pilot appeared to pay little or no attention to the matter. When he had enough of the music he tapped the bell to lay in the leads, and nothing was said as to the results. Yet if asked at St. Paul by a brother pilot how much water he found on any one of a hundred crossings of average depth, he could tell, without hesitation, just where he found the lowest cast of the lead.

In my experience as a printer I have stood at the case and set up an editorial out of my head (how "able" I will not pretend to say), at the same time keeping up a spirited argument on politics or religion with a visitor. The thinking appeared to be all devoted to the argument; it was probably the talking only. To set the type required no thought at all; that was purely mechanical; and to compose the editorial was the unconscious operation of the mind, accustomed to doing just this sort of thing, until the framing of words into sentences became more or less mechanical. Certainly the mental drill of a river pilot along a very few lines, developed a memory for the things pertaining to his profession which was wonderful, when you sit down and attempt to analyze it. To the men themselves it was not a wonder — it was the merest commonplace. It was among the things which you must acquire before you could pilot a steamboat; and for a consideration they would covenant to teach any boy of average mental ability and common sense all these things, provided always that he had the physical ability to handle a wheel, and provided also, that he demonstrated in time of trial that he had the "nerve" necessary for the business. A timid, cowardly, or doubting person had no business in the pilot house. If it were possible for him to acquire all the rest, and he lacked the nerve to steady him in time of danger, he was promptly dropped out of the business.

I saw this illustrated in the case of a rapids pilot between St. Paul and St. Anthony. We always made this trip when a cargo of flour was offered by the one mill which in that early day represented all there was of that great interest which now dominates the business of Minneapolis. While our pilots were both capable of taking the boat to St. Anthony and back, the underwriters required that we should take a special pilot for the trip — one who made a specialty of that run. On the occasion in point we had taken an unusually heavy cargo, as the river was at a good stage. At that time the channel was very crooked, winding about between reefs of solid rock, with an eight to ten mile current. It required skilful manipulation of the wheel to keep the stern of the boat off the rocks. In going downstream it is comparatively easy to get the bow of a steamer around a crooked place; it is not easy to keep the stern from swinging into danger. In this case the stern of the steamer struck a rock reef with such force as to tear one of the wing rudders out by the roots, in doing which enough noise was made to warrant the belief that half the boat was gone. The special pilot was satisfied that such was the case, and exclaimed: "She is gone!" at the same time letting go the wheel and jumping for the pilot house door. She would have been smashed into kindlings in a minute if she had been left to herself, or had the engines been stopped even for an instant. Fortunately the rapids pilot was so scared by the noise of rending timbers and wheel-buckets that he did not have nerve enough left to ring a bell, and the engineer on watch was not going to stop until a bell was rung, as he knew that the drift of a minute in

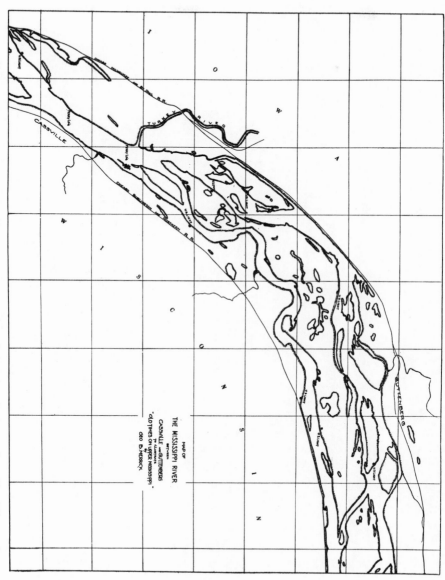

TYPICAL PORTION OF THE UPPER MISSISSIPPI. Map of the river between Cassville, Wis., and Guttenberg, Iowa, showing the characteristic winding of the stream.

that white water, would pile us up on the next reef below. Fortunately for the "Fanny Harris", Tom Cushing was in the pilot house, as well as myself. When the other man dropped the wheel Cushing jumped for it, and fired an order to me to get hold of the other side of the wheel, and for the next six miles he turned and twisted among the reefs, under a full head of steam, which was necessary to give us steerageway in such a current. We never stopped until we reached St. Paul, where we ran over to the west shore, it being shallow, and beached the boat. When she struck land the captain took the special pilot by the collar and kicked him ashore, at the same time giving him the benefit of the strongest language in use on the river at that time. Beyond the loss of a rudder and some buckets from the wheel, the boat was not seriously damaged, and we continued the voyage to Galena as we were. Had Tom Cushing not been in the pilot house at the time, she would have been a wreck in the rapids a mile or so below St. Anthony Falls. The rapids pilot lost his certificate.

Chapter XII

The Art of Steering

Every pilot must of necessity be a steersman; but not every steersman is of necessity a pilot. He may be studying to become a pilot, and not yet out of the steersman stage. "Cubs" begin their studies by steering for their chiefs. Many boys become quite expert in handling a boat, under the eyes of their chiefs, before they are sufficiently acquainted with the river to be trusted alone at the wheel for any length of time.

At first thought, one might imagine a number of favorable conditions as prerequisite to the ideal in steering: a straight piece of river, plenty of water, and an average steamboat. These would indeed guarantee leaving a straight wake; but under such conditions a roustabout might accomplish this. The artistic quality is developed in the handling of a boat under the usual conditions — in making the multitudinous crossings, where the jack staff is continually swinging from side to side as the boat is dodging reefs and hunting the best water. In doing this, one man puts his wheel so hard down, and holds it so long, that he finds it necessary to put the wheel to the very opposite to check the swing of the boat and head it back to its proper course, in which evolution he has twice placed his rudder almost squarely across the stern of his boat. If this athletic procedure is persevered in at every change of course, it will materially retard the speed of the steamer and leave a wake full of acute angles, besides giving the steersman an unnecessary amount of work.

The skilled steersman, combining his art with his exact knowledge of the bottom of the river, will give his boat only enough wheel to lay her into her "marks", closely shaving the points of the reefs and bars, and will "meet her" so gradually and so soon as to check the swing of the jack staff at the exact moment when

THE ART OF STEERING

the "marks" are reached. There is then no putting the wheel over to bring the boat back, after having overreached her marks, and the rudders have at no time been more than a quarter out of line with the hull of the boat. It is this delicate handling of the wheel, which differentiates between the artist and the athlete.

Steamboats have their individuality, the same as pilots and steersmen. There are boats (or have been), that would almost steer themselves, while there are others so perverse and tricky that no one could feel sure of keeping them in the river for any consecutive two miles. The "Ocean Wave" was, perhaps, the most unreliable and tricky of all the craft on the upper river — or any river. In low water no one man ever thought of standing a watch alone at the wheel, and at times she would run away with two men at the wheel. She was short, "stubby", and narrow; and when she smelt a reef she would, unless very carefully handled, under a slow bell, run away from it, often with one paddle wheel backing while the other was coming ahead, and the rudder standing squarely across the stern. Many times she has plumped into the bank under these conditions, and nothing less than the bank would stop her. The "City Belle", the "Favorite", and the "Frank Steele" were built much like the "Ocean Wave", but were not quite so unreliable in steering. She was in a class by herself. On the other hand, the "Key City", one of the largest, longest, and finest of the up-river packets, was so well-balanced, and her hull so finely moulded, that it was a delight to handle her, even under otherwise unfavorable conditions, such as low water, or high winds.

A stern-wheel boat going downstream when the wind was blowing up the river, was about as helpless a craft to handle as could well be imagined. After she was once "straightened down" she was all right; but in attempting to get her nose pointed down river, after having made a landing, there were more profane possibilities than the uninitiated ever dreamed of. The current, acting on the stern of the boat and the partially-submerged wheel, was all the time pulling that end of the boat downstream; while the wind, acting upon the tall chimneys and the pilot house and "Texas", was at the same time pushing the bow of the boat upstream; and the pilot was all the while endeavoring to reverse this position, and get the bow of his boat pointed in the direction in which he wished to go. It sometimes took hours to accomplish this, particularly if caught in places where the river was narrow and correspondingly swift, and the wind strong and contrary. The only way to swing a stern-wheel boat was, to put the steering wheel hard over, throwing the four rudders as far to one side as possible, and then back strongly against them. Under this leverage if there was no wind, the boat would swing easily and promptly, until her head was pointed downstream; and then by coming ahead and gaining steerageway, the boat was under perfect control. But when the wind was blowing upstream, it was often found impracticable to back fast and far enough to gain the necessary momentum to swing her in a narrow place; the engines would have to be stopped before the boat was swung to more than a right angle with the river, and then, before steerageway was gained after coming ahead, the bow of the boat would again be pointing upstream, and the same performance would have to be gone through with — sometimes a dozen or twenty times, before the boat would get under way in the proper direction.

In 1881 I saw Henry Link, after having made a landing at Newport, back the "Mary Morton", of the Diamond Jo Line, more than five miles down the river, she having swung stern-down at that place. He see-sawed back and forth across the stream, first in one direction and then in another, and failed at last to swing his boat against the strong south wind which was blowing. He finally gave it up and ran ashore, and getting out a line to a big tree, backed his craft around until her bow was pointed downstream, and then made a start from a broadside position against the bank. I happened to be a passenger on the boat at the time. His remarks on that occasion were unprintable. A side-wheel boat, under the same conditions, would have backed out into the river, come ahead on one wheel while backing on the other, and in two or three minutes would have been going full speed ahead on the desired course. That is the beauty of the independent side-wheel system. It is a great saving of labor and morality for the steersman, and a great saving of time for the owners.

It would seem that if you could get the bow of your boat clear of the bank, or of an overhanging tree, after pointing in pretty close, that the rest of the boat would follow the bow and

likewise come out, without any undue intimacy with the trees
or bank. It takes only one trial to disabuse a beginner of this
notion. The balance of the boat does not follow the bow out of
such a position; and while every pilot knows the immutable
laws of physics which operate upon his boat under such circumstances, most of them, sooner or later, get caught, either through
carelessness or recklessness, just as the green cub does through
ignorance.

In running downstream, when you point into the bank, and
shave it closely, you pull the bow of the boat away, and then
there are two forces over which you have no control with your
steering wheel: the impetus of the after half of your boat is still
in the direction of the bank, after the forward half has begun
to swing away; which would also be the case in a perfectly dead
lake. In the river, you have the second force in the current
which is pressing against the whole of the hull, but more particularly against the after part, and this is pushing the boat in
toward the bank after you have pulled her bow away from it.
The result is, that while you may clear the bank with the bow
of the boat, the stern swings in and gets the punishment.

Because of these two laws of physics, it was almost impossible
to run a stern-wheel boat around the sharp bend in Coon Slough,
a feat which "Tom" Burns performed several times without
stopping a wheel. "Jack" Harris tried it with the big side-
wheeler, the "Northern Light", late in the fall, when the anchor
ice was running. Her bow got around all right; but her stern
swung into the ice which had lodged in the bend, with the result
that the whole stern was torn away, and she sank in twenty
feet of water. "Ned" West tried a similar experiment at Dayton
Bluff, just below St. Paul, with the "Key City". He ran in very
close to the rocky shore, under full headway. He got her head
out in good shape, but the stern struck the rocks, tearing out the
rudder and smashing the deadwood. He worked her back to
St. Paul with the wheels alone, and there the damage was repaired.
I doubt if he was even reprimanded, for he was the "fastest"
pilot on the upper river, as well as one of the best, and getting
eight hundred dollars a month for his services. He could get
a boat over the course from St. Louis to St. Paul, in less time
than any other pilot could take the same boat, and that of course

carried with it the supposition that he knew the river as well as any man.

I learned the lesson myself through inattention. I was well acquainted with the principle through precept, and had been very careful not to run too near the bank. Coming down from St. Croix Falls with the "H. S. Allen", on reaching the mouth of the Apple River, I saw a school of black bass lying on the white sandy bottom where the Apple River empties into the St. Croix. The inflow from Apple River sets almost squarely across the St. Croix, and when the former is in flood the current sets nearly across the channel. To meet it, it is necessary to point toward the incoming current, to prevent being thrown against the opposite bank. Being an ardent fisherman I was deeply interested in the scores of fine fish plainly distinguishable from the height of the pilot house. The result was inevitable. I neglected to point the bow of the boat sufficiently against the inflow, and she took a sheer for the opposite bank the instant she struck the cross current. I pulled the wheel hard over in an instant, and got the bow clear of the overhanging timber, but the stern went under, and when it came out the "H. S. Allen" lacked two escape pipes and half of the washroom and laundry. The stewardess herself was short about half her senses, and all her temper. The captain had seen the same trick performed by older and better pilots than myself, and was not unduly distressed. It took about one hundred dollars to make the boat presentable. I did not tell about the black bass for some time after the incident occurred — long enough after so that there would be no obvious connection between the fish and the missing laundry.

The man who has once mastered the art of steering a steamboat on Western waters, never loses his love for it. Whatever may have been his occupation after leaving the river, his hands instinctively reach out for the wheel if fortune so favors him as to place the opportunity within his reach. I mean, of course, the man who sees and feels more than the mere turning of the wheel so many hours a day, for so much money to be paid at the completion of his task. It may be work, and hard work, for the enthusiast as well as for the hireling; but with the man who puts his spirit into the task, it is work ennobled by painstaking devotion, and glorified by the realization of work artistically and lovingly done.   To such a man there is an exhilaration about the handling of a big steamboat in the crooked channels of the Great River, akin to that felt by the accomplished horseman when guiding a spirited team of roadsters, or that of the engineer, holding the throttle of a great locomotive rushing over the rails at a speed of sixty miles an hour.   However long the hands of the horseman or the engineer may have been divorced from reins or throttle, there is the same longing to grasp the one or the other when the opportunity offers.   It is a wholly natural craving of the inner being; and however inexplicable it may be, it is there.

For forty years, since leaving the river for other pursuits, often harassing and full of care, I have dreamed, time and again, of holding a wheel on one of the old-time boats on which I served as a boy.   In my sleep I have felt again the satisfaction in work well done, the mortification of failure, and have felt again the cares and responsibilities that weighed so heavily when beset with difficulties and dangers.   It is all as real as though I again stood at the wheel, doing real work, and achieving real victories over besetting difficulties and dangers.   Mere work, as a means of earning a living, would not take such hold upon one's nature. It is the soul of the artist incarnate in the pilot.

Chapter XIII

An Initiation

I have said that in addition to "knowing the river", and knowing that he knows it, the young pilot must also be fortified with a large measure of self-reliance, or all else will go for nothing. The time of trial comes to every one, sooner or later, and the manner in which it is met usually determines the standing of the young novitiate in the estimation of river men. The reputation of every man on the river is common property the length of his run, from St. Louis to St. Paul. It was proverbial that river men "talked shop" more than any others, in those early days, probably because they were more interested in their own business than they were in that of other men. Possibly because, as one government engineer stated it, they didn't know anything else. However, the doings of all the river men were pretty thoroughly discussed sooner or later, from the latest dare-devil exhibition of fancy piloting by "Ned" West, to the mistakes and mishaps of the youngest "cub". Sooner or later, each and all were served up at the casual meetings of river men, at whatever port they might foregather.

My own "baptism" — not of "fire", but of water and lightning — came on the very first trip I made alone on a steamboat. I had been running with Charley Jewell on the "H. S. Allen", from Prescott to St. Croix Falls. Mr. Jewell fell sick and was laid off at Prescott. On the levee, the day he went home, was a steamboat load of rope, rigging, boats, and camp-equipage, together with a couple of hundred raftsmen landed from a down-river packet that did not care to make the run up the lake. The disembarked men were anxious to reach Stillwater with their cargo, that night. Our regular starting time, as a United States mail boat, was at 7 o'clock in the morning. They offered extra compensation if we would take them up that night, and the proposition was accepted by Captain Gray. All hands were set to work loading the stuff. I felt quite elated at the prospect, as it was a bright evening, and I felt sure of finding my way, for there were only three or four close places to run in the thirty miles of lake navigation between Prescott and Stillwater.

We got everything aboard, and I backed her out and started up the lake. There had been some lightning in the north, where there was a bank of low-lying clouds. So far away were they, apparently, that no one thought of a storm, certainly not a serious one. We were running toward it, however, and as we soon discovered, it was coming to meet us at a rattling pace. We met when about six miles above Prescott. First a terrific wind out of the north, followed by torrents of rain, and incessant lightning, which took on the appearance of chain-mail as it shimmered and glittered on the falling rain drops. I put up the breast-board, and let down the head-board as far as I could and still leave room between to look out ahead; but the fierce wind drove the rain in sheets into the pilot house, and in a minute's time I was completely soaked. The lightning and thunder were terrifying in brilliancy and in sharpness of sound, the flash and the report coming so closely together as to leave no doubt that the bolts were getting seriously close to the smokestacks. The pilot house was not the place I would have chosen from which to enjoy these effects, had I my choice. The place I really longed for was somewhere down below, where I would have felt less conspicuous as a target.

I managed to work my way around the Kinnickinnic bar, and made the run up to the Afton (or "Catfish") bar, around which the channel was quite narrow and wofully crooked. Thus far, the high banks had sheltered us somewhat from the wind. Here, however, the low-lying prairie came down to the water's edge. The sweep of the wind was terrific, while the downpour of rain was such that at times it was impossible to see any landmarks a hundred feet away. Captain Gray, wrapped in his storm clothes, who had, since the tempest broke, staid on the roof, one eye on the banks, when he could see them, and the other on the young man at the wheel, finally called up and wanted to know if I did not think we had better feel our way ashore and tie up until the storm abated, even at the risk of being late in getting back to Prescott to take up our regular trip in the morning. I was shivering so that my teeth chattered, and the captain would have been fully justified in assuming that I was shaking as much from fear as from cold. I had a deal of pride in those days, however, and a fair allowance of inherited courage, with perhaps a dash of pig-headedness. I did not wish to have it bulletined from one end of the river to the other that the first time I was left in charge of a steamboat, I had hunted a tree to tie up to because it happened to thunder and rain a little. That would have been the popular version of the incident, in any case. I replied, therefore, that if Captain Gray would send his waiter up with a glass of brandy, I would take the steamer to Hudson levee before taking out a line, and from there to Stillwater and back to Prescott in time for our morning run. The captain said nothing, then or thereafter, but sent his "boy" up with the brandy. This was applied inwardly, and served to take the chill off.

Thus fortified — temperance people will please not be horrified at this depravity of a nineteen-year-old novice, under such extraordinary provocation — I worked around "Catfish" and followed along the west shore as far as Lakeland. From Lakeland across the lake to the Hudson levee, is about three-quarters of a mile. It was still blowing a gale, and the rain came down in torrents, so that the opposite shore could not be seen — in fact one could not distinguish an object ten rods ahead. I had felt my way along, sometimes under the "slow bell", until the present. I must now cut loose from the west shore, and make the crossing to Hudson. There was plenty of water everywhere; but I could not see any landmarks on the opposite side of the lake. I got a stern bearing, however, and headed across. In a minute's time I could see nothing, either ahead or astern, and having no compass I had to rely on the "feel" of the rudders to tell me which way she was swinging. As it turned out, this was of little value, owing to the strength of the wind. For five minutes I ran under full head, and then slowed, trying to get a glimpse of the east bank, and "find myself". When I did, the "H. S. Allen" was headed squarely down the lake, and fully a mile below the Hudson landing. The force of the wind on the chimneys had turned her bow down-wind and downstream. As the rain began to slacken and I could see my marks, it took but a few minutes to straighten her up and make the run to the landing.

On leaving Hudson there were two ways of running the big bar opposite and below the mouth of Willow River. One, the longest, was to cross back to Lakeland and then run up the west shore — all of it straight work. The other, was to run squarely out into the middle of the lake, turn north and run half a mile, then quartering west-north-west across the lake to the opposite shore. This crossing saved a mile or more of steaming over the other course; but it was crooked and narrow, and the possibility of hanging up was much greater. Captain Gray asked me, when backing out, which crossing I would make. I replied that I was going to take the upper to save time. He said nothing, but again took his place by the bell. He made no suggestion, nor offered any opinion as to my decision. That was a part of the river etiquette, which he adhered to even in the case of a boy; for which I sincerely thanked him in my inner being, while accepting it outwardly quite as a matter of course — which it would have been, with an older and more experienced man at the wheel.

I made the crossing without calling for leads, or touching bottom, and the rest of the way was easy. When we made Still-water the stars were out, and the storm-clouds hung low on the southern horizon. I went below and got into dry clothes, and had a few hours sleep while the freight was being put ashore. Along about two o'clock in the morning I started back, with the mate on the roof. In confidence he confided to me the gratifying news that the "old man says you're all right. He says that you've got nerve enough to last you through". As "nerve" was one of the things needed in the business, I was certainly proud that my night's work, alone on a heavily-loaded boat, in one of the worst of storms, had given me a standing with the "old man"; and I felt reasonably certain that his report would carry weight among the river men who might chance to discuss the merits of the young "cub", and his equipment for serious work.

I may, I hope, be pardoned for dwelling at such length upon an incident of such common occurrence on the river as to attract little or no attention when the man at the wheel was an old and experienced pilot. But this was my "trying-out" time, which made a difference. Even if no one else ever gave the incident a second thought, I should have felt the shame of it to this day, had I "craw-fished" on that first trial.

I have never seen or heard anything to compare with the storms we used to have on the river. The river men had a theory of their own — not very scientific, and probably without foundation in fact — that the vapors from the lowlands and islands formed clouds which were more than ordinarily charged with electricity. *Why* they should be more highly charged than vapors arising from lowlands or islands elsewhere, they did not attempt to explain, and could not had they attempted. The fact remains, that our thunder storms were something out of the ordinary, and were so regarded by people from the East who experienced them for the first time. Many steamboats were struck by lightning, but few were burned, the electrical bolt being diffused through the iron of the boilers and machinery, and finding ready escape through the water-wheel shafts into the river. I have heard it stated that engineers have often received serious shocks from bolts thus passing from the chimneys to the water, by way of the machinery, but I never heard of one being killed. I do know that when these pyrotechnics were going on, the engineers kept their hands off the throttle-wheel, except in cases of dire necessity. The pilot was seemingly in more, but really less danger than the engineers. However, under such circumstances, a man had to hang on to his nerve as well as his wheel; and I doubt if many pilots ever became so hardened as not to feel "creepy" when the storm was on.

Chapter XIV

Early Pilots

"How did the first steamboats find their way up the hundreds of miles of water heretofore unbroken by steam-driven wheel?" No voice out of the past will give an answer to this query. The imagination of the trained pilot, however, needs no written page to solve the problem of how it might have been done; and he can picture to himself the satisfaction, akin to joy, of the man at the wheel, picking his way amid the thousand islands and snag-infested channels innumerable, guided only by his power to read the face of the water, and his knowledge of the basic principles that govern the flow of all great rivers. Standing thus at his wheel, with new vistas of stream and wood and bluff opening to him as he rounded each successive bend, choosing on the instant the path as yet uncharted; unhampered by time-honored "landmarks", with "all the world to choose from", none might be so envied as he. But we will never know who had this pleasure all his own.

In thus picturing the passage of pioneer steamboats up the Mississippi, there is danger that we may inject into the scene the image of the modern floating palace, with her three decks, her tall chimneys, her massive side-wheels, her "Texas", and her pilot house, fully equipped with spars, gang planks, jack staff, and all the paraphernalia of the beautiful and speedy "packets" of our day. Upon no such craft, however, did the early navigators pick their way into the solitudes of the upper river. Their boats were little better than the keel boats which they superseded — in fact they were keel boats operated by steam. The cargo-box afforded shelter for passengers, merchandise, and machinery. There was no pilot house in which to stand, fifty feet above the water, from that height to study the river bottom. The steersman stood at the stern, and manipulated his tiller by main strength and awkwardness, while the captain stood at the bow and studied the river, and gave his orders to "port" or "starboard", as the case required. As the boat drew less than three feet of water, the necessity for fine judgment in choosing the channel was not as necessary as in guiding a craft drawing twice as much. Nevertheless, it did call for judgment and decision; and these qualities were inherent in the men who made the navigation of Western waters their occupation in the early decades of the nineteenth century.

Long years before the advent of steam, the fur-traders of the upper river were running their heavily-laden canoes, bateaux, and Mackinac boats from St. Anthony Falls to Prairie du Chien, and thence up the Wisconsin and down the Fox to Green Bay and Mackinac; or, farther down the Mississippi to St. Louis. To guide these boats, with their valuable cargoes of peltries, pilots were as necessary as on the larger craft that later were to supersede them. A man standing in the stern, with ready paddle in hand, was the forerunner of the pilot of civilization. In his veins the blood of sunny France mingled with that of a tawny mother from Huron, Chippewa, or Dakota wigwams. His eye was quick to read the dimpling waters, and his arm strong to turn the prow of his craft aside from threatening snag or sand-bar.

The transition from bateaux paddle and sweep to the steamboat wheel was not great, and it followed that the names of the earliest recorded members of the profession are such as to leave no room for doubt as to nationality or pedigree. Louis DeMarah heads the list of upper Mississippi River pilots who handled steamboats prior to 1836. There were steamers running between St. Louis and Fort Snelling from the year 1823, with more or less regularity. The "Virginia" (Captain Crawford) was the first steamboat to reach Fort Snelling, May 10, 1823. While we have the name of the captain, we have no mention of her pilots and engineers. It is probable that the master did his own piloting. Nearly all historical references to the early navigation of the upper Mississippi or Missouri Rivers speak of the master as also the pilot of his craft. Occasionally, however, we read of a pilot, but do not learn his name, his office being his only individuality.

Lumbering operations had already begun on the Black, Chippewa, and St. Croix Rivers prior to 1836, and pilots were in demand to run the timber rafts down the river. No doubt De-Marah began his professional life in this trade, if not in the earlier life of the *voyageur*. He is mentioned as being an old man in 1843, his home being then in Prairie du Chien, where, in the census of Crawford County, in the new Territory of Wisconsin, he is listed with a family of eight — probably a Chippewa wife and seven "breeds" of varying attenuations. With the phonetic freedom exercised by our forefathers, his name appears as Louis "Demerer".

In connection with DeMarah's name there is associated in the earliest annals of the river that of Louis Moro (or Morrow), evidently a corruption of Moreau, a name not appearing on the census roll of Crawford County. Evidently a *protegé* of De-Marah's, he probably was taught the science of piloting by the elder man, as the names are nearly always spoken of in connection. Evidently they were partners, so far as that was possible in the days when steamboats took but one pilot, running only by day, and lying at the bank at night. Captain Russell Blakeley, who began life on the river in the early '40's, speaks of these men as the first who engaged in steamboat piloting as a business.

It may only be an accidental coincidence of names, and yet it is more than possible that Louis Moreau, of Prairie du Chien in 1836, was a descendant of the Pierre Moreau, the noted *courier du bois*, and adventurous trader who befriended Father Marquette, patron saint of Wisconsin, as he lay sick, slowly dying, in his squalid hut on the portage between the Chicago River and the Des Plaines, one hundred and fifty years earlier, as recorded in the pages of Parkman's *La Salle and the Discovery of the Great West*.

Another of the earliest pilots was Pleasant Cormack, also a Frenchman with possibly a slight dash of Indian blood in his composition. He is in the records as an intelligent, trustworthy pilot, and held the wheels of many of the largest and finest of upper river boats during the flush times between 1850 and 1862.

DeMarah and Moreau were so far ahead of my generation on the river, that I never saw either of them. My own acquaintance with the half-breed pilot of tradition, was confined to the person of Joe Guardapie, a St. Croix and Mississippi River raftsman. He filled the bill completely, however, and having seen and known him the type was fully identified. A lithe savage, about five feet ten inches in height, and a hundred and sixty-five or seventy pounds in weight, his color exhibited more of the traits of his Chippewa mother than of his French father. In facial expression, however, the mercurial disposition of his father's kindred supplanted the stolidity of his Indian forbears. As quick as a panther, and as strong in nerve and sinew, he could whip any member of his crew, single-handed. In case of necessity he could put to rout a dozen of them — else he could not have run a raft to St. Louis; in fact, had it been otherwise he could not have started a raft from the landing at Prescott. Several times he made the return trip from below on our boat, taking cabin passage while his crew went "deck passage". He loafed in the pilot house most of the time on the up trip, as was the custom of the craft, and occasionally took a trick at the wheel to relieve the regular pilots. I never heard of his doing regular steamboat work, however, his tastes and education tying him to rafting.

It was interesting to listen to his broken English, freely mingled with borderland French, the whole seasoned with unmistakable Anglo-Saxon profanity. It is curious to note that the untutored Indian has no profanity at all; and that of the Frenchman is of such mild-mannered texture as to be quite innocuous. Any one acquainted with modern polite literature must have observed that the French brand of profanity is used to flavor popular novels treating of life in high society, and the *mon Dieus* and *sacres* are not considered at all harmful reading, even for boarding school misses. It follows that the Frenchman who wishes to lay any emphasis upon his orders to a mixed crew of all nationalities — English, Irish, Dutch, Yankee, and Norwegian, with a sprinkling of French and Indian, must resort to Anglo-Saxon for effective expressions. And even this must often be backed with a ready fist or a heavy boot, properly to impress the fellow to whom it is directed. Joe Guardapie had the whole arsenal with him, all the time, largely accounting, I fancy, for his success as a raft pilot.

Another old-time raftsman was Sandy McPhail. He piloted log and lumber rafts from the Chippewa to Prairie du Chien, and further down, in the days when Jefferson Davis, as a lieutenant in the regular army, was a member of the garrison at Fort Crawford. Whether "Sandy" was the name conferred upon him at the baptismal font, or gratuitously bestowed by an appreciative following on account of the color of his hair and beard, which were unmistakably red, will never be known. He certainly had no other name on the river. He was a good pilot, and a great handler of men, as well, which made him a model raftsman. He never took to the milder lines of steamboat piloting, so far as there is any record to be found.

Still another was Charles LaPointe, who ran rafts from the Chippewa to lower river ports prior to 1845 — how much earlier, it is now impossible to learn. He also was of the typical French half-breed *voyageur* pioneers of the West, and handed down a record as a competent navigator of rafts on the river when it was almost unknown and entirely undeveloped.

When I was pantry boy on the "Kate Cassell", my first venture aboard, we had a pilot picked up "above the lake", when we started out in the spring, a raftsman named McCoy — J. B., I think he signed himself. He was from Stillwater, and made but few trips on the steamer before taking up his regular work in rafting. A Scotchman, very quiet and reserved, so far as his deportment went while on the "Kate Cassell", he had, nevertheless, the reputation of being exceedingly handy with his fists when on his native saw-logs. This reputation led to an impromptu prize fight, which was "pulled off" at a woodyard near Hastings, Minnesota. A St. Louis bruiser named Parker, who had fought several battles on Bloody Island, opposite that city, was on board. Having heard of McCoy's reputation as a fighter, he lost no opportunity to banter and insult him, especially when he (Parker) was in liquor, which was most of the time. This lasted for several days, from Galena to Hastings, where it reached a climax. McCoy told him he would settle it with him at the next wood-pile, so that they might not go into St. Paul with the question in doubt. When the wood-pile was reached the officers of the boat, with most of the passengers, and as many of the crew as could abandon their posts, adjourned to the woods a few rods from the landing. A ring was roped off, seconds were chosen, and bottle-holders and sponge-bearers detailed. The men stripped to their trousers and went in. There was not as much science exhibited, probably, as in some of our modern professional "mills", but there was plenty

of good, honest slugging.   Both men were well punished, especially
about the head and face.   So equally were they matched, that
neither suffered a knock-out, and when the bell struck for starting
they had to quit without either getting the decision.   This happened in the days when the Heenan-Sayre international bout was
one of the prime topics of public interest, and it was noticeable that
any number of our men were well enough posted in the rules of the
P. R. to serve as officials in all departments.   McCoy lost no
caste among crew or passengers on account of this incident.   There
were neither kid gloves nor silk stockings among the pioneers
who were pushing into Minnesota in 1856, and an incident of this
sort was diverting rather than deplorable.

Other pilots whose names appear very early in the annals
of steamboating on the upper river, and whose fame as masters of
the art will ever remain green among members of the craft so
long as pilots turn a wheel on the river, were William White,
Sam Harlow, Rufus Williams, George Nichols, Alex. Gody, and
Hugh White, all of whom appear to have been in service in
1850 or before.   These were followed by John Arnold, Joseph
Armstrong, John King, Rufus Williams, Edward A. West, E.
V. Holcomb, Hiram Beadle, William Cupp, Jerome Smith,
William Fisher, Stephen Dalton, Jackson Harris, Henry Gil-
patrick, James Black, Thomas Burns, T. G. Dreming, Harry
Tripp, William Tibbles, Seth Moore, Stephen Hanks, Charley
Manning, Thomas Cushing, Peter Hall, and fifty others equally
as good.   All of those named, served in the Minnesota Packet
Company in the days of its prosperity, some of them for many
years.   All were experts in their profession, and some of them,
as "Ned" West and John King, were entitled to the highest
encomium known on the river — that of being "lightning pilots".

Chapter XV

Incidents of River Life

Captain William Fisher, of Galena, Illinois, is probably the oldest living pilot of the upper Mississippi. At the time of this writing (1908), he is spending the closing years of his life in quiet comfort in a spot where he can look down upon the waters of "Fevre" River, once alive with steamboats, in the pilot houses of which he spent over thirty years in hard and perilous service.

As a young man Captain Fisher had served five years on the Great Lakes on a "square rigger", at a time when full-rigged ships sailed the inland waters. Coming to Galena just as the great boom in steamboating commenced, and following the opening of Minnesota Territory to settlement, he naturally gravitated toward the life of a steamboatman, taking his first lessons in piloting in 1852, on the "Ben Campbell", under the tutelage of Captain M. W. Lodwick. The next season (1853), he worked on the "War Eagle", under William White and John King, two of the best pilots on the upper river. Under their teaching he soon obtained his license, and henceforth for thirty years he piloted many of the finest boats running between St. Louis and St. Paul. His crowning achievement was the taking of the "City of Quincy" from St. Louis to St. Paul, Captain Brock being his partner for the trip. The "City of Quincy" was a New Orleans packet, that had been chartered to take an excursion the length of the river. Of sixteen hundred tons burden, with a length of three hundred feet and fifty feet beam, she was the largest boat ever making the trip above Keokuk Rapids.

Two or three incidents of his river life, among the many which he relates, are of interest as showing the dangers of that life. One, which he believes was an omen prophetic of the War of Secession, he relates as follows:

"I'm going to tell you this just as it happened. I don't know whether you will believe me or not. I don't say that I would believe it if I had not seen it with my own eyes. If some one else had told it to me, I might have set it down as a 'yarn'. If they have never had any experiences on the river, some men would make yarns to order; it is a mighty sight easier to make them than it is to live them — and safer.

"When this thing happened to me, I was entirely sober, and I was not asleep. If you will take my word for it, I have never been anything else but sober. If I had been otherwise, I would not be here now, telling you this, and eighty-two years old. [4]

"Whiskey always gets 'em before they see the eighty mark. And you know that a man can't run a steamboat while asleep — that is, very long. Of course he can for a little while, but when she hits the bank it wakes him up.

"This story ought to interest you, because I was on your favorite boat when it happened. The "Fanny Harris" was sold in 1859, in May or June, to go South. She came back right away, not going below St. Louis, after all. I took her down to that port. Joseph Jones of Galena had just bought the bar for the season when she was sold, and lost thirty dollars in money by the boat being sold. [5]

"Captain W. H. Gabbert was in command, and I was pilot. We left Galena in the evening. It was between changes of the moon, and a beautiful starlight night — as fine as I ever saw. By the time we got down to Bellevue, the stars had all disappeared, and it had become daylight, not twilight, but broad daylight, so bright that you couldn't see even the brightest star, and from 11:30 to 12:30, a full hour, it was as bright as any day you ever saw when the sun was under a cloud. At midnight I was right opposite Savanna. Up to this time Captain Gabbert had been asleep in the cabin, although he was on watch. We were carrying neither passengers nor freight, for we were just taking the boat down to deliver her to her new owners. He

---

[4] This was told in 1903.

[5] Observe the minuteness with which the Captain remembers the small and insignificant details of this trip. It is a guarantee that his memory is not playing any tricks in his narrative of the more important happenings.

Steamer "War Eagle," 1852; 296 tons.
Steamer "Milwaukee," 1856; 550 tons.

woke up, or was called, and when he saw the broad daylight, yet saw by his watch that it was just midnight, he was surprised, and maybe scared, just as every one else was. He ran up on to the roof and called out: 'Mr. Fisher, land the boat, the world is coming to an end'!

"I told him that if the world were coming to an end we might as well go in the middle of the river as at the bank, and I kept her going. It took just as long to get dark again as it took to get light — about half an hour. It began to get light at half-past eleven, and at twelve (midnight) it was broad daylight; then in another half hour it was all gone, and the stars had come out one by one, just as you see them at sunset — the big, bright ones first, and then the whole field of little ones. I looked for all the stars I knew by sight, and as they came back, one by one, I began to feel more confidence in the reality of things. I couldn't tell at all where the light came from; but it grew absolutely broad daylight. That one hour's experience had more to do with turning my hair white than anything that ever occurred to me, for it certainly did seem a strange phenomenon."

"Was it worse than going into battle?" I asked.

"Yes, a hundred times worse, because it was different. When you go into battle you know just what the danger is, and you nerve yourself up to meet it. It is just the same as bracing up to meet any known danger in your work — wind, lightning, storm. You know what to expect, and if you have any nerve you just hold yourself in and let it come. This was different. You didn't know what was coming next; but I guess we all thought just as the Captain did, that it was the end of the world.

"I confess that I was scared, but I had the boat to look out for, and until the world really did come to an end I was responsible for her, and so stood by, and you know that helps to keep your nerves where they belong. I just hung on to the wheel and kept her in the river, but I kept one eye on the eastern sky to see what was coming next. I hope when my time comes I shall not be scared to death, and I don't believe I shall be. It will come in a natural way, and there won't be anything to scare a man. It is the unknown and the mysterious that shakes him, and this midnight marvel was too much for any of us. We had a great many signs before the war came, and I believe this marvel on the night in question, was one of them, only we didn't know how to read it."

"How about the narrow escapes, Captain?"

"Well, I have had a number of them. In 1871 I was running a towboat with coal barges. Twelve miles below Rock Island, we were struck by a cyclone. It took the cabin clean off the boat, and of course the pilot house went with it. My partner was with me in the pilot house, having seen the storm coming up, with heavy wind, so he came up to help me keep her in the river. At this time we were pushing a lumber raft downstream. Both of us were blown into the river. My partner got hold of the raft and pulled himself out, but I went under it. I thought that it was the end of piloting; but Providence was with me. I came up through an aperture where four cribs of lumber cornered — a little hole not over three feet square. My partner saw me and ran and pulled me out, and we both got back on the dismantled hull of our boat. I could not have helped myself, as I was too near strangled. The force of the cyclone must have stopped the current of the river for the time or I would never have come up where I did. The shock and the wetting laid me up for six weeks.

"When I was able to resume work, Dan Rice happened to come along with his circus boat. He wanted a pilot to take his craft not only up the great river, but also, so far as possible, up such tributaries as were navigable, he wishing to give exhibitions at all the towns alongshore. I shipped with him for $300 a month and had an easy time during the rest of the season, running nights, mostly, and laying up daytimes while the show was exhibiting.

"The next year I was engaged on the "Alex. Mitchell." We had left St. Paul at 11 o'clock in the forenoon, on Saturday, May 6, 1872. I am particular about this day and date, for the point of this story hinges on the day of the week (Sunday). In trying to run the Hastings bridge we were struck by a squall that threw us against the abutment, tearing off a portion of our starboard guard. We arrived at La Crosse, Sunday morning, and took on two hundred excursionists for Lansing. They wanted to dance, but it being Sunday Captain Laughton hesitated for some time about giving them permission, as it was contrary to the known wishes, if not the rules, of Commodore Davidson to have dancing or games on board of his boats on Sunday. The passengers were persistent, however, and at last Captain Laughton yielded, saying that he couldn't help it! Of course he might have helped it. What is a captain for, if not to run his boat, no matter if everybody else is against him? That was where he was weak. He finally yielded, however, and they danced all the way to Lansing. When we arrived there it was raining, and the excursionists chartered the boat for a run back to Victory, about ten miles, and they were dancing all the time.

"Leaving them at Victory we proceeded on our way down the river. When about twelve miles above Dubuque, a little below Wells's Landing, at three o'clock Monday morning, we were struck by a cyclone. We lost both chimneys, the pilot house was unroofed, and part of the hurricane deck on the port side was blown off. Mr. Trudell, the mate, was on watch, and standing on the roof by the big bell. He was blown off, and landed on shore a quarter of a mile away, but sustained no serious injuries. The port lifeboat was blown a mile and a half into the country. Following so soon after the Sunday dancing, I have always felt that there was some connection between the two."

Captain Fisher is a very conscientious man — a religious man, and he believes in observing Sunday — that is, keeping it as nearly as is possible on a steamboat running seven days in the week. The dancing was wholly unnecessary, if not in itself immoral, and its permission by Captain Laughton was in direct contravention of the known wishes if not orders of the owners. Hence the conclusion that Providence took a hand in the matter and meted out swift punishment for the misdoing. I did not argue the matter with the Captain; but I could not reconcile the unroofing of Commodore Davidson's steamboat, or the blowing away of Mr. Trudell, who had no voice in granting license to the ungodly dancers, with the ordinary conception of the eternal fitness of things. If it had blown Captain Laughton a mile and a half into the country, as it did the port lifeboat, or even a quarter of a mile, as it did Mr. Trudell, and had left Commodore Davidson's steamboat intact, the hand of Providence would have appeared more plainly in the case. As it was, Captain Laughton slept serenely in his berth while Mr. Trudell and the lifeboat were sailing into space, and he did not get out until all was over. It is pleasant to be able to relate that although Providence appears to have miscarried in dealing out retribution, Commodore Davidson did not. Captain Davis was put in charge of the "Alex. Mitchell" as soon as she struck the levee at St. Louis.

William F. Davidson — "Commodore", from the fact that he was at the head of the greatest of upper river packet lines — had been converted after many years of strenuous river life. He was as strong a man, affirmatively, after he began living religiously, as he had been negatively before that time. He abolished all bars from his steamboats, at great pecuniary loss to himself and the other stockholders; forbade Sunday dancing and other forms of Sunday desecration; stopped all gambling, and instituted other reforms which tended to make his steamboats as clean and reputable as the most refined ladies or gentlemen could wish. The promptitude with which he cashiered Captain Laughton, on account of the foregoing incident, was in keeping with his character as a man and as a manager. It was an evidence that he meant all that he said or ordered in the ethical conduct of his steamboats.

The Commodore had a brother, Payton S. Davidson, who had the well-earned reputation of being one of the best steamboatmen on the Mississippi. Superintendent of the Northwestern Line, he prided himself upon the regularity with which his boats arrived at or departed from landings on schedule time. He was a driver, and the captains and pilots who could not "make time" under any and all conditions of navigation, were *persona non grata* to "Pate", and when they reached this stage they went ashore with scant notice. In other ways he was equally efficient.

One of the Northwestern Line, the "Centennial", was caught in the great ice gorge at St. Louis, in 1876. She was a new boat, costing $65,000, just off the ways, and a beauty. She was stove and sank, as did a dozen other boats at the same time. All the others were turned over to the underwriters as they lay, and were a total loss. Not so the "Centennial". Superintendent Payton S. Davidson was on hand and declared that the beautiful new boat could and should be raised. Putting on a force of men — divers, wreckers, and other experts — under his personal supervision and direction, he did get her afloat, although in a badly damaged condition, and that at a cost of only $5,000. Twice she sank, after being brought to the surface; but the indomitable energy of Davdison, who worked night and day, sometimes in the water up to his middle, and in floating ice, finally saved the steamer. She was one of the finest boats that ever plied the upper river. Payton S. was famous for his pugnacity as well as his pertinacity, and there is no record of his repentance or conversion. He lived and died a typical steamboat captain of the olden time.

Chapter XVI

Mississippi Menus

It was a saying on the river that if you wished to save the meals a passenger was entitled to on his trip, you took him through the kitchen the first thing when he came aboard. The inference was, that after seeing the food in course of preparation he would give it a wide berth when it came on the table. It would be unfair to the memory of the average river steward to aver that this assertion was grounded upon facts; but it would be stretching the truth to assert that it was without foundation. Things must be done in a hurry when three meals a day are to be prepared and served to three or four hundred people; and all the work had to be accomplished in two kitchens, each ten by twenty-feet in area — one for meats and vegetables, and the other for pastry and desserts.

The responsibility of providing for meals at stated times, with a good variety, cooked and served in a satisfactory manner, devolved upon the steward. Under him were two assistants, with meat cooks, vegetable cooks, pastry cooks, and bread makers, and a force of waiters and pantrymen conditioned upon the boat's capacity for passengers. While the steward was in the thought of outsiders rated as an officer of the second class, he was as a matter of fact in the first class. When the pay of the captain was three hundred dollars per month, and that of the mate two hundred, the average steward of any reputation also commanded two hundred, while a man with a large reputation commanded three hundred, the same as the captain, and his services were sought by the owners of a dozen boats. Likewise, he earned every cent of his salary, whatever it might be.

Unlike the other officers he had no regular watch to stand, after which he might lay aside his responsibility and let the members of the other watch carry the load while he laid off and watched them sweat. He was on duty all the time, and when and how he slept is to this day a mystery to me. He might have slept in the morning, when the cooks were preparing breakfast, had he felt quite confident that the cooks were not likewise sleeping, instead of broiling beefsteaks and making waffles. This being a matter of some doubt, and of great concern, he was usually up as soon as the cooks, and quietly poking about to see that breakfast reached the table promptly at seven o'clock. If the floor of the cabin was covered with sleepers, it was the steward who must awaken them, and, without giving offense, induce them to vacate the premises that the tables might be set. This was a delicate piece of business. To send a "nigger" to perform that duty, would be to incur the risk of losing the "nigger". The steward also saw that the assistant in charge of the waiters was on hand with all his crew, to put the cabin to rights, set the tables, and prepare to serve breakfast, while the cabin steward and the stewardess, with their crews, were making up the berths, sweeping, dusting, and "tidying up".

As soon as breakfast was out of the way, the menu for dinner was prepared and handed to the chief cook. Shortages in provisions were remedied at the first landing reached, and stocks of fish, game, fresh eggs, and fresh vegetables were bought as offered at the various towns. While there was a cold-storage room on all first-class packets, its capacity was limited, and with a passenger list of two hundred and fifty or three hundred in the cabin, it was often found necessary to lay in additional stocks of fresh meats between Galena and St. Paul. Often, a dozen lambs could be picked up, or a dozen "roaster" pigs, and these were killed and dressed on the boat by one of the assistant cooks. Live poultry was always carried in coops, and killed as wanted. Perhaps the poultry killing, if witnessed by the passenger, would come as near curing him of the dinner habit as anything else he might see about the cook's galley. A barrel of scalding hot water, drawn from the boiler, stands on the guard. A coop of chickens is placed near the master of ceremonies, and two or three assistants surround the barrel. The head dresser grasps a chicken by the head, gives it a swing from the coop to the barrel, bringing the chicken's neck on to the iron rim of the barrel. The body goes

into hot water and the head goes overboard. Before the chicken
is dead he is stripped of everything except a few pin feathers —
with one sweep of the hand on each side of the body and a dozen
pulls at the wing feathers. The yet jerking, featherless bodies
are thrown to the pin-feather man, who picks out the thickest
of the feathers, singes the fowls over a charcoal grate-fire and
tosses them to one of the under-cooks who cuts them open, cuts
them up, and pots them, all inside of two minutes from the coop.
A team of three or four expert darkies will dispose of one hundred
and fifty chickens in an hour. Are they clean? I never stopped
to inquire. If they were *dead* enough to stay on the platter when
they got to the table that was all any reasonable steamboatman
could ask.

However, the live chicken business is about the worst feature
of the cook-house operations. Of course the darkies are not the
cleanest-appearing people aboard the boat, but if the steward is
up in his business he sees to it that a reasonable degree of clean-
liness is maintained, even in the starboard galley. On the opposite
side of the steamer is the pastry-cook's domain, and that is usually
the show place of the boat. Most stewards are shrewd enough
to employ pastry cooks who are masters of their profession, men
who take a pride not only in the excellence of their bread, biscuit,
and pie crust, but also in the spotlessness of their workshops.
They are proud to receive visits from the lady passengers, who
can appreciate not only the out-put but the appearance of the
galley. It is a good advertisement for a boat, and the steward
himself encourages such visits, while discouraging like calls at
the opposite side.

In old, flush times in the steamboat business, pastry cooks
generally planned to give a surprise to the passengers on each
up trip of the steamer. I remember one such, when no less than
thirteen different desserts were placed in front of each passenger
as he finished the hearty preliminary meal. Six of these were
served in tall and slender glass goblets — vases, would more nearly
describe them — and consisted of custards, jellies, and creams
of various shades and flavors; while the other seven were pies,
puddings, and ice creams. The passenger was not given a menu
card and asked to pick out those that he thought he would like,
but the whole were brought on and arranged in a circle about

his plate, leaving him to dip into each as he fancied, and leave such as did not meet his approval. It was necessary to carry an extra outfit of glass and china in order to serve this bewildering exhibition of the pastry cook's art, and it was seldom used more than once on each trip.

Serving such a variety of delicacies, of which but a small portion was eaten by any person at the table, would seem like an inexcusable waste; but the waste on river steamers was really not as great in those days as it is in any great hotel of our day. Each steamer carried forty or more deck hands and "rousters". For them, the broken meat was piled into pans, all sorts in each pan, the broken bread and cake into other pans, and jellies and custards into still others — just three assortments, and this, with plenty of boiled potatoes, constituted the fare of the crew below decks. One minute after the cry of "Grub-pile"! one might witness the spectacle of forty men sitting on the bare deck, clawing into the various pans to get hold of the fragments of meat or cake which each man's taste particularly fancied. It certainly wasn't an appetizing spectacle. Only familiarity with it enabled an onlooker fully to appreciate its grotesqueness without allowing the equilibrium of his stomach to be disturbed. It usually had but one effect upon such lady passengers as had the hardihood to follow the cry of "Grub-pile"! and ascertain what the thing really was.

Altogether the duties of the steward were arduous and tormenting. The passengers expected much; and after getting the best, if any slip occurred they were sure to enter complaint — a complaint so worded as to convey the impression that they never had anything fit to eat while on the boat, nor any service that white men were justified in tolerating. The fact was, that most of the passengers so served had never in all their lives lived so well as they did on the trip from Galena to St. Paul on one of the regular boats of the Minnesota Packet Company. Certainly, after reaching their destination in the Territory of Minnesota, the chances were that it would be many long years, in that era of beginnings, before they would again be so well fed and so assiduously cared for, even in the very best hotels of St. Paul.

This chapter on Mississippi menus would be incomplete without some reference to the drinkables served on the steamboat tables.

These were coffee, tea, and river water. Mark Twain has described the ordinary beverage used on the river, as it is found on the Missouri, or on the Mississippi below the mouth of the "Big Muddy":

"When I went up to my room, I found there the young man called Rogers, crying. Rogers was not his name; neither was Jones, Brown, Baxter, Ferguson, Bascom, nor Thompson; but he answered to either of them that a body found handy in an emergency; or to any other name, in fact, if he perceived that you meant him. He said:

" 'What is a person to do here when he wants a drink of water? drink this slush?'

" 'Can't you drink it?'

" 'I would if I had some other water to wash it with.'

"Here was a thing which had not changed; a score of years had not affected this water's mulatto complexion in the least; a score of centuries would succeed no better, perhaps. It comes out of the turbulent bank-caving Missouri, and every tumblerful of it holds nearly an acre of land in solution. I got this fact from the bishop of the diocese. If you will let your glass stand half an hour, you can separate the land from the water as easy as Genesis; and then you will find them both good; the one good to eat, the other good to drink. The land is very nourishing, the water is thoroughly wholesome. The one appeases hunger, the other, thirst. But the natives do not take them separately, but together, as nature mixed them. When they find an inch of mud in the bottom of the glass, they stir it up, and then take the draught as they would gruel. It is difficult for a stranger to get used to this batter, but once used to it he will prefer it to water. This is really the case. It is good for steam-boating, and good to drink; but it is worthless for all other purposes, except baptizing."

The above sketch had not been written in 1860, as Mark Twain was himself piloting on the lower river at that time. It could not, therefore, have been this description which prejudiced many eastern people against Mississippi River water as a beverage. But that prejudice did exist, away back in the fifties, and the fame of the yellow tipple had reached even to the fastnesses of the Vermont hills at that early day. Many emigrants from the old New England states provided themselves with kegs, jugs or "demijohns", and before embarking at Rock Island or Dunleith for the river trip, would fill these receptacles with water from the nearest well, or even cistern, and drink such stuff, warm, and sometimes putrid, rather than drink the life-giving elixir which had welled up from springs nestled in the shadows of the everlasting hills, or had been distilled by the sun from the snowbanks and ice fields of the unspoiled prairies and azure lakes of the great northwest.

One old Yankee would pin his faith to nothing less than the water from his own spring or well at home, away back in old Vermont, and brought, at infinite pains and labor, a five-gallon demijohn all the way from his native state, drinking it on the cars en route, and on the boat after reaching the river.

It wasn't as bad as that. The river water was as pure and healthful as any water on the footstool — *then*. It may not be so now — it *isn't, now*. Then there were no great cities on the river banks, pouring thousands of gallons of sewage and all manner of corruption into the stream, daily. There was very little land under cultivation even, and few farmyards, the drainage from which might contaminate the feeders of the great river. It was good, clean, healthful, spring and snow water. Above the mouth of the Missouri, in any ordinary stage of water, especially with a falling river, the water was but slightly discolored with the yellow sediment with which the river itself is always tinged; and this sediment was so fine that there was no suspicion of grit about it. When properly stirred up and evenly mixed, as those to the manner born always took it, it was an invigorating potion, and like good old Bohea, it would cheer but not inebriate.

Since the advent of sewage in the river and with it the popular superstition that everything, liquid or solid, is permeated with pernicious microbes, it is possible that it has lost something of its pristine purity, and it is certain that it has lost something of its reputation; but river men still drink it from preference, and passengers, unless they revert to the Yankee method, must drink it perforce, or go dry.

Chapter XVII

Bars and Barkeepers

In the old days on the river, whiskey was not classed as one of the luxuries. It was regarded as one of the necessities, if not the prime necessity, of life. To say that everybody drank would not be putting much strain upon the truth, for the exceptions were so few as scarcely to be worth counting. It was a saying on the river that if a man owned a bar on a popular packet, it was better than possessing a gold mine. The income was ample and certain, and the risk and labor slight. Men who owned life leases of steamboat bars willed the same to their sons, as their richest legacies. Ingenious and far-seeing men set about accumulating bars as other men invested in two, three, or four banks, or factories.

"Billy" Henderson of St. Louis was the first financier to become a trust magnate in bars. He owned the one on the "Excelsior", on which boat he ran between St. Louis and St. Paul. Later, he bought the lease of the bar on the "Metropolitan", and still later, when the Northern Line was organized, he bought the bars on all the boats, putting trusty "bar-keeps" aboard each, he himself keeping a general oversight of the whole, and rigorously exacting a mean average of returns from each, based upon the number of passengers carried. This system of averages included men, women, and children, and "Indians not taxed", presupposing that a certain percentage of the passengers' money would find its way into his tills, regardless of age, sex, or color. What his judgment would have been had one of the craft been chartered to carry a Sunday school picnic from St. Louis to St. Paul, will never be known. Such an exigency never confronted him, in those days. The judgment rendered was, that he was not far off in his conclusions as to the average income from the average class of passengers carried.

WINONA, MINNESOTA. The Levee in the 1870s.

Ordinarily, the bartenders were young men "of parts". None of them, so far as I know, were college graduates; but then college graduates were then mighty few in the West in any calling — and there were bars in plenty. It was required by their employers that they be pleasant and agreeable fellows, well dressed, and well mannered. They must know how to concoct a few of the more commonplace fancy drinks affected by the small number of travellers who wished such beverage — whiskey cocktails for the Eastern trade, and mint juleps for the Southern. The plain, everyday Western man took his whiskey straight, four fingers deep, and seldom spoiled the effect of his drink by pouring water on top of it. The "chaser" had not, at that early day, become fashionable, and in times of extreme low water it was not permitted that water should be wasted in that manner when all was required for purposes of navigation.

The barkeeper was also supposed to know how to manufacture a choice brand of French brandy, by the judicious admixture of burnt peach stones, nitric acid, and cod-liver oil, superimposed upon a foundation of Kentucky whiskey three weeks from the still. He did it, too; but judicious drinkers again took theirs straight, and lived the longest.

I flatter myself that I can recall the name of but one bartender with whom I sailed. While I had no very strong scruples about drinking or selling liquor, I seldom patronized the bar beyond the purchase of cigars and an occasional soft drink. I remember one dispenser, however, from his short but exceedingly stormy experience on the "Fanny Harris". He was an Irish lad, about twenty or twenty-one years of age, and not very large. He was sent on board by the lessee of the bar, who lived in Dubuque.

Charley Hargus, our chief clerk, did not like the Irish. He had personal reasons for disliking some member of that nationality, and this dislike he handed on to all its other members with whom he came in contact. There were no Irishmen among the officers of the "Fanny Harris", and when Donnelly came aboard to take charge of the bar Hargus strongly objected, but without avail. He then set himself about the task of making life so uncomfortable for the lad that he would be sure to transfer to some other boat, or quit altogether, an end accomplished within three months. The process afforded rare amusement to such witnesses as happened to see the fun, but there was no fun in it for Donnelly; and in later years, when I came to think it over, my sympathy went out to the poor fellow, who suffered numberless indignities at the hands of his tireless persecutor. If Donnelly — who was not at all a bad fellow, was earning his living honestly, and never did anything to injure Hargus — had had the spirit common to most river men in those days, he would have shot the chief clerk and few could have blamed him.

Bars are not looked upon with the same favor in our day, as in the past. It is claimed that upon some of the boats plying upon the upper river there are now no bars at all. If a person thinks he must have liquor on the trip, he must take it with his baggage. It is further credibly asserted that many of the officers handling the steamers are teetotalers; further, that there is no more profit in the bar business, and that investors in that kind of property are becoming scarce. Modern business conditions are responsible for much of the change that has taken place, especially in the transportation business, within the last twenty-five years. Railroad and steamboat managers do not care to intrust their property to the care of drinking men, and it is becoming more and more difficult for such to secure positions of responsibility. As the display of liquor in an open bar might be a temptation to some men, otherwise competent and trusty officers, the owners are adopting the only consistent course, and are banishing the bar from their boats.

This does not apply in all cases, however. A few years ago I took a trip from St. Paul to St. Louis on one of the boats of the Diamond Jo Line. There was a bar on the boat, but it seemed to depend for its patronage upon the colored deck crew. They were pretty constant patrons, although their drinking was systematically regulated. A side window, opening out upon the boiler deck promenade, was devoted to the deck traffic. If a rouster wanted a drink he must apply to one of the mates, who issued a brass check, good for a glass of whiskey, which the deck hand presented at the bar, and got his drink. When pay day came, the barkeeper in his turn presented his bundle of checks and took in the cash. How many checks were issued to each man on the trip from St. Louis to St. Paul and return, I do not know; but it is safe to say that the sum total was not permitted to exceed the amount of wages due the rouster. Some of the "niggers" probably had coming to them more checks than cash, at the close of the voyage. The regulation was effective in preventing excess, which would demoralize the men and render them less valuable in "humping" freight.

The bartender always poured out the whiskey for the "coons", and for the latter it was not a big drink. It was, likewise, not a good drink for a white man, being a pretty tough article of made-up stuff, that would burn a hole in a sheet-iron stove. If it had been less fiery the rousters would have thought they were being cheated.

While on this trip, I never saw an officer of the boat take a drink at the bar, or anywhere else, and but few of the passengers patronized it. It accentuated as much as any other one thing the fact that the "good old times" on the river were gone, and that a higher civilization had arisen. But peddling cheap whiskey to "niggers"! What would an old-time bartender have thought of that? The bare insinuation would have thrown him into a fit. But we are all on an equality now, black and white — before the bar.

Chapter XVIII

Gamblers and Gambling

Volumes have been written, first and last, on the subject of gambling on the Mississippi. In them a small fraction of truth is diluted with a deal of fiction. The scene is invariably laid upon a steamboat on the lower Mississippi. The infatuated planter, who always does duty as the plucked goose, invariably stakes his faithful body servant, or a beautiful quadroon girl, against the gambler's pile of gold, and as invariably loses his stake. Possibly that may occasionally have happened on the lower river in ante-bellum days. I never travelled the lower river, and cannot therefore speak from actual observation.

On the upper river, in early times, there were no nabobs travelling with body servants and pretty quadroons. Most of the travellers had broad belts around their waists, filled with good honest twenty-dollar gold pieces. It was these belts which the professional gamblers sought to lighten. Occasionally they did strike a fool who thought he knew more about cards than the man who made the game, and who would, after a generous baiting with mixed drinks, "set in" and try his fortune. There was, of course, but one result — the belt was lightened, more or less, according to the temper and judgment of the victim.

So far as I know, gambling was permitted on all boats. On some, there was a cautionary sign displayed, stating that gentlemen who played cards for money did so at their own risk. The professionals who travelled the river for the purpose of "skinning suckers" were usually the "gentlemen" who displayed the greatest concern in regard to the meaning of this caution, and who freely expressed themselves in the hearing of all to the effect that they seldom played cards at all, still less for money; but if they did feel inclined to have a little social game it was not the business of the boat to question their right to do so, and if they lost their money they certainly would not call on the boat to restore it.

After the expression of such manly sentiments, it was surprising if they did not soon find others who shared with them this independence. In order to convey a merited reproof to "the boat", for its unwarranted interference with the pleasure or habits of its patrons, they bought a pack of cards at the bar and "set in" to a "friendly game". In the posting of this inconspicuous little placard, "the boat" no doubt absolved itself from all responsibility in what might, and surely did follow in the "friendly games" sooner or later started in the forward cabin. Whether the placard likewise absolved the officers of the boat from all responsibility in the matter, is a question for the logicians. I cannot recollect that I had a conscience in those days; and if a "sucker" chose to invest his money in draw poker rather than in corner lots, it was none of my business. In that respect, indeed, there was little choice between "Bill" Mallen on the boat with his marked cards, and Ingenuous Doemly at Nininger, with his city lots on paper selling at a thousand dollars each, which to-day, after half a century, are possibly worth twenty-five dollars an acre as farming land.

Ordinarily, the play was not high on the upper river. The passengers were not great planters, with sacks of money, and "niggers" on the side to fall back upon in case of a bluff. The operators, also, were not so greedy as their real or fictitious fellows of the lower river. If they could pick up two or three hundred dollars a week by honest endeavor they were satisfied, and gave thanks accordingly.

Probably by some understanding among themselves, the fraternity divided themselves among the different boats running regularly in the passenger trade, and only upon agreement did they change their boats; nor did they intrude upon the particular hunting ground of others.

The "Fanny Harris" was favored with the presence, more or less intermittently, of "Bill" Mallen, "Bill" and "Sam" Dove, and "Boney" Trader. "Boney" was short for Napoleon Bonaparte. These worthies usually travelled in pairs, the two Dove brothers faithfully and fraternally standing by each other, while Mallen and "Boney" campaigned in partnership.

These men were consummate actors. They never came aboard the boat together, and they never recognized each other until introduced — generally through the good offices of their intended victims. In the preliminary stages of the game, they cheerfully lost large sums of money to each other; and after the hunt was up, one usually went ashore at Prescott, Hastings, or Stillwater, while the other continued on to St. Paul. At different times they represented all sorts and conditions of men — settlers, prospectors, Indian agents, merchants, lumbermen, and even lumber-jacks; and they always dressed their part, and talked it, too. To do this required some education, keen powers of observation, and an all-around knowledge of men and things. They were gentlemanly at all times — courteous to men and chivalrous to women. While pretending to drink large quantities of very strong liquors, they did in fact make away with many pint measures of quite innocent river water, tinted with the mildest liquid distillation of burned peaches. A clear head and steady nerves were prerequisites to success; and when engaged in business, these men knew that neither one nor the other came by way of "Patsey" Donnelly's "Choice wines and liquors". They kept their private bottles of colored water on tap in the bar, and with the uninitiated passed for heavy drinkers.

The play was generally for light stakes, but it sometimes ran high. Five dollars ante, and no limit, afforded ample scope for big play, provided the players had the money and the nerve. The tables were always surrounded by a crowd of lookers-on, most of whom knew enough of the game to follow it understandingly. It is possible that some of the bystanders may have had a good understanding with the professionals, and have materially assisted them by signs and signals.

The chief reliance of the gamblers, however, lay in the marked cards with which they played. No pack of cards left the bar until it had passed through the hands of the gambler who patronized the particular boat that he "worked". The marking was called "stripping". This was done by placing the high cards— ace, king, queen, jack, and ten-spot — between two thin sheets of metal, the edges of which were very slightly concaved. Both edges of the cards were trimmed to these edges with a razor; the cards so "stripped" were thus a shade narrower in the middle than those not operated upon; they were left full width at each end. The acutely sensitive fingers of the gamblers could distinguish between the marked and the unmarked cards, while the other players could detect nothing out of the way in them. "Bill" Mallen would take a gross of cards from the bar to his stateroom and spend hours in thus trimming them, after which they were returned to the original wrappers, which were carefully folded and sealed, and replaced in the bar for sale. A "new pack" was often called for by the victim when "luck" ran against him; and Mallen himself would ostentatiously demand a fresh pack if he lost a hand or two, as he always did at the beginning of the play.

I never saw any shooting over a game, and but once saw pistols drawn. That was when the two Doves were holding up a "tenderfoot". There was a big pile of gold on the table — several hundred dollars in ten and twenty dollar pieces. The losers raised a row and would have smashed the two operators but for the soothing influence of a cocked Derringer in the hands of one of them. The table was upset and the money rolled in all directions. The outsiders decided where the money justly belonged, in their opinion, by promptly pocketing all they could reach while the principals were fighting. I found a twenty myself the next morning.

I saw "Bill" Mallen for the last time under rather peculiar and unlooked-for circumstances. It was down in Virginia, in the early spring of 1865. There was a review of troops near Petersburg, preparatory to the advance on Lee's lines. General O. B. Wilcox and General Sam. Harriman had sent for their wives to come down to the front and witness the display. I was an orderly at headquarters of the First Brigade, First Division, Ninth Army Corps, and was detailed to accompany the ladies, who had an ambulance placed at their disposal. I was mounted, and coming alongside the vehicle began to instruct the driver where to go to get the best view of the parade. The fellow, who was quite under the influence of liquor, identified himself as Mallen, and sought to renew acquaintance with me.

It went against the grain to go back on an old messmate, but the situation demanded prompt action. "Bill" was ordered to attend closely to his driving or he would get into the guard-house, with the displeasure of the division commander hanging over him, which would not be a pleasant experience. He knew enough about usages at the front, at that time, to understand this, and finished his drive in moody silence. After the review was over he went back to the corral with his team, and I to headquarters. I never saw or heard of him again, the stirring incidents of the latter days of March, 1865, eclipsing everything else. I presume he was following the army, nominally as a mule driver, while he "skinned" the boys at poker as a matter of business. The whiskey had him down for the time being, however, otherwise I would have been glad to talk over former times on the river.

Chapter XIX

Steamboat Racing

It is popularly supposed that there was a great deal of racing on Western rivers in the olden time — in fact, that it was the main business of steamboat captains and owners, and that the more prosaic object, that of earning dividends, was secondary. There is a deal of error in such a supposition. At the risk of detracting somewhat from the picturesqueness of life on the upper Mississippi as it is sometimes delineated, it must in truth be said that little real racing was indulged in, as compared with the lower river, or even with the preconceived notion of what transpired on the upper reaches. While there were many so-called steamboat races, these were, for the most part, desultory and unpremeditated. On the upper river, there never was such a race as that between the "Robert E. Lee" and the "Natchez", where both boats were stripped and tuned for the trial, and where neither passengers nor freight were taken on board to hinder or encumber in the long twelve hundred miles between New Orleans and St. Louis, which constituted the running track.

It is true, however, that whenever two boats happened to come together, going in the same direction, there was always a spurt that developed the best speed of both boats, with the result that the speediest boat quickly passed her slower rival, and outfooted her so rapidly as soon to leave her out of sight behind some point, not to be seen again, unless a long delay at some landing or woodyard enabled her to catch up. These little spurts were in no sense races, such as the historic runs on the lower waters. They were in most cases a business venture, rather than a sporting event, as the first boat at a landing usually secured the passengers and freight in waiting. Another boat, following so soon after, would find nothing to add to the profits of the voyage.

Racing, as racing, was an expensive if not a risky business. Unless the boats were owned by their commanders, and thus absolutely under their control, there was little chance that permission would be obtained for racing on such a magnificent and spectacular scale as that usually depicted in fiction.

The one contest that has been cited by every writer on upper river topics, that has ever come under my observation, was the one between the "Grey Eagle" (Captain D. Smith Harris), and the "Itasca" (Captain David Whitten); and that was not a race at all. It is manifestly unfair to so denominate it, when one of the captains did not know that he was supposed to be racing with another boat until he saw the other steamer round a point just behind him. Recognizing his rival as following him far ahead of her regular time, he realized that she was doing something out of the ordinary. He came to the conclusion that Captain Harris was attempting to beat him into St. Paul, in order to be the first to deliver certain important news of which he also was the bearer. When this revelation was made, both boats were within a few miles of their destination, St. Paul.

Here are the details. In 1856, the first telegraphic message was flashed under the sea by the Atlantic cable — a greeting from Queen Victoria to President Buchanan. Captain D. Smith Harris had, the year before, brought out the "Grey Eagle", which had been built at Cincinnati at a cost of $60,000. He had built this boat with his own money, or at least a controlling interest was in his name. He had intended her to be the fastest boat on the upper river, and she was easily that. As her captain and practically her owner, he was at liberty to gratify any whim that might come into his head. In this case it occurred to him that he would like to deliver in St. Paul the Queen's message to the President ahead of any one else.

There was at that time no telegraph line into St. Paul. Lines ran to Dunleith, where the "Grey Eagle" was taking in cargo for St. Paul, and also to Prairie du Chien, where the "Itasca" was loading. Both boats were to leave at six o'clock in the evening. Captain Harris had sixty-one miles farther to run than had Captain Whitten. But Harris knew that he was racing, and Whitten did not, which made all the difference in the world.

Whitten soldiered along at his usual gait, stopping at every

THE LEVEE AT ST. PAUL, 1859. Showing the Steamer "Grey Eagle" (1857; 673 tons), Capt. Daniel Smith Harris, the fastest and best boat on the Upper River, together with the "Jeanette Roberts" (1857; 146 tons), and the "Time and Tide" (1855; 131 tons), two Minnesota River boats belonging to Captain Jean Robert, an eccentric Frenchman and successful steamboatman. (Reproduced from an old negative in possession of Mr. Edward Bromley of Minneapolis, Minn.)

landing, putting off all cargo at each place, and taking on all that offered, and probably delayed to pass the compliments of the day with agents and other friends, as well as discuss the great message that he was bearing. The "Grey Eagle", on the contrary, stopped at only a few of the principal landings, and took on no freight after leaving Dunleith. She did not even put off freight that she was carrying, but took it through to St. Paul and delivered it on her return trip. She carried the mail, but in delivering it a man stood on the end of one of the long stages run out from the bow, from which he threw the sacks ashore, the boat in the meantime running along parallel with the levee, and not stopping completely at any landing. Running far ahead of her time, there were no mail sacks ready for her, and there was no reason for stopping. The "Grey Eagle" had the best of soft coal, reinforced by sundry barrels of pitch, from which the fires were fed whenever they showed any signs of failing. With all these points in her favor, in addition to the prime fact that she was by far the swiftest steamboat that ever turned a wheel on the upper river, it was possible for her to overtake the slower and totally unconcerned "Itasca", when only a few miles from St. Paul.

The race proper began when Whitten sighted the "Gray Eagle" and realized that Harris was trying to beat him into St. Paul in order to be the first to deliver the Queen's message. Then the "Itasca" did all that was in her to do, and was beaten by less than a length, Harris throwing the message ashore from the roof, attached to a piece of coal, and thus winning the race by a handbreadth.

The time of the "Grey Eagle" from Dunleith, was eighteen hours; the distance, two hundred and ninety miles; speed per hour, 16 1/9 miles.

The "Itasca", ran from Prairie du Chien to St. Paul in eighteen hours; distance, two hundred and twenty-nine miles; speed, 12 2/3 miles per hour.

The "Itasca" was far from being a slow boat, and had Whitten known that Harris was "racing" with him, the "Grey Eagle" would not have come within several hours of catching her.

As a race against time, however, the run of the "Grey Eagle" was really something remarkable. A sustained speed of over sixteen miles an hour for a distance of three hundred miles, upstream, is a wonderful record for an inland steamboat anywhere, upper river or lower river; and the pride which Captain Harris had in his beautiful boat was fully justified. A few years later, she struck the Rock Island Bridge and sank in less than five minutes, a total loss. It was pitiful to see the old Captain leaving the wreck, a broken-hearted man, weeping over the loss of his darling. and returning to his Galena home, never again to command a steamboat. He had, during his eventful life on the upper river, built, owned, or commanded scores of steamboats; and this was the end.

The "Northerner", of the St. Louis Line, was a fast boat, and an active contestant for the "broom". The boat that could, and did run away from, or pass under way, all other boats, signalized her championship by carrying a big broom on her pilot house. When a better boat passed her under way, the ethics of the river demanded that she pull the broom down and retire into seclusion until she in turn should pass the champion and thus regain her title. The struggle on the upper river lay between the "Northerner" and the "Key City". The "Grey Eagle" was in a class by herself, and none other disputed her claims, while actively disputing those of all others of the Minnesota Packet Company, of which the "Key City" was the champion and defender.

The two rivals got together at Hudson, twenty miles up Lake St. Croix — whether by accident or agreement it is impossible to say, but probably by agreement. They had twenty miles of deep water, two miles wide, with only four close places to run. It was a fair field for a race, and they ran a fair and a fine one. For miles they were side by side. Sometimes a spurt would put one a little ahead; and again the other would get a trifle the most steam and the deepest water, and so creep ahead a little. When they came into Prescott, at the foot of the lake, the "Key City" was a clear length ahead, her engineers having saved a barrel or two of resin for the home stretch. With this lead she had the right of way to turn the point and head up the river. Ned West was at the wheel, with an assistant to "pull her down" for him, and he made a beautiful turn with his long and narrow craft; while the "Northerner" had to slow down and wait a minute or two before making the turn. In the meantime the "Key City's" whistles were blowing, her bell ringing, and her passengers and crew cheering, while a man climbed to the roof of the pilot house and lashed the broom to the finial at the top, the crown of laurels for the victor.

The lower river stern-wheel steamer "Messenger" was also a very fast boat. On one occasion she came very near wresting the broom from the "Key City", in a race through Lake Pepin, where also there was plenty of water and sea room. The "Key City" had a barge in tow and thus was handicapped. The "Messenger" seemed, therefore, likely to win the race, as she had passed the former under way. Within four miles of the head of the lake, Captain Worden of the "Key City" ordered the barge cast adrift, having placed a few men on board of it, with an anchor and cable to use in case of necessity. Thus freed from the encumbrance, he put on steam and passed his rival before reaching Wacouta, in spite of the most strenuous efforts on the part of the latter to retain her lead. Running far enough ahead of the "Messenger" to render the maneuver safe, Worden crossed her bow, and circling around her ran back and picked up his barge.

In this race, it was said by passengers who were on board the two boats, that the flames actually blazed from the tops of the tall chimneys on both craft; and on both, men were stationed on the roof playing streams of water from lines of hose on the chimney breechings, to prevent the decks from igniting. Under such conditions it is easy to see how a boat might catch fire and burn. And yet the passengers liked it. Had they been the owners of casks of hams, as legend relates of a passenger on a lower river boat under like circumstances, there is no doubt they would have made an oblation of them to the gods of heat and steam, rather than have the other boat win.

The earliest recorded race run on the upper river was that between the "Nominee", owned and commanded by Captain Orren Smith, and the "West Newton" (Captain Daniel Smith Harris), in 1852. In this event but one boat actually ran, for Harris had no confidence in the ability of his boat to win, and not possessing the temper that would brook defeat, he declined to start. The "Nominee" completed the run from Galena to St. Paul and return, a distance of seven hundred miles, making all landings and handling all freight and passengers, in fifty-five hours and forty-nine minutes, an average rate of speed of 12½ miles an hour, half of it against and half with the current. This was good running, for the boats of that time. As there was no other boat to compete for the honor, the "Nominee" carried the broom until she sank at Britt's Landing, below La Crosse, in 1854.

Bunnell, in his very interesting *History of Winona*, says:

"Captain Orren Smith was a very devout man; and while he might indulge in racing, for the honor of his boat, he believed in keeping the Sabbath; and as long as he owned the boats which he commanded he would not run a minute after twelve o'clock Saturday night, but would tie his boat to the bank, wherever it might be, and remain at rest until the night following at twelve o'clock, when he would resume the onward course of his trip. If a landing could be made near a village or settlement where religious services could be held, the people were invited on board on Sunday, and if no minister of the gospel was at hand, the zealous Captain would lead in such service as suited his ideas of duty. But the Captain's reverence and caution did not save his boat, and she sank below La Crosse in the autumn of 1854."

Two of the boats on which I served, the "Kate Cassell" and the "Fanny Harris", while not of the slow class, yet were not ranked among the fast ones; consequently we had many opportunities to pass opposition boats under way, and to run away from boats that attempted to so humiliate us.

There was a great difference in boats. Some were built for towing, and these were fitted with engines powerful enough, if driven to their full capacity, to run the boat under, when the boat had no barges in tow. Other boats had not enough power to pull a shad off a gridiron. It was the power that cost money. A boat intended solely for freighting, and which consequently could take all the time there was, in which to make the trip, did not require the boilers and engines of a passenger packet in which speed was a prime factor in gaining patronage.

There is great satisfaction in knowing that the boat you are steering is just a little faster than the one ahead or behind you. There is still more satisfaction in feeling, if you honestly can, that you are just a little faster as a pilot than the man who is running the other boat. The two combined guarantee, absolutely, a proper ending to any trial of speed in which you may be engaged. Either one of them alone may decide the race, as a fast pilot is able to take his boat over a long course at a better rate of speed than a man not so well up in his business. If both men are equally qualified, then it is certain that the speediest boat will win.

What conditions determine the speed of two boats, all observable terms being equal? Nobody knows. The "Key City" and the "Itasca" were built for twins. Their lines, length, breadth, and depth of hold were the same; they had the same number and size boilers, and the parts of their engines were interchangeable; yet the "Key City" was from one to three miles an hour the faster boat, with the same pilots at the wheel. It was a fruitful topic for discussion on the river; but experts never reached a more enlightening conclusion than, "Well, I don't know". They didn't.

The boats of the old Minnesota Packet Company averaged better than those of a later era. In the run from Prairie du Chien to St. Paul, as noted above, the "Itasca" averaged twelve miles an hour, upstream, handling all her freight and passengers. The schedule for the Diamond Jo Line boats, in 1904, allowed eight miles an hour upstream, and eleven downstream, handling freight and passengers.

Chapter XX

Music and Art

In the middle of the nineteenth century, many an artist whose canvases found no market in the older cities, found ready bidders for his brush, to decorate the thirty-foot paddle-boxes of the big side-wheelers with figures of heroic size; or, with finer touch, to embellish the cabins of Western steamboats with oil paintings in every degree of merit and demerit.

The boat carrying my father and his family from Rock Island to Prescott, upon my first appearance on the Father of Waters, was the "Minnesota Belle". Her paddle-boxes were decorated with pictures the same on each side, representing a beautiful girl, modestly and becomingly clothed, and carrying in her arms a bundle of wheat ten or twelve feet long, which she apparently had just reaped from some Minnesota field. In her right hand she carried the reaping-hook with which it was cut.

All the "Eagles" were adorned with greater than life-size portraits of that noble bird. Apparently all were drawn from the same model, whether the boat be a Grey-, Black-, Golden-, War-, or Spread-Eagle.

The "Northern Belle", also had a very good looking young woman upon her paddle-boxes. Evidently she exhibited herself out of pure self-satisfaction, for she had no sheaf of wheat, or any other evidence of occupation. She was pretty, and she knew it.

The "General Brooke" showed the face and bust, in full regimentals, of the doughty old Virginian for whom it was named.

Later, the "Phil Sheridan" boasted an heroic figure of Little Phil, riding in a hurry from Winchester to the front, the hoofs of his charger beating time to the double bass of the guns at Cedar Creek, twenty miles away.

The "Minnesota" reproduced the coat-of-arms of the state

STEAMER "KEY CITY," 1857; 560 tons.
STEAMER "NORTHERN LIGHT," 1856; 740 tons.

whose name she bore — the ploughman, the Indian, and the motto "L'etoile du Nord". But the majority of the side-wheel boats boasted only a sunburst on the paddle-boxes, outside of which, on the perimeter of the wheel-house circle, was the legend showing to what line or company the boat belonged. The sunburst afforded opportunity for the artist to spread on colors, and usually the effect was pleasing and harmonious.

It was the inside work wherein the artists in oil showed their skill. Certainly there were many panels that showed the true artistic touch. The "Northern Light", I remember, had in her forward cabin representations of Dayton Bluff, St. Anthony Falls, Lover's Leap, or Maiden Rock, drawn from nature, for which the artist was said to have been paid a thousand dollars. They were in truth fine paintings, being so adjudged by people who claimed to be competent critics. On the other hand there were hundreds of panels — thousands, perhaps, in the myriad of boats that first and last plied on the river — that were the veriest daubs. These were the handiwork of the house painters who thought they had a talent for higher things, and who had been given free hand in the cabin to put their ambitions on record.

There was one case, however, which appealed to the humorous side of every one who was fortunate enough to see it. It was not intended that it should strike just this note. The artist who put it on the broad panel over the office window of the little stern-wheel "dinkey" from the Wabash, intended to convey a solemn note of warning to all who might look upon it to flee temptation. As the painting very nearly faced the bar, it required no very great stretch of imagination to read into the picture the warning to beware of the tempter, strong drink, particularly the brand served out on a Hoosier packet hailing from the Wabash.

In the centre was a vividly-green apple tree, bearing big red fruit. Our beloved Mother Eve, attired in a white cotton skirt that extended from waist to knee, was delicately holding a red scarf over her left shoulder and bosom. Confronting her was a wofully weak-minded Adam, dressed in the conventional habit of a wealthy first century Hebrew. The Satanic snake, wearing a knowing grin on his face, balanced himself on the tip of his tail.

Thirty years or more after the little boat from the Wabash

introduced this artistic gem to travellers on the upper river, I saw a copper-plate engraving two centuries old, from which the Hoosier artist had painted his panel. It was all there, except the colors — the tree, the apples, Eve in her scarf and skirt, Adam as a respectable Hebrew gentleman, and Satan balanced on the turn of his tail and leering with a devilish grin at the young woman who wanted to know it all, and at the lily-livered Adam who then and there surrendered his captaincy and has been running as mate ever since.

In the flush times on the river all sorts of inducements were offered passengers to board the several boats for the up-river voyage. First of all, perhaps, the speed of the boat was dwelt upon. It was always past my comprehension why any one who paid one fare for the trip, including board and lodging as long as he should be on the boat, and who had three good, if not "elegant", meals served each day without extra charge, should have been in such a hurry to get past the most beautiful scenery to be found anywhere under the sun. I would like nothing better than to take passage on the veriest plug that ever made three miles an hour, and having full passage paid, dawdle along for a week, and thus be enabled to enjoy in a leisurely manner, all the beauties of river, bluff, and island.

After speed came elegance — "fast and elegant steamer" — was a favorite phrase in the advertisement. An opportunity to study Eve and her apple, instead of the wealth of beauty which the Almighty has strewn broadcast over the Mississippi Valley, was an inducement carrying weight with some. It was a matter of taste.

After elegance came music, and this spoke for itself. The styles affected by river steamers ranged from a calliope on the roof to a stringed orchestra in the cabin. My recollection is, that most of us thought the name "calliope" was derived from some mechanical appliance in connection with music, with which we were as yet unfamiliar, the fame of Jupiter's daughter not yet having extended to the headwaters of the Mississippi. The question as to what relation this barbaric collection of steam whistles bears to the epic muse, that it should have appropriated her name, is still an open question. The "Excelsior", Captain Ward, was the first to introduce the "steam piano" to a long-suffering passenger list. Plenty of people took passage on the "Excelsior" in order to hear the calliope perform; many of them, long before they reached St. Paul, wished they had not come aboard, particularly if they were light sleepers. The river men did not mind it much, as they were used to noises of all kinds, and when they "turned in" made a business of sleeping. It was different with most passengers, and a steam piano solo at three o'clock in the morning was a little too much music for the money. After its introduction on the "Excelsior", several other boats armed themselves with this persuader of custom; but as none of them ever caught the same passenger the second time, the machine went out of fashion. Other boats tried brass bands; but while these attracted some custom they were expensive, and came to be dropped as unprofitable.

The cabin orchestra was the cheapest and most enduring, as well as the most popular drawing card. A band of six or eight colored men who could play the violin, banjo, and guitar, and in addition sing well, was always a good investment. These men were paid to do the work of waiters, barbers, and baggagemen, and in addition were given the privilege of passing the hat occasionally, and keeping all they caught. They made good wages by this combination, and it also pleased the passengers, who had no suspicion that the entire orchestra was hired with the understanding that they were to play as ordered by the captain or chief clerk, and that it was a strictly business engagement. They also played for dances in the cabin, and at landings sat on the guards and played to attract custom. It soon became advertised abroad which boats carried the best orchestras, and such lost nothing in the way of patronage.

Some of the older generation yet living, may have heard Ned Kendall play the cornet. If not, they may have heard of him, for his fame was at this time world-wide, as the greatest of all masters on his favorite instrument. Like many another genius, strong drink mastered him, and instead of holding vast audiences spell-bound in Eastern theatres, as he had done, he sold his art to influence custom on an Alton Line boat. It was my good fortune to have heard him two or three times, and his music appeals to me yet, through all the years that lie between. The witchery and the pathos of "Home, Sweet Home", "Annie Laurie", the "White Squall", and selections from operas of which I had then never even heard the names, cast such a spell that the boat on which he travelled was crowded every trip. Pity 'tis that one so gifted should fall into a slavery from which there was no redemption. He died in St. Louis, poor and neglected, a wreck infinitely more pitiable than that of the finest steamboat ever cast away on the Great River.

One of the boats on which I served employed a sextet of negro firemen, whose duty, in addition to firing, was to sing to attract custom at the landings. This was not only a unique performance, but it was likewise good music — that is, good of its kind. There was nothing classic about it, but it was naturally artistic. They sang plantation melodies — real negro melodies; not the witless and unmusical inanities which under the name of "coon songs" pass with the present generation for negro minstrelsy. Of course these darkies were picked for their musical ability, and were paid extra wages for singing.

The leader, Sam Marshall, received more than the others, because he was an artist. This term does not do him justice. In addition to a voice of rare sweetness and power, Sam was a born *improvisatore*. It was his part of the entertainment to stand on the capstan-head, with his chorus gathered about him, as the boat neared the landing. If at night, the torch fed with fatwood and resin threw a red glow upon his shining black face, as he lifted up his strong, melodious voice, and lined out his improvised songs, which recited the speed and elegance of this particular boat, the suavity and skill of its captain, the dexterity of its pilots, the manfulness of its mate, and the loveliness of Chloe, its black chambermaid. This latter reference always "brought down the house", as Chloe usually placed herself in a conspicuous place on the guards to hear the music, and incidentally the flatteries of her coal-black lover. As each line was sung by the leader the chorus would take up the refrain:

> De Captain stands on de upper deck;
> (Ah ha-a-a-ah! Oh ho-o-o-o-ho!)
> You nebber see 'nudder such gentlehem, *I* 'spec;
> (Ah ha-a-a-ah, Oh ho-o-o-ho.)

and then would follow, as an interlude, the refrain of some old plantation melody in the same key and meter, the six darkies singing their parts in perfect time and accord, and with a melody that cannot be bettered in all the world of music.

> De pilot he twisses he big roun' wheel;
> (Ah ha-a-a-ah, Oh ho-o-o-oh.)

> He sings, and he whissels, and he dance Virginia reel,
> (Ah ha-a-a-ah, Oh ho-o-o-ho), —

an undoubted reference to Tom Cushing, who, before his promotion to the pilot house was said to have been a tenor in grand opera in New York. He was a beautiful singer at any rate; could whistle like a New York newsboy, and dance like a coryphée. The "Old Man" would have been willing to take his oath that Cushing could and did do all three at the same time, in the most untimely hours of the morning watch, at the same time steering his steamboat in the most approved fashion.

The next stanza was:

> " 'Gineer in the engin' room listenn' fo' de bell;
> He boun' to beat dat oder boat or bus' 'em up to — *heb'n*,"

was accepted as a distinct reference to Billy Hamilton, as the manner of stating his intention to win out in a race was peculiar to the junior engineer, and the proposition was accepted without debate.

> "De Debbel he come in the middle of de night;
> Sam, dere, he scairt so he tuhn *mos'* white — Jes like dat white man out dere on de lebbee",

pointing at some one whom he deemed it safe to poke fun at, and of course raising a laugh at the expense of the individual so honored.

> "Des *look* at dem white fokses standin' on de sho';
> Dey la-a-aff, and dey la-a-aff, till dey cain't laff no mo' — ha-ha-ha-ha-ha",

and Sam would throw back his head and laugh a regular contagion into the whole crowd — on the boat and "on de sho'", opening a mouth which one of the darkies asserted was "de biggest mouf dis nigger ebber saw on any human bein' 'cept a aligator"; or, as the mate expressed it: "It was like the opening of navigation."

> "Dish yer nigger he fire at the middle do';
> Shake 'em up libely for to make de boat go",

was a somewhat ornate description of Mr. Marshall's own duties on board the boat. As a matter of fact he did very little firing, personally, although when a race was on he could shovel coal or pitch four-foot wood into the middle door with the best of them, at the same time, singing at the top of his voice. Upon ordinary occasions he let the other darkies pitch the cord wood while he exercised a general supervision over them, as became an acknowledged leader.

To hear these darkies sing the real slave music, which was older than the singers, older than the plantation, as old as Africa itself, wherein the ancestors of some of them at least, might have been kings and princes as well as freemen, was better than the fo'c'sle comedies enacted for the amusement of the passengers. These minor chords carried a strain of heartbreak, as in the lines:

> "De night is dark, de day is long
> And we are far fum home,
> Weep, my brudders, weep!"

And the closing lines:

> "De night is past, de long day done,
> An' we are going home,
> Shout, my brudders, shout!"

were a prophecy of that day of freedom and rest, after centuries of toil and bondage, the dawn of which was even then discernible to those who, like Abraham Lincoln, were wise to read in the political heavens the signs of its coming.

Chapter XXI

Steamboat Bonanzas

How it was possible to derive any profit from an investment of from $20,000 to $40,000, the principal of which had an average tenure of life of but five years, has puzzled a great many conservative business men from "down east", where "plants" lasted a lifetime, and the profits from which may have been sure, but were certain to be small. A man educated in such an atmosphere would hesitate long, before investing $25,000 in a steamboat that was foreordained to the scrap pile at the end of five summers; or where one out of every two was as certainly predestined to go up in smoke or down into the mud of the river bottom at the end of four years — these periods representing the ordinary life of a Mississippi River steamboat.

From 1849 to 1862 the shipyards of the Ohio, where nine out of ten Western boats were built, could not keep up with the orders. Every available shipwright was employed, and on some boats gangs worked at night by the light of torches at double wages, so great was the demand. Every iron foundry was likewise driven to the limit to turn out engines, boilers, and other machinery with which to give life to the hulls that were growing as if by magic in every shipyard.

If there had not been profit in the business, the captains and other river men who gave orders for these craft would not have given them. By far the greater number of boats were built for individual owners — practical river men who navigated the boats, and who knew just what they were about. Many of the orders were given to replace vessels that had been snagged or burned within the past twenty-four hours — for time was money, and a man could not afford to be without a steamboat many weeks, when twenty weeks or less represented a new boat in net earnings.

These men knew from actual experience that if they could keep their craft afloat for two years they could build a new boat from the profits made with her, even if she sank or burned at the end of that time. If she kept afloat for four years, they could buy or build two or three new ones from the profits, even without the aid of insurance. As a matter of fact the boats carrying insurance in those days were the exceptions. It came high, and owners preferred to take their own chances rather than indulge to any great extent in that luxury. How such profits were earned and such results obtained, it will be the object of this chapter to disclose.

In those days every boat made money. A big and fast one made a great deal; those small and slow made little as compared with their larger rivals, but plenty as compared with their own cost. Perhaps most vessel owners began on a small scale. A little boat might cost $5,000. She would run on some tributary of the Great River, and in the absence of any railroads might control all the traffic she was capable of handling, and at her own rates. In the course of two or three years her owner was able to build a bigger and a better boat. By combining with some other river man, the two might build one costing $25,000, and carrying from a hundred and fifty to two hundred tons of freight, and passengers in proportion. With such an equipment there was a fortune in sight at any time between 1849 and 1862, provided always that the boat was not snagged or burned on her first trip.

The doctrine (or science) of averages, is peculiar. In order to get an average of four years for a steamboat's life, it is necessary to keep some of them afloat for nine or ten; while on the other hand you are certain to "kill" a lot of them within a year after they touch water. When the latter happens, the investment is lost and the owner is probably ruined.

For purposes of illustration we will take as a sample one from the best class of money-makers on the upper river, in the flush times of 1857. Minnesota was organized as a territory in 1849, and admitted as a state in 1858. From 1852 to 1857 there were not boats enough to carry the people who were flocking into this newly-opened farmers' and lumbermen's paradise. There were over a hundred and twenty-five different steamboats registered at St. Paul in the latter year. The boats carrying good cargoes all through the season were the money-makers. Some of the larger ones were unable to get over the sand-bars after the midsummer droughts began. The stern-wheel boat of two hundred to three hundred tons was the one that could handle a good cargo on little water, and represented the highest type of profit-earning craft.

Such a boat would be about 200 feet long, 30 feet beam, and five feet depth of hold. She would have three large iron boilers (steel not having entered largely into boiler construction at that time), and fairly large engines, giving her good speed without an excessive expenditure for fuel. She would cost from $25,000 to $30,000, and accommodate two hundred cabin passengers comfortably, with a hundred second-class people on deck.

With such a boat furnished and ready for business, it is the duty of the captain to go out and hire his crew, and fit her out for a month's work. Such an investment in 1857, on the upper river, would approximate the following figures:

	Per month
Captain	$ 300.00
Chief clerk	200.00
Second clerk	100.00
Chief mate	200.00
Second mate	100.00
Pilots (2 at $500.00)	1,000.00
Chief engineer	200.00
Second engineer	150.00
Firemen (8 at $50.00)	400.00
Steward	200.00
Carpenter	150.00
Watchman	50.00
Deck hands (40 at $50.00)	2,000.00
Cabin crew	800.00
Food supplies ($75.00 per day, 30 days)	2,250.00
Wood (25 cords per day, 30 days, at $2.50)	2,000.00
Sundries	1,400.00
	$11,500.00

With this wage-list and expense-account before them, the captain and his chief clerk, who may also be a part owner in the boat, are face to face with the problem of meeting such expenses from passenger and cargo lists, and at the same time providing a sinking fund with which to build another craft within four years. To the uninitiated this would seem a somewhat appalling problem; with these old hands, the question would no doubt resolve itself down to the number of round trips that they would have to make to pay for their boat. The question of years never enters their heads.

In 1857 there were three principal points of departure on the upper river, above St. Louis. At that time St. Louis itself was the great wholesale centre, but it was not so important as an initial point for passengers for the upper Mississippi. The flood of immigration from St. Louis was for many reasons up the Missouri: furs and gold could be found in the mountains; there was a possible slave state in the farming regions below the mountains. The people who settled Minnesota and northern Wisconsin came from the East, and reached the river at three points — Rock Island, Dunleith (or Galena), and Prairie du Chien. Taking the point with which I am most familiar, we will start the new boat from Galena.

At that time Galena was, next to St. Louis, the principal wholesale *entrepôt* in the West. It was a poor trip for the boat which I have taken as a model, when she did not get a hundred tons of freight at Galena from the wholesale houses there. The balance was found at Dunleith, the terminus of what is now the Illinois Central Railway (then the Galena & Western Union); at Dubuque, which was also a big wholesale town; and at Prairie du Chien, the terminus of the Milwaukee & Mississippi Railway.

The freight rates on the river ran from 25 cents per hundred for short distances, to $1.50 per hundred from Galena to Stillwater, or St. Paul. No package was taken at less than 25 cents, however small it was, or how short the distance. In order not to overstate, we will take fifty cents per hundred as the average, and three hundred tons of cargo as the capacity of the two hundred-ton boat. [6] This is relatively the capacity of a vessel of that tonnage after deducting for passengers and fuel, and the

---

[6] A boat *measuring* 200 tons would carry from 300 to 350 tons weight in cargo. The tonnage of all boats is given by measurement, while the cargo is always in hundredweights.

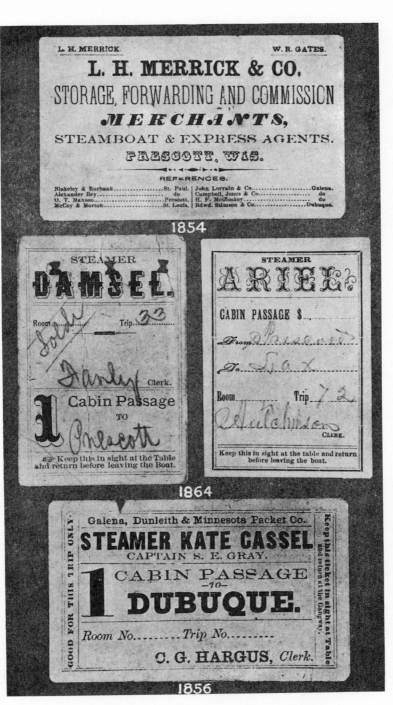

FACSIMILES OF EARLY TICKETS AND BUSINESS CARD.

space occupied by deck passengers. This latter item did not seriously count, for the freight was usually taken first and the deck passengers were then piled on top of it. Their comfort or convenience was never taken into consideration.

The boat can carry two hundred cabin passengers, and a hundred on deck. We will assume that there is another boat competing for this trip, and we do not fill up to the capacity. The clerk studies the rate sheets in vogue in 1857, and finds the following:

UP-STREAM RATES

30 miles or under (no charge less than 25c) .	6c per mile
30 to 60 miles	5c per mile
Over 60 miles	4c per mile

GALENA OR DUNLEITH TO —	Miles	Cabin passage	Deck passage
Cassville . . .	30	$ 2.00	$1.25
Prairie du Chien . .	66	3.50	2.00
La Crosse . . .	150	6.00	3.25
Red Wing . . .	256	10.00	3.50
Stillwater and St. Paul .	321	12.00	6.00

Galena or Dunleith to St. Paul	321	$12.00	$6.00
Prairie du Chien to St. Paul	255	10.00	5.00
La Crosse to St. Paul .	175	7.00	4.00

In 1904, the cabin passage on the Diamond Jo Line boats from Dunleith to St. Paul, was $8.00; from Prairie du Chien, $6.75; from La Crosse, $4.75. This is in competition with six railroads practically paralleling the river. In 1857 there was no railroad competition, and practically none from steamboats. Every boat attained a full passenger list, and was at liberty to charge whatever the conscience of the captain dictated — assuming a conscience. I have known a boat to fill up at Dunleith at the rate of $16.00 to St. Paul, and contract that all the men should sleep on the cabin floor, leaving staterooms for the women. And the passengers were glad enough to accept such conditions, for a detention of two days at Dunleith would cost a far greater sum than the overcharge exacted by the steamboat officers.

In the foregoing table I have included La Crosse, which,

however, was not an active factor in river rates until 1859. Before then, hundreds of passengers were landed there from Rock Island, Dunleith, and Prairie du Chien; but as the railroad had not yet reached the river at that point, there were but few passengers from La Crosse for landings farther up the river. When our boat leaves Prairie du Chien, then, the following business is in sight:

150 passengers from Dunleith or Galena, at an average of $8.00	$1,200.00
50 deck passengers at an average of $5.00 . .	250.00
300 tons freight, 6,000 cwts. at an average of 50c	3,000.00
	$4,450.00

A boat leaving Galena on Friday evening usually arrived at St. Paul in time to have her cargo all ashore and ready to start on the return trip sometime on Tuesday — usually about noon. At that time we shall find the chief clerk studying the downstream rate sheets. These differ somewhat from the up-stream and are like this, a few principal points being taken to illustrate:

DOWN-STREAM RATES

30 miles or under (no charge less than 25c.) .	5c per mile
30 to 60 miles	4c per mile
Over 60 miles	3c per mile

ST. PAUL OR STILLWATER TO—	Miles	Cabin passage	Deck passage
Hastings . . .	32	$1.50	$1.00
Red Wing . . .	65	2.50	2.00
Winona . . .	146	4.50	2.50
La Crosse . . .	175	5.00	3.00
Prairie du Chien . .	255	7.00	3.50
Dunleith or Galena . .	321	8.00	4.00

Down-stream rates are somewhat less than the up-stream, because, for one reason, it costs less to get a boat downstream. There is a four-mile current pushing the boat along, in addition to the applied power. Going upstream the boat had had this current to overcome before she gained an inch. A four-mile current is one-third of an average steamboat's progress. Again, the passengers do not get a chance to eat as much, and very often they were not served as well, on the down trip. Then, there were fewer people who wished to go down river, with the result that there were many boats bidding for the patronage of those who did make the trip. All these elements, with possibly others, entered into the cutting of the rates by about one-third on the down trip.

The only item besides passengers to be depended upon on the return trip, was wheat. There may have been some potatoes or barley, or, if fortune favored, some tons of furs and buffalo robes from the "Red River train", or some flour from the one mill at St. Anthony (now Minneapolis), or perhaps woodenware from the same point. There was always a more or less assorted cargo, but the mainstay was wheat. We will assume, in order to simplify this illustration, that there was nothing but wheat in sight at the time. There was no question about getting it. Every boat got all the wheat it could carry, and the shippers begged, almost on bended knees, for a chance to ship five hundred sacks, or a hundred, or fifty — any amount would be considered a great favor. Wheat was shipped at that time in two-bushel sacks, each weighing a hundred and twenty pounds. Three hundred tons, dead weight, is a pretty good cargo for a two-hundred ton boat. Wheat is dead weight, and a boat goes down into the water fast, when that is the sole cargo. We get five thousand sacks, all of which is unloaded at Prairie du Chien. The down trip foots up somewhat like this:

80 passengers at $8.00	$ 640.00
5,000 sacks of wheat at 12c	600.00
	$1,240.00

Arriving in Galena Friday morning, the clerk figures up his receipts with the following result:

Up trip	$4,450.00
Down trip	1,240.00
	$5,690.00

The boat makes four trips during the month, leaving out the extra two or three days, which may have been spent on some sand-bar. At the end of the month the clerk again does some figuring, with this result:

Income from four trips, at $5,690.00 . . .	$22,760.00
Less wages, fuel, provisions, etc. . . .	11,500.00
Net profit for month	$11,260.00

A stern-wheel, light-draught boat such as we have taken for this illustration, was quite certain to get five months' service — between the middle of April and the middle of October. In order not to put too great tension upon the credulity of modern readers, we will assume that she gets only five months of navigation. At the close of the season the captain and his clerk figure up the receipts and expenses, and strike a balance like this:

Receipts, 5 months, at $22,760.00 . . .	$113,800.00
Expenses, 5 months, at $11,500.00 . . .	57,500.00
Net earnings for the season	$ 56,300.00

This is enough to buy a new boat, and have something over for pin money. No one knows better than the writer the elusiveness, not to say the mendacity, of figures. He has often figured out greater profits than this in the nebulous schemes which have from time to time seduced him from the straight and narrow path of six per cent investment — and had them come out the other way. In steamboating in the fifties, this occurred very often. The most careful captain, employing the highest-priced pilots and engineers, would often lose his boat the first season; a snag or a lighted match, or a little too much steam, dissipating the best-laid plans in a few minutes of time. But the figures given above are conservative — made so purposely. The truth lies at the opposite extreme.

If the books of some of the boats of the old Minnesota Packet Company could be resurrected, they would show earnings and profits far greater than I have ventured to claim in my illustration. The "Fanny Harris", for instance, was a boat of 279 tons. Her wage-list and expense-account have been taken as a basis of the illustration above given, partly from recollection, and partly from figures which I made when I was second clerk, and which I have had before me in writing this chapter. We used to tow one barge all the time — most of the time two barges, and both boat and barges loaded to the water line, both ways, nearly every trip.

Of course we sometimes missed it. We landed ten thousand sacks of wheat at Prairie du Chien on one trip. Instead of a hundred and fifty cabin passengers, she often carried three hundred, "sleeping them" on the cabin floor three deep — at stateroom rates; and under such conditions the fortunate winners of such a chance to get into the promised land have risen up and called the whole outfit blessed, when in fact it was the other thing. I have heard of other boats claiming that they had to tow an extra barge to carry the money which they took in on the trip. I have always thought that these men were slightly overstating the case — but maybe not.

An item in one of the St. Paul papers of the time, states that the "Excelsior" arrived from St. Louis November 20, 1852, with two hundred and fifty cabin passengers, one hundred and fifty deck passengers, and three hundred tons of freight. For which freight she received "one dollar per hundred for any distance"; and the net profits of the up trip on freight alone were over $8,000. For two hundred and fifty cabin passengers she would receive $16 each, or $4,000; for the deck passengers, $8 each, or $1,200. These sums added to the $8,000 received for freight, would aggregate $13,200. The "Excelsior" cost not to exceed $20,000 — probably not over $16,000. Two trips like this would build a better boat. As this was the last trip of the season, she probably did not get such another. Under that freight rate — "one dollar per hundred for any distance" — a shipment of a hundred pounds from Prescott to Point Douglass, one mile, would cost the shipper a dollar. There were possibilities in such conditions.

Another item, also from a St. Paul paper, states that the "Lady Franklin" arrived May 8, 1855, from Galena, with five hundred passengers. She would accommodate a hundred and fifty cabin people, ordinarily. Figure this trip down to the probabilities, and the net result would be about as follows:

300 cabin passengers at $12 .   .   .   .   . $3,600
200 deck passengers at $6   1,200
                                                         ———————
                                                         $4,800

Or, reversing it:

200 cabin passengers at $12	$2,400
300 deck passengers at $6	1,800
	$4,200

The "Lady Franklin" cost about $20,000. Two months' work at this rate would buy a new and better boat. If I remember aright, the "Lady Franklin" was sunk in 1856 or 1857, but not until she had earned money enough to buy two new boats, each costing twice as much as she did. At the time she carried five hundred passengers she undoubtedly carried a full cargo of freight, worth at least two thousand dollars more to the boat.

An item in a St. Louis paper of that date, announces the departure of the side-wheel steamer "Tishomingo" (Jenks, master), for St. Paul on April 14, 1857, with 465 cabin passengers, 93 deck passengers and 400 tons of assorted freight. This trip would figure somewhat like this:

465 cabin passengers at an average of $16 . .	$7,440.00
93 deck passengers at an average of $8 . .	744.00
400 tons freight at 75c per hundred . . .	6,000.00
	$14,184.00

These rates are estimated at a very low figure. The regular cabin rate at that time, St. Louis to St. Paul, was, for cabin, $24; deck, $12; freight, $1.50 per hundredweight. It is not necessary to amplify at all. The "Tishomingo" had been bought in the spring of 1857, within a month, for $25,000. She paid one-half her purchase price on her first trip that season.

I would not have it understood that all boats made these phenomenal earnings; but many boats did, and all those of the Minnesota Packet Company were in this favored class. There were several conditions precedent, which made these results possible with the boats of this line. It controlled, absolutely, the freighting from the Galena and Dubuque jobbing houses; it controlled, absolutely, the freight business of the Dunleith and Prairie du Chien railroads, and practically all the passenger business of the two roads, as steamboat tickets were sold on the train, good only on the boats of the Minnesota Packet Company. These conditions insured a full cargo for every boat, and a full passenger list every trip. Outside boats did not have such a "cinch", but each had a source of revenue of its own, equally satisfactory. Even the "wild" boats had no difficulty in getting cargoes, and every vessel in that busy era had all the business it could handle.

The term "Company" was something of a misnomer. It was not at first a stock company, in the modern sense of the word. Each boat was owned by its captain, or a number of persons acting individually. In organizing the company, instead of capitalizing it with a certain amount of stock, the controlling parties simply put in their steamboats and pooled their earnings. Each boat had an equal chance with all the others for a cargo; and when the dividends were declared each one shared according to the earnings of his boat. A big boat could earn more than a smaller or slower one, and such a boat got a larger percentage than the latter. The particular advantage, in fact the only advantage, in pooling lay in securing a monopoly of the railroad and jobbing business. In order to do this it was necessary to have boats enough to handle the business at all times, and to have a general manager who would place the craft so as to give the most effective service.

One of the beauties of the pooling system was, that if a captain or owner became dissatisfied and desired to pull out, he could take his boat and the share of profits due him, and leave at any time. A few years later the company was reorganized as a joint stock company. After that, if one wished to get out he was lucky if he could get clear with the clothes on his back. The financiers who controlled fifty-one per cent of the stock retained all the steamboats and all the profits.

Chapter XXII

Wild-cat Money and Town-sites

Both of these specimens of natural history were bred, nurtured, and let loose in countless numbers to prey upon the people in the early days that witnessed the opening of the Northwestern territories to settlement. The wild-cat dollars waxed fat upon the blood and brawn of the settlers who had already arrived; wild-cat town-sites found ready victims in the thousands of Eastern people who desired to better their fortunes, and who lent ready ears to the golden tales of unscrupulous promoters, that told of wonderful cities in the West, whose only reality was that blazoned in the prospectuses scattered broadcast through the East.

The younger generation, whose only acquaintance with the circulating symbols of wealth that we call "money", is confined to the decades since the close of the War of Secession, can have no idea of the laxity of banking laws of the fifties, in the Northwestern states and territories, nor of the instability of the so-called "money" that conprised nine-tenths of the medium of exchange then in use in the West. Nowadays, a bank bill stands for its face value in gold, if it be a National Bank issue. If a state bank — and bills of this sort are comparatively few in these days — they are also guaranteed, in a measure, by the laws of the state in which the bank is situated. In the days of which I am writing, and especially in the unsettled and troublesome times just before the war (from 1856 to 1862), the money that was handled on the river in the prosecution of business, except of course the small proportion of gold that was still in circulation, had little or no backing, either by federal or state enactments.

A man went into an embryo city, consisting in that day of two or three thousand town lots, and from fifty to a hundred inhabitants, with an iron box costing twenty-five dollars. In this box he had ten, twenty, or thirty thousand "dollars" in new bank bills purporting to have been issued from two, three, or four banks doing business in other equally large, populous, and growing cities, situated elsewhere in Wisconsin, or preferably in Illinois, Indiana, or Michigan. How did he become possessed of all this wealth? Was it the savings of years? The iron box was, perhaps; perhaps he got trusted for that. The money was not usually the savings of any time at all; it was simply printed to order.

Five or six persons desirous of benefitting their fellow men by assisting them in opening their farms and "moving their crops", would get together in Chicago, Cincinnati, or St. Louis, wherever there was an establishment capable of engraving and printing bank bills — and not very elegant or artistic printing was required, or desired. These men propose to start as many banks, in as many "cities" in the West. They have money enough, each of them, to buy a safe, an iron box into which any carpenter could bore with an ordinary brace and bit, and enough over to pay for the printing of twenty thousand dollars' worth of bills in denominations of one, two, five and ten dollars. The printing finished, each man would sign his own bills as president, and one of the others would add the final touch of authenticity by signing a fictitious name to the same bills as cashier. Then it was "money".

But it would have been overloading the credulity of even the most gullible denizens of his adopted city to ask them to accept his own bills as legal tender; so a swap was made all around, and when the requisite amount of shuffling was completed, each man had his twenty thousand dollars in bills on four or five banks, but none of his own issue. There was a double incentive in this transaction: first, it inspired the utmost confidence in the minds of the men who were to borrow this money. How could this banker who had come among them for their good, have acquired this money by any other than legitimate transactions? If it were bills on his own bank that he proposed to put into circulation, there might be some question as to their guaranty; but he could not get this money by merely going to the printing office and ordering it, as he might in case of bills on his own institution. It certainly must be good money. Secondly, by distributing his bills in as many different localities as possible, the chances of its never being presented for redemption were greatly multiplied; it might be burned, or lost overboard, or worn out, in which case he would be just so much ahead, and no questions asked.

The foregoing may be a somewhat fanciful statement of the way in which the bankers proceeded, but in essence it is a true picture. They may not have all met in Chicago, or anywhere else, to perfect these arrangements, but the arrangements were all perfected practically as stated: "You put my bills into circulation, and I will put out yours; and in each case the exchange will greatly assist each and all of us in hoodwinking our victims into the belief that it is money, and not merely printed paper which we are offering them".

Equipped with these goods, and with a charter from the state in which he proposed to operate — a charter granted for the asking, and no questions raised — the banker transports himself and his box of money to his chosen field of operations. The newspaper which has already been located in the new city heralds the coming of Mr. Rothschild, our new banker, more or less definitely hinting at the great wealth lying behind the coming financier. A bank building is rented, a sign hung out, and he begins to loan his money at five per cent per month on the partially-improved farms of his neighbors, or the house and lot of his "city" friends. He is a liberal man, and if it is not convenient for you to pay the interest as it accrues, he will let it stand — but he does not forget to compound it every month. The result is inevitable. The debt mounts up with a rapidity that paralyzes the borrower, and in the end a foreclosure adds farm and improvements to the growing assets of the banker. Within a very few years he is the owner of eight or ten of the best farms in the county, and perhaps half a dozen houses and lots in the village, and all with the investment of less than a hundred dollars invested in printing, and an iron box, and without the expenditure of an ounce of energy or a legitimate day's work. And the victims break up and start anew for the still farther West, to take new farms, to be engulfed in the maws of other sharks. One may not greatly pity the men themselves, for men are born to work and suffer; but the women! God pity them. Worn, tired, broken-hearted, they must leave that which is dearest to them in all the world, their homes, and fare forth again into the wilderness, to toil and suffer, and at last, blessed release, to die.

McGregor, Iowa.   Looking north, up the river.

And the bankers? They were counted honest. If by any chance one of their bills came to hand and was presented for payment at the home counter, it was promptly redeemed, sometimes in gold or silver, but oftener with another bill on some other bank belonging to the syndicate. I personally knew some of these bankers. Some of them were freebooters without conscience and without shame. Under color of law, they robbed the settlers of their lands and improvements, and defied public opinion. Others put on a cloak of righteousness; they were leaders in the love-feasts and pillars in the church; and they also had their neighbors' lands and improvements. Their descendants are rich and respected to-day in the communities where their fathers plied their iniquitous trade; and these rule where their fathers robbed.

As a clerk on the river, I had some experience in handling the wild-cat money. At Dunleith, before starting on the up-river trip, we were handed by the secretary of the company, a *Thompson's Bank Note Detector*, and with it a list of the bills that we might accept in payment for freight or passage. We were also given a list of those that we might not accept at all; and still another list upon which we might speculate, at values running from twenty-five to seventy-five per cent of their face denominations. Thus equipped we started upstream, and the trouble started with us. At McGregor we put off a lot of freight, and were tendered money. We consulted our lists and cast into outer darkness that which had upon it the anathema of Mr. Jones, the secretary. We accepted all on the list of the elect, and compromised upon enough more to balance our freight account. The agent at McGregor had a list of his own which partly coincided with ours but in general disagreed. In the meantime another boat of our line had arrived from up river, and we get from her clerk fifteen or twenty lists of bills which would be taken or rejected at as many landings above. This helps somewhat, as we see our way clear to get rid of some of our twenty-five per cent stuff at par in exchange for cord wood or stores on the upper river, and we sort our stock out into packages which are reported current at each landing. We also see an opportunity to swap at Dunleith some bills which are not current there at all, but which are taken at par at Prescott or Stillwater, for other bills which they do not want but which will be taken at the company's office at Dunleith in settlement of our trip.

It required a long head to figure it out. Mine was long enough, but unfortunately it had the same dimensions both ways, and was not to be depended upon in these finer transactions. Mr. Hargus labored with the problem, studying lists until he came nigh to the point of insanity, with the result that when we "cashed in" on our return it was usually found that we had from five hundred to a thousand dollars that was not acceptable. This we kept, and the boat was debited with the amount on the company's books. On the next trip we would usually be able to work off some of this stuff. At the end of one season I recollect that we had some two thousand dollars, face estimate, of this paper on hand, which the treasurer would not accept, for the banks on which the bills were drawn had gone out of existence.

The town-site industry was on the same plane of deception and robbery as the banking frauds, but it found its victims "back East", instead of close at hand. Being Easterners, who had been educated to suppose that integrity and honesty were the basis of all business confidence, and themselves practiced these old-fashioned virtues, they all too readily accepted the assurances of the land-sharks, and invested their money without seeing the property which was so glowingly described in the prospectuses sent out by the Western promoters. The result was, that they were "taken in and done for" by the hundreds of town-site sharks who were operating all along the river, between Dunleith and St. Paul. I shall refer to but one of which I had personal knowledge, and to another described to me by Captain Russell Blakeley.

The city of Nininger, as delineated on the large and beauti-fully-engraved and printed maps issued by Ingenuous Doemly, was a well-built metropolis capable of containing ten thousand people. As delineated, it had a magnificent court house, this city being the county seat of Dakota County, Minnesota. Four or five church spires sprang a hundred feet each into the atmosphere. It had stores and warehouses, crowded with merchandise, and scores of drays and draymen were working with feverish energy to keep the levee clear of the freight being landed from half a dozen well-known steamboats belonging to the Minnesota Packet Company or the St. Louis & St. Paul Packet Company. An imposing brick structure with cut stone trimmings, four stories high, housed the plant of the Nininger *Daily Bugle*.

This last-mentioned feature of the prospectus was the only one that had the remotest semblance of foundation in fact.   There certainly was a *Daily Bugle*, issued once a week, or once in two or three weeks, depending upon the energy of the printer and his "devil", who jointly set the type, and the assiduity of the editors who furnished them with copy.   This paper was printed upon the first power press that ever threw off a printed sheet in the Territory of Minnesota.   It was a good press, and the paper printed upon it was a monument to the shrewdness and ingenuity of the honorable proprietor of the Nininger town-site.   The sheet was filled with a wealth of local advertising — drygoods, groceries, hardware, millinery, shoe stores, blacksmith shops — every class of business found in a large and prosperous city, was represented in those columns.   But every name and every business was fictitious, coined in the fertile brain of this chief of all promoters.   It was enough to deceive the very elect — and it did.   When the Eastern man read that there were six or eight lots, lying just west of Smith & Jones's drygoods store, on West Prairie Street, that could be had at a thousand dollars per lot if taken quickly, and that they were well worth twice that money on account of the advantageous situation, they were snapped up as a toad snaps flies on a summer day.

The paper was filled with local reading matter, describing the rush at the opening of the latest emporium; that Brown had gone East to purchase his spring stock; that Mrs. Newbody entertained at her beautiful new residence on Park Avenue, and gave the names of fifty of her guests.   The whole thing was the plan of a Napoleonic mind, being carried out to the minutest detail with painstaking care by a staff of able workers, with the result that the whole prairie for two miles back from the river was sold out at the rate of ten thousand dollars an acre or upwards, and that before the proprietor had himself perfected his legal rights to the land which he was thus retailing.

Henry Lindergreen, the printer who did the mechanical work on the Nininger paper, was a chum of mine, we having set type in the same "alley" elsewhere, and that winter I went up to Nininger to help him out.   The four-story brick block of the wood-cuts shrunk into a little frame building, the sides of which were made of inch boards set up on end and battened on the outside. Inside, it was further reinforced with tarred paper; and while I was there a pail of water ten feet from a red-hot stove, froze solid in a night, and the three printers had all they could do to feed the fire fast enough to keep themselves from freezing also, with the mercury down to forty degrees below zero. The editor who, in the absence of the promoter himself, in the East disposing of lots, was hired to improvise facts for the columns of this veracious sheet, lived in St. Paul, and sent his copy down to Hastings, as there was no postoffice at Nininger. If the editor or the proprietor had been found at Nininger in the following spring when the dupes began to appear, one or two of the jack oaks with which the city lots were plentifully clothed, would have borne a larger fruit than acorns. Even the printer who set the type, was forced to flee for his life.

One of the boldest-faced swindles I ever heard of, was the so-called Rolling Stone colony. In the spring of 1852, some three or four hundred people, chiefly from New York city, came to seek their purchased lands in Rolling Stone. They brought with them beautiful maps and bird's-eye views of the place, show-ing a large greenhouse, lecture hall, and library. Each colonist was to have a house lot in town and a farm in the neighboring country. The colony had been formed by one William Haddock, and none of the members had the faintest shadow of experience in farming. Boarding steamers at Galena, they expected to be put off at the Rolling Stone levee, for the views represented large houses, a hotel, a big warehouse, and a fine dock. But the steam-boat officers had never heard of such a place. Careful question-ing, however, seemed to locate the site three miles above Wabasha Prairie, on land then belonging to the Sioux Indians. As they insisted on landing, they were put off at the log cabin of one John Johnson, the only white man within ten miles. They made sod houses for themselves, or dug shelter burrows in the river banks; sickness came; many died during the summer and autumn; and when winter set in the place was abandoned. The people suffered severely, and the story of Rolling Stone makes a sad chapter in the early history of Minnesota.

While the craze was on, some made fortunes, while thousands of trusting men and women lost the savings of years. After the fever of speculation had burned itself out, the actual builders

of the commonwealth came in and subdued the land.   Nininger
and Rolling Stone are still on the map, and that is about all there
is of them — a name.   La Crosse, Winona, St. Paul and Minneapolis have superseded them, and the population, wealth, and
commerce of these are greater in reality than were the airy figments
of the brain which they have supplanted.

Chapter XXIII

A Pioneer Steamboatman

The same year and the same month in the year that witnessed the advent of the first steamboat on the Upper Mississippi, likewise witnessed the arrival in Galena of one who was destined to become the best known of all the upper river steamboatmen. In April, 1823, James Harris [7] accompanied by his son, Daniel Smith Harris, a lad of fifteen, left Cincinnati on the keel boat "Colonel Bumford", for the Le Fevre lead mines (now Galena),

---

[7] Captain Daniel Smith Harris was born in the state of Ohio in 1808. He came with his parents to Galena, Ill., in 1823, where he attended the frontier schools, and worked in the lead mines until 1836, when he commenced his career as a steamboatman, which was developed until he should become known as the greatest of all the upper river steamboat owners and captains. In the year 1836, in company with his brother, R. Scribe Harris, who was a practical engineer, he built the steamer "Frontier," which he commanded that season. In 1837 the two brothers brought out the "Smelter," which was commanded by Daniel Smith Harris, Scribe Harris running as chief engineer. In 1838 they built the "Pre-Emption," which was also run by the two brothers. In 1839 they built the "Relief," and in 1840 the "Sutler," both of which he commanded. In 1841 they brought out the "Otter," which Captain Harris commanded until 1844, when the two brothers built the "War Eagle" (first), which he commanded until 1847. In 1848 he commanded the "Senator"; in 1849 the "Dr. Franklin No. 2"; in 1850 and 1851 the "Nominee"; in 1852 the "Luella," "New St. Paul" and "West Newton"; in 1853 the "West Newton"; 1854, 1855 and 1856 the "War Eagle" (second), which he built. (See picture of "War Eagle" on page 120.) In 1857 Captain Harris built the "Grey Eagle," the largest, fastest and finest boat on the upper river up to that time, costing $63,000. He commanded the "Grey Eagle" until 1861, when she was lost by striking the Rock Island Bridge, sinking in five minutes. Captain Harris then retired from the river, living in Galena until his death in 189-. As a young man he took part, as a Lieutenant of Volunteers, in the battle of Bad Axe, with the Indians under Chief Black Hawk.

where they arrived June 20, 1823, after a laborious voyage down the Ohio and up the Mississippi.

A word in passing, regarding the keel boat. Few of the men now living know from actual observation what manner of craft is suggested by the mere mention of the name. None of this generation have seen it. A canal boat comes as near it in model and build as any craft now afloat; and yet it was not a canal boat. In its day and generation it was the clipper of the Western river to which it was indigenous. Any sort of craft might go downstream; rafts, arks, broadhorns, and scows were all reliable down-stream sailers, dependent only upon the flow of the current, which was eternally setting toward the sea. All of this sort of craft did go down, with every rise in the Ohio, in the early days of the nineteenth century, from every port and landing between Pittsburg and Cairo, to New Orleans. They were laden with adventurers, with pioneers, with settlers, or with produce of the farms already opened along the Ohio and its tributaries; corn, wheat, apples, live-stock — "hoop-poles and punkins", in the slang of the day — in fact anything of value to trade for the merchandise of civilization which found its *entrepôt* at New Orleans from Europe or the Indies. The craft carrying this produce was itself a part of the stock in trade, and when unloaded was broken up and sold as lumber for the building of the city, or for export to Cuba or other West Indian ports. The problem was to get back to the Ohio with the cargo of merchandise bought with the produce carried as cargo on the down trip. The broad horns and arks were an impossibility as up-stream craft, and thus it came about in the evolution of things required for specific purposes, that the keel boat came into being.

This boat was built to go upstream as well as down. It was a well-modelled craft, sixty to eighty feet long, and fifteen to eighteen feet wide, sharp at both ends, and often with fine lines — clipper-built for passenger traffic. It had usually about four feet depth of hold. Its cargo box, as it was called, was about four feet higher, sometimes covered with a light curved deck; sometimes open, with a "gallows-frame" running the length of the hold, over which tarpaulins were drawn and fastened to the sides of the boat for the protection of the freight and passengers in stormy weather. At either end of the craft was a deck for eight

or ten feet, the forward or forecastle deck having a windlass
or capstan for pulling the boat off bars, or warping through swift
water or over rapids.

Along each side of the cargo box ran a narrow walk, about
eighteen inches in width, with cleats nailed to the deck twenty-
eight or thirty inches apart, to prevent the feet of the crew from
slipping when poling upstream. Of the motive power of these
boats, Captain H. M. Chittenden, U. S. A., in a recent work
on the navigation of the Missouri River in early days, says:

"For the purposes of propulsion the boat was equipped with nearly all
the power appliances known to navigation, except steam. The cordelle
was the main reliance. This consists of a line nearly a thousand feet
long, fastened to the top of a mast which rose from the centre of the
boat to the height of nearly thirty feet. The boat was pulled along with
this line by men on shore. In order to hold the boat from swinging
around the mast, the line was connected with the bow of the boat by
means of a "bridle", a short auxiliary line fastened to a loop in the
bow, and to a ring through which the cordelle was passed. The bridle
prevented the boat from swinging under force of wind or current when
the speed was not great enough to accomplish this purpose by means of
the rudder. The object in having so long a line was to lessen the tendency
to draw the boat toward the shore; and the object in having it fastened
to the top of the mast was to keep it from dragging, and to enable it to
clear the brush along the bank. It took from twenty to forty men to
cordelle the keel boat along average stretches of the river [the Missouri],
and the work was always one of great difficulty."

For poling the men were provided with tough ash poles,
eighteen or twenty feet long, with a wooden or iron shoe or
socket to rest on the bottom of the river, and a crutch or knob
for the shoulder. In propelling the boat, ten or a dozen men
on each side thrust the foot of their poles into the bottom of the
river, and with the other end against their shoulders, walked
toward the stern of the boat, pushing it upstream at the same
rate of speed with which they walked toward the stern. As
each pair — one on each side of the boat — reached the stern,
they quickly recovered their poles, leaped to the roof of the cargo
box, and running forward jumped to the deck and replanted their
poles for a new turn of duty. By this means an even speed was
maintained, as in a crew of twenty there were always sixteen
men applying motive power, while four others were returning to
the bow for a new start. The writer, in his childhood, has stood
for hours on the banks of the St. Joseph River, in Niles, Michigan,

watching the crews of keel boats thus laboriously pushing their craft up the river from St. Joseph, on the lake, to Niles, South Bend, and Mishawaka. They were afterward to float back, laden with flour in barrels, potatoes and apples in sacks, and all the miscellaneous merchandise of the farm, destined for Detroit, Buffalo, and the East, by way of the Great Lakes.

In addition to cordelling, as described above, the long line was also used in warping the boat around difficult places where the men could not follow the bank. This was accomplished by carrying the line out ahead in the skiff as far as possible or convenient, and making it fast to trees or rocks. The men on the boat then hauled on the line, pulling the boat up until it reached the object to which the line was attached. The boat was then moored to the bank, or held with the poles until the line was again carried ahead and made fast, when the process was repeated. In this manner the greatest of up-river steamboatmen, Captain Daniel Smith Harris, prosecuted his first voyage from Cincinnati to Galena, in the year 1823. It probably required no more than four or five days to run down the Ohio, on the spring flood, to Cairo; from Cairo to Galena required two months of cordelling, poling, and warping.

About the time the keel boat "Colonel Bumford" was passing St. Louis, the steamer "Virginia" departed for the upper river with a load of supplies for the United States military post at Fort Snelling. She had among her passengers Major John Biddle and Captain Joseph P. Russell, U. S. A., and Laurence Talliaferro, United States Indian Agent for the Territory of Minnesota. The "Virginia" arrived at Fort Snelling May 10, 1823, the first boat propelled by steam to breast the waters of the upper Mississippi. She was received with a salute of cannon from the fort, and carried fear and consternation to the Indians, who watched the smoke rolling from her chimney, the exhaust steam shooting from her escape pipe with a noise that terrified them. The "Virginia" was scarcely longer than the largest keel boat, being about a hundred and twenty feet long, and twenty-two feet beam. She had no upper cabin, the accommodations for the passengers being in the hold, in the stern of the boat, with the cargo-box covering so common to the keel boats of which she herself was but an evolution.

What did the young steamboatman see on his voyage from
Cairo to Galena in 1823? In his later years, in speaking of this
trip, he said that where Cairo now stands there was but one log
building, a warehouse for the accommodation of keel-boat navigators of the Ohio and Mississippi Rivers. Cape Girardeau, St.
Genevieve, and Herculaneum were small settlements averaging
a dozen families each. St. Louis, which was built almost entirely
of frame buildings, had a population of about five thousand. The
levee was a ledge of rocks, with scarcely a fit landing place on
the whole frontage. Alton, Clarksville, and Louisiana were minor
settlements. What is now Quincy consisted of one log cabin only,
which was built and occupied by John Woods, who afterwards
became lieutenant-governor of the State of Illinois, and acting
governor. This intrepid pioneer was "batching it", being indus-
triously engaged in clearing a piece of land for farming purposes.
The only settler at Hannibal was one John S. Miller, a blacksmith, who removed to Galena in the autumn of 1823. In later
years, Hannibal was to claim the honor of being the birthplace
of "Mark Twain", the historian of the lower Mississippi pilot
clans. The last farm house between St. Genevieve and Galena
was located at Cottonwood Prairie (now Canton), and was occupied by one Captain White, who was prominently identified with
the early development of the Northwest. There was a government garrison at Keokuk, which was then known as Fort Edwards,
and another at Fort Armstrong, now Rock Island. The settlement at Galena consisted of about a dozen log cabins, a few
frame shanties, and a smelting furnace.

If he were looking only for the evidence of an advancing
civilization, the above probably covers about all he saw on his
trip. Other things he saw, however. The great river, flowing
in its pristine glory, "unvexed to the sea"; islands, set like emer-
alds in the tawny flood, the trees and bushes taking on their
summer dress of green in the warm May sunshine; prairies
stretching away in boundless beauty, limited only by his powers
of vision. Later, as his craft stemmed the flood and advanced
up the river, he saw the hills beginning to encroach upon the
valley of the river, narrowing his view; later, the crags and
bastions of the bluffs of the upper river, beetling over the very

Alton, Illinois. Looking down the river.

channel itself, and lending an added grandeur to the simple beauty of the banks already passed.

His unaccustomed eyes saw the wickyups and tepees of the Indians scattered among the islands and on the lowlands, the hunters of the tribe exchanging the firelock for the spear and net as they sought to reap the water for its harvest of returning fish. It was all new to the young traveller, who was later to become the best known steamboatman of the upper river, the commander of a greater number of different steamboats than any of his compeers, and who was to know the river, in all its meanderings and in all its moods, better than any other who ever sailed it — Daniel Smith Harris, of Galena, Illinois.

Chapter XXIV

A Versatile Commander; Wreck of the "Equator"

While some men were to be found on the Mississippi in the sixties who did not hesitate to avow themselves religious, and whose lives bore witness that they were indeed Christians, the combination of a Methodist preacher and a steamboat captain was one so incongruous that it was unique, and so far as I know, without a parallel on the river. There appeared to be no great incompatibility between the two callings, however, as they were represented in the person of Captain Asa B. Green. He was a good commander, as I had personal opportunity of observing at the time of the incident described in this chapter; and a few years later, when the great drama of the Civil War was on, I again had an opportunity to observe Captain Green in his alternate rôle of minister of the gospel, he having been appointed chaplain of the Thirtieth Wisconsin Infantry in which I served as a private soldier. In this capacity he showed rare good sense and practical wisdom. He preached to the boys when a favorable opportunity offered on a Sunday, when there was not too much else going on; but his sermons were short, and as practical as was the man himself.

Of his conversion, or early life, on the river as a missionary, little seemed to be known by any one whom I ever met. He ran the Chippewa in the early days, during the summer months, and in the winter did missionary work among the lumbermen, following them to their camps in the woods, preaching and ministering to them; not as an alien, and in an academic fashion, but as one "to the manner born". It is likely that his young manhood was passed on the river and in the lumber camps, and when he was converted his thoughts turned naturally to the needs of these particular classes, for none knew better than he just how great their needs were. Of how or where he was ordained to preach I know nothing; but as he was in good standing with the Methodist conference there is no question as to the regularity of his commission. His master's certificate authorizing him to command a steamboat certified to his standing as a river man.

Probably he divided his time between commanding a steamboat and preaching the gospel, two callings so dissimilar, because the river work was quite remunerative, financially, while the other was quite the reverse. It probably took all the money he earned during the summer to support himself and his philanthropies during the winter. If his expenditures among the boys in the lumber camps were as free-handed as were his gifts to poor, sick, wounded, and homesick soldiers during his service with the Thirtieth Wisconsin during the war, it would easily require the seven months' pay of a river captain to sustain the other five months' liberality of the quondam preacher. Certain it is, that after three years' service as chaplain he came out as poor as he went in — in money. If the respect and high regard of his brother officers were worth anything; or better yet, if the love and gratitude of hundreds of plain boys in blue, privates in the ranks, might be counted as wealth, then Captain Green was rich indeed. And that was what he did count as real wealth. To be hugged by one of his "boys" at a Grand Army reunion, one whom he had nursed back to life in an army hospital by his optimistic cheerfulness and Christian hope and comfort — was to him better than gold or silver. He has gone to his reward; and whether he now is telling the "old, old story" to other men in other spheres, or pacing the deck of a spectre steamboat on the River of Life — whichever may be his work — beyond a peradventure he is doing that work well.

In the spring of 1858, in April, in his capacity as captain, Asa B. Green was commanding the steamer "Equator". She was a stern-wheel boat of about a hundred and twenty tons, plying on the St. Croix between Prescott and St. Croix Falls. The lake opened early that season, but the opening was followed by cold and stormy weather, with high winds. There was some sort of celebration at Stillwater, and as was customary in those days an excursion was organized at Hastings and Prescott to attend the "blow-out". About three hundred people crowded the little steamer, men, women, and children. She started off up the lake in the morning, fighting her way against a high wind right out of the north. Charley Jewell was pilot, the writer was "cub", John Lay was chief engineer. I have forgotten the name of the mate, but whatever may have been his name or nationality, he was the man for the place. He was every inch a man, as was the captain on the roof, and so in fact was every officer on the boat.

Everything went well until we had cleared Catfish bar, at Afton. From there to Stillwater is about twelve miles, due north. The wind had full sweep the whole length of this reach. The lake is two and a half miles wide just above Catfish bar. The sweep of the wind had raised a great sea, and the heavily-laden boat crawled ahead into the teeth of the blizzard — for it began to snow as well as blow. We had progressed very slowly, under an extra head of steam, for about three miles above the bar, when the port "rock-shaft", or eccentric rod, broke with a snap, and the wheel stopped instantly; in fact, John Lay had his hand on the throttle wheel when the rod broke, and in an instant had shut off steam to save his cylinders.

As soon as the wheel stopped the boat fell off into the trough of the sea. The first surge caught her on the quarter, before she had fully exposed her broadside, but it rolled her lee guards under water, and made every joint in her upper works creak and groan. The second wave struck her full broadside on. The tables had just been set for dinner. As the boat rolled down, under stress of wind and wave, the tables were thrown to leeward with a crash of broken glass and china that seemed to be the end of all things with the "Equator". Women and children screamed, and many women fainted. Men turned white, and some went wild, scrambling and fighting for life preservers. Several persons — they could hardly be called men — had two, and even three, strapped about their bodies, utterly ignoring the women and children in their abjectly selfish panic. The occasion brought out all the human nature there was in the crowd, and some that was somewhat baser than human.

As a whole, however, the men behaved well, and set about doing what they could to insure the safety of the helpless ones before providing for their own safety. It has always been a satisfaction to me that I had this opportunity, while a boy, to witness and take part in an accident which, while it did not result in the loss of a single life, had every element of great danger, and the imminent probability of the loss of hundreds of lives. It was an object lesson in what constituted manhood, self-reliant courage, official faithfulness, and the prompt application of ready expedients for the salvation of the boat.

When the crash came, Mr. Lay called up through the speaking-tube, stating the nature and extent of the accident. Mr. Jewell reported it to Captain Green, who ordered him to go to the cabin and attempt to allay the fright of the passengers, and to prevent a panic. As he started, Jewell ordered me to remain in the pilot house and listen for calls from the engine-room.

In the meantime the deck hands, or many of them, were in a panic, some of them on their knees on the forecastle, making strong vows of religious reformation should they come safe to land. This was a commendable attitude, both of body and spirit, had there been nothing else to do. In this particular province it would seem that much might have been expected from a captain who was also a preacher. On the contrary his manner of meeting the exigency was decidedly and profoundly out of drawing with preconceived notions of what might be expected from such a combination. An old man from Prescott, the richest man in town, and also one of the meanest, nearly seventy years old, crept up the companion way to the upper deck, and clasping Captain Green about the legs cried: "Save me! for God's sake save me! and I will give you a thousand dollars"!

"Get away you d——d cowardly old cur. Let go of me and get down below or I will throw you overboard", was Captain Green's exhortation as he yanked him to his feet by his collar and kicked him to the stairway. Both the language and the action were uncanonical in the extreme; but then, he was acting for the time in his capacity as captain, and not as preacher. I didn't laugh at the time, for I was doing some thinking on my own hook about the salvation business; and my estimate of the chances for getting to the shore, two miles away, in that wind and sea, was not flattering. I have laughed many times since, however, and wondered what the old miser thought of the orthodoxy of Chaplain Green when he answered his prayer.

The deck hands also met with a surprise from the mate, and that in less than a minute.   Men think fast in such an emergency, especially those schooled amid dangers and quickened in mind and body by recurring calls for prompt action.   A dozen seas had not struck the "Equator" before the mate was on the forecastle, driving the panic-stricken deck hands to work.   Dropping the two long spars to the deck, with the assistance of the carpenter and such men as had gathered their wits together, he lashed them firmly together at each end.   Then bending on a strong piece of line extending from end to end, and doubled, he made fast the main hawser, or snubbing line, to the middle, or bight of the rope attached to the spars, and then launched the whole overboard, making a "sea-anchor" that soon brought the bow of the vessel head to sea, and eased the racking roll of the hull, steadying the craft so that there was little further danger of her sinking.   In the ten or fifteen minutes that it had taken to get the drag built and overboard, the waves had swept over the lower deck and into the hold, until there was a foot of water weighing her down, which the bilge pumps operated by the "doctor" were unable to throw out as fast as it came in.   Had it continued to gain for fifteen minutes longer, the boat would have gone to the bottom with all on board.   The drag saved the vessel; the coolness and quickness of the mate and carpenter were the salvation of the steamer and its great load of people.

In the meantime other incidents were occurring, that made a lasting impression upon my mind.   I did not witness them myself, but I learned of them afterwards.   All this time I stood at the side of the useless wheel in the pilot house, listening for sounds from the engine-room.   Mr. Lay was doing all that was possible to remedy the break.   He cut off the steam from the useless cylinder, and with his assistant and the firemen, was at work disconnecting the pitman, with the intent to try to work the wheel with one cylinder, which would have been an impossibility in that sea.   In fact it would have been impossible under any circumstances, for the large wheel of a stern-wheel boat is built to be operated by two engines; there is not power enough in either one alone to more than turn it over, let alone driving the steamboat.   When the crash came, Engineer Lay's wife, who was on board as a passenger, ran immediately to the engine-room to be with her husband when the worst should come. He kissed her as she came, and said: "There's a dear, brave, little woman. Run back to the cabin and encourage the other women. I must work. Good-bye". And the "little woman" — for she was a little woman, and a brave little woman, also — without another word gave her husband a good-bye kiss, and wiping away the tears, went back to the cabin and did more than all the others to reassure the frightened, fainting women and little children — the very antithesis of the craven old usurer who had crept on his knees begging for a little longer lease of a worthless life.

It took an hour or more to drift slowly, stern first, diagonally across and down the lake to the shore above Glenmont, on the Wisconsin side, where she struck and swung broadside onto the beach. The men carried the women ashore through four feet of water, and in another hour the cabin was blown entirely off the sunken hull, and the boat was a total wreck. Her bones are there to-day, a striking attestation of the power of wind and wave, even upon so small a body of water as Lake St. Croix.

Big fires were built from the wreckage to warm the wet and benumbed people. Runners were sent to nearby farm houses for teams, as well as to Hudson, seven or eight miles way. Many of the men walked home to Prescott and Hastings. Captain Green, who owned the boat, stayed with his crew to save what he could from the wreck, in which he lost his all; but he had only words of thanksgiving that not a life had been lost while under his charge. Through it he was cool and cheerful, devoting himself to reassuring his passengers, as soon as the drag was in place, and giving orders for getting the women and children ashore as soon as the boat should strike. His only deviation from perfect equipoise was exhibited in his treatment of the old man, a notoriously mean, and exacting money-lender, with whom he had no sympathy at any time, and no patience at a time like this.

Chapter XXV

A Stray Nobleman

Of the many men whom it was my good fortune to meet while on the river as a boy, or as a young man, there was none who came nearer to filling the bill as a nobleman than Robert C. Eden, whose memory suggests the title of this chapter. Just what constitutes a nobleman in the college of heraldry, I am not qualified to assert. "Bob" Eden, as his friends fondly called him — Captain Eden, as he was known on the river, or Major Eden as he was better known in the closing days of the War of Secession — was the son of an English baronet. There were several other sons who had had the luck to be born ahead of "Bob", and his chance for attaining to the rank and title of baronet was therefore extremely slim. However, his father was able to send him to Oxford, from which ancient seat of learning he was graduated with honors. As a younger son he was set apart for the ministry, where he finally landed after sowing his wild oats, which he did in a gentlemanly and temperate manner that comported well with the profession for which he was destined, all his studies having been along theological lines. The *wanderlust* was in his blood, however, and he declined taking holy orders until he had seen something of the unholy world outside. Accordingly he took the portion due him, or which his father gave him, and departed for Canada. Not finding things just to his taste in that British appanage, possibly not rapid enough for a divinity student, he promptly crossed the line and began making himself into a Yankee, in all except citizenship.

In his wanderings he finally reached Oshkosh, attracted no doubt by the euphony of the name, which has made the little "saw dust city of the Fox" one of the best known towns, by title, in the world. If there was any one place more than another cal-

RED WING, MINNESOTA. Showing Barn Bluff in the background, with a glimpse of the river on the left.

culated to educate and instruct an embryo clergyman in the ways
of the world, and a particularly wicked world at that, it was
Oshkosh before the war. That he saw some of the "fun" which
the boys enjoyed in those days was evidenced by the fund of stories
relating to that place and that era, which he had in stock in later
years.

I do not know how long he remained there on his first
visit. When I made his acquaintance he was journeying up the
river by easy stages on a little side-wheel steamer, having both
wheels on a single shaft — a type of steamboat which I had
known on the St. Joseph River in Michigan, but which was not
common on the Mississippi. This class was used on the Fox and
Wolf Rivers, and on Lake Winnebago. Captain Eden had bought
this little steamboat, of perhaps eighty tons burden, for the purpose
of exploring at his leisure the upper Mississippi and its tributaries.
He had sailed up the Fox River to Portage, through the canal
to the Wisconsin, and down that stream to the Mississippi, and
had reached Prescott, where I met him. He wanted to go up the
St. Croix to the Falls, stopping at all the towns, and at places
where there were no towns, at his own sweet will. First-class
pilots were getting six hundred dollars a month wages in those
days. Eden's boat was not worth two months' pay of such a pilot,
and he was on the lookout for a cheaper man when he found me.

His crew consisted of himself, acting in the capacity of
captain and first and second mates; an engineer and fireman in
one person; a deck hand, and a cook. The cook is named last, but
he was by no means the least personage aboard the "Enterprise".
As this was a sort of holiday excursion, the cook was about the
most important official about the boat. He was fully up in his
business, and could cook all kinds of game and fish to perfection,
as well as the ordinary viands of civilization. It was a privilege
to be catered to by this master of his art. The captain had under
him, therefore, three men, in addition to the pilot for temporary
service from time to time as he journeyed up the river. The
"Enterprise" was not a speedy boat. She could make four or
five miles an hour upstream if the current was not too strong, and
double that downstream if the current was strong enough. She
had no upper cabin answering to the "boiler deck" of the river
boats — only a little box of a pilot house on the roof, big enough

to contain a little wheel and the man who turned it. This wheel was only about a third the diameter of a real steamboat wheel, and instead of wheel-ropes it had chains, large enough for a man-of-war. When the wheel was put hard up or hard down, the chains responded with a series of groans and squeaks not unmusical, but new and novel to one used only to the noiseless operation of the well-oiled wheel-ropes of the river steamers. The chains were part of the fire-proof outfit required by regulations on the great lakes. The "Enterprise" was from Winnebago. To pull the little three-foot wheel hard down, and hold the stumpy little steamer up to a reef from which she wanted to run away, required the expenditure of as much muscle as was demanded to cramp a four-hundred ton steamer over the same bar by the use of the larger wheel and easier-running wheel-ropes.

The cabin of the "Enterprise" was all aft of the paddle-boxes. It was so divided as to afford sleeping quarters for the crew at the forward part, next the engine, while Captain Eden occupied the after part, which was fitted up as a boudoir, with a little side niche, in which he slept. His pointer dog and his retriever also slept in the same niche. There was a fine library in the cabin — not a great number of books, but the best books, some English, some French, some German, and several Greek and Latin, for Captain Eden was a polyglot in his reading. There was also a gun rack with several rifles, three or four shot guns of big and little calibre, and a pair of duelling pistols. Likewise there were rods, reels, landing nets, and fly-hooks without number, rubber boots and mackintoshes for rough weather, and all the paraphernalia of a gentleman sportsman. It was evident at a glance that Captain Eden was not in financial straits, and it was equally evident that he was not steamboating for profit.

As I knew the St. Croix River well enough to navigate it with a far larger boat than Captain Eden's, and in addition knew also a great deal more about the haunts of bear, deer, prairie chickens, brook trout, and indeed all species of fish inhabiting the waters of the Mississippi River and its tributaries; and further, had a speaking and dining acquaintance with sundry red men, both Sioux and Chippewa, with whom Captain Eden also wished to become acquainted for purposes of original investigation and study, I was deemed a valuable acquisition. On my side a reasonable salary as pilot, with a free run of the guns, fishing tackle, and books was an attractive presentation of the case, and it took but a short time to arrange the details of an engagement.

A day's work on this model craft consisted in steering the boat five or six miles up or down the river or lake to the most inviting hunting or fishing grounds, or to the vicinity of an Indian camp, finding a sheltered place in which to tie up, and then taking a tramp of ten or a dozen miles after deer, bear, or prairie chickens, or a walk of three or four miles up some favorite trout stream, and fishing back to the boat. In that day bear and deer abounded within a very few miles of Prescott, Hudson, or other points. Indeed, as late as 1876 bears were quite common about River Falls, one or two having come right into the village to pick up young pigs and lambs; and deer were also numerous within a few miles of the same place.

This in itself was an ideal occupation. But added to it was the privilege of an intimate association with, and the conversation of, a man from across the ocean, whose father was a baronet, who had himself been schooled in Oxford, who had lived in London, and Paris, and Berlin, and had seen men and things of whom and which I had read in books, but which were all very far removed from the backwoods farm of Michigan where I was born, and from the still wilder surroundings of the upper Mississippi in the middle fifties.

I had been a persistent reader from the time I had learned my letters, and was now seventeen years old. The volumes to which I had had access were principally school books, with here and there a history or biography, and an occasional novel. At one period only, while working in the printing office, had I the run of a well-chosen library belonging to the lawyer-editor. Here, however, was something better than books. I could question this man on points that the books might have passed over, and he could answer. His mind was quick, his powers of observation trained, his brain well stored with the lore of books — history, poetry, eloquence, and in addition he had seen much of the world which lay so far beyond and outside the life of a Western-bred country lad. It was better than any school I had ever attended, and he was a rare teacher. He didn't realize that he was teaching, but I did.

It was not a case of absorption alone on my part, however. In my own field I had much to communicate — the lore of woods and streams, the ways of the red men, the moods and legends of the Great River, matters which seemed of little value to me, but which this stranger from an older civilization was as solicitious to hear about as I was to listen to the stories of his larger life. While I deemed myself fortunate indeed in making the acquaintance of this cosmopolitan man of the world, I was pleased to know that there were some things that I knew better than my more widely-travelled employer. One of these things, insignificant in itself, was the fact that the pilot could catch ten trout to the captain's one, after giving him all possible advantages of first chances at good "holes", and likely riffles, and the first chance in wading ahead down the stream. This was for a long time one of the mysteries to the captain — why a trout would not bite at one man's hook just as readily as at another's, when they were exactly alike as to lures, whether natural or artificial. The fact remains that there is a difference in the manner in which you approach them with the temptation; until you get the "hang of the thing" you will not catch the trout that the more astute disciple of the good Walton catches out of the same stream, in the same hour.

Thrown together as we both were on board the boat and on these excursions, the relation of employer and servant was soon forgotten, and the closer and more intimate relation of friend to friend was established, a relation which lasted as long as Captain Eden remained in America. Two months were passed in idling along the St. Croix, in hunting, fishing, exploring, studying the beautiful, if not grand, rock formations of the Dalles, and in visiting the Indians in their haunts around Wood Lake and the upper St. Croix. Then Captain Eden turned the prow of his little steamboat toward home, descending the river to Prairie du Chien, ascending the Wisconsin, portaging through the canal to the Fox, and thence steaming down to Oshkosh. Disposing of his steamboat there, he entered the office of the *Northwestern* newspaper, first as a reporter and later as an editorial writer. Not many suburban newspapers fifty years ago could boast of an Oxonian among their editorial writers. But very few people outside of his immediate friends ever knew that the quiet man who represented the *Northwestern* was either an Oxonian or the son of an English baronet.

In the autumn of 1863 the men of the North were gathering themselves together for the mightiest struggle of modern times — the battle summer of 1864. In Wisconsin, the Thirty-seventh Regiment of Infantry was in process of enrollment, and the whilom Englishman was one of those engaged in recruiting for this regiment, putting his money as well as his time into the work. Captain Eden was so successful in enlisting men for the service, that when the regiment was organized he was commissioned as major. In the strenuous days immediately following the battle of Cold Harbor the writer again met his old employer. The difference in rank between the enlisted man and the commissioned officer was no bar to the recognition of the former friendship existing between the steamboat captain and his pilot — friendship broadened and strengthened by companionship in woods and along streams by mutual interest and respect.

Major Robert C. Eden, or "Bob" Eden, as he was called at the front, was a model officer. His family had for generations been furnishing officers for the British army, and the fighting blood ran in his veins. His regiment was in the hottest of the fight at the Petersburg mine disaster, and he was at the head of his men. Through all the long siege following the first repulse, from June, 1864, until April, 1865, constantly under fire, he proved the metal that was in his composition. When he left England to seek his fortune, he was engaged to a Scotch lassie from one of the old families of the borderland. After a summer's experience of Yankee warfare, pitted against the "Johnnies" under Lee, Longstreet, Gordon, and Wise — men of equal courage, tenacity, and fighting ability — "Bob" concluded that another summer of the same sort as the last might prove too much for him, and that he might lose the number of his mess, as hundreds of his comrades had in the summer just closed. If he hoped or wished to leave a widow when he was called, he had better clinch the contract at once. And so he did.

His fiancée, who also came of fighting stock, promptly responded to the challenge and came overseas to meet her hero. They were married across a stump in the rear of Fort Haskell (Fort Hell, the boys called it, as opposed to Fort Damnation,

immediately opposite, in the Confederate line of works). Chaplain Hawes read the full Church of England service for the occasion, the regiment formed in hollow square about them, and the
brigade band played the wedding march, while an occasional shell
from the Confederate works sang overhead. Major-General O.
B. Wilcox, commanding the division, gave away the bride, and
all went merry despite the warlike surroundings.

After the war, Major Eden returned to Oshkosh and resumed
his editorial labors, in which he persisted for several years. Finally the home hunger came upon him, or perhaps more strongly
upon his wife. The wild Western society of the swiftest town of
its size in the state was not so much to her liking as that of the
slower but more refined surroundings of the land of her birth.
Severing all ties, business and otherwise, they returned to England.
Once there the influence of English kin and early associations was
too strong to permit of his return to Yankee land, and Major
"Bob" assumed the canonical robes which had so long awaited
his broad shoulders.

"And now, instead of mounting barbéd steeds
To fright the souls of fearful adversaries",

he ministers at the altar of the Prince of Peace, the calling toward
which his early education tended. His excursion into the wilds
of the Northwest, his steamboat trip up the Great River, his
experience as the editor of a frontier newspaper, and his service
in an alien army — all must have had an influence in broadening
his view and enriching his preaching.

One incident which occurred in our rambles was somewhat
amusing. We had tied up in the mouth of the Kinnickinnic
River, and had walked up the stream some eight or ten miles to
the little village of River Falls, where I was very well acquainted,
and where the trout .fishing was excellent. It had been Eden's
request that I should introduce him simply as Captain Eden, without going into any particulars of parentage, education, or nationality. As he wore a suit of Scotch tweeds somewhat the worse
for wear from numerous excursions after deer, prairie chickens,
and trout, there was nothing suggestive of the Oxonian about him.
In River Falls lived the only really educated man of that locality —
a graduate from Yale, both in law and divinity. We called upon
him and while discussing the country, its beauty, its game, and

its fishing, Captain Eden was toying with a book of Greek tragedies, that lay open on the table. His apparent interest in the
strange characters in which the book was printed tempted the
scholar to remark, possibly with a slightly ironical inflection:

"I presume you read Greek on the river, Captain?"

"Oh, yes", was Captain Eden's response, "I am very fond
of the Greek tragedies, and I have read a good deal to keep in
practice. I like this passage that you were reading when we
came in."

Taking the book, Captain Eden read in a beautifully modu-
lated voice, and with probably a perfect accent, the passage which
the scholar had marked, and which he had been reading when
we called. I say, "probably perfect accent". I had never seen
a printed page of Greek before, much less had I ever heard it
read as fluently as I could read English. The *amende* which the
scholar instantly made, and the praises which he bestowed on the
marine prodigy who captained a little steamboat on the river, wore
rough clothes, and read Greek like a native, convinced me that his
ministerial preparation had been laid upon solid foundations, and
that his accent was above criticism, out in that country at least.

It was during this visit to River Falls that Captain Eden
made the acquaintance of Ellsworth Burnett, another nobleman,
born among the hills of Vermont, at whose farm we were guests
while loading our baskets with trout from the south fork of the
Kinnickinnic, which flowed through his farm and past his door.
The friendship thus begun undoubtedly led to Eden's going into
the army, for Burnett was largely instrumental in raising one
of the companies of the regiment in which Major Eden was
commissioned, himself going out as a captain, and returning at the
close of the war as major.

Chapter XXVI

In War Time

In the early spring of 1861 the "Fanny Harris" was chartered by the United States government to go to Fort Ridgeley, up the Minnesota River, and bring down the battery of light artillery stationed at that post, known as the Sherman Battery, Major T. W. Sherman having been in command long enough to have conferred his name upon the organization, and by that it was known at the time of which I write. It is three hundred miles from St. Paul to Fort Ridgeley by the river; as a crow flies, the distance is about half of that. A little more than one year after our visit there was business at and near the fort for many crows — the gruesome occupation of picking the bones of a thousand white people (men, women, and children) murdered by the crafty Sioux, who saw in the withdrawal of the troops an opportunity to avenge all their wrongs, real or imaginary, and to regain the lands which had been sold under treaty, or which had been stolen from them by the fast encroaching white population of the state.

The Minnesota River is the worst twisted water course in the West. No other affluent of the Mississippi can show as many bends to the mile throughout its course. It is a series of curves from start to finish, the river squirming its way through an alluvial prairie from Beaver Falls, the head of navigation, to Mendota at its mouth. Up this crooked stream it was the problem to force the largest boat that had ever navigated it, and a stern-wheeler at that. At the time the trip was made, there was a nineteen-foot rise in the river, resulting from the melting of the snow after an exceptionally hard winter. This precluded any danger of touching bottom anywhere, but it added ten fold to the difficulties of navigating a two hundred-foot steamboat around the short bends for the reason that the water did not follow the regular channel, but cut right across bends and points, so that most of the time the current was setting squarely across the river, catching the steamer broadside on, and driving her into the woods, and when there holding her as in a vise. Being a stern-wheeler it was impossible, by going ahead on one wheel and backing on the other, as would have been done by a side-wheeler, to keep her head clear of the bank. All this work had to be done by the men at the wheel, and they very soon found their work cut out for them, in handling the boat by the steering wheel and rudders alone. We had a Minnesota River pilot on board to assist our men in steering; it was an impossibility to lose one's self, so that his services were confined almost exclusively to steering, and not to piloting, in its true sense. We also had an army officer from Fort Snelling on board, to see that all possible speed was made. His orders were to "push her through" at whatever cost, regardless of damage.

The boat was coaled at St. Paul for the round trip, for the woodyards were all under water, and the cord wood was adrift on its way to St. Louis, derelict. From the time we entered the river at Fort Snelling, two men were at the wheel all the time. I was sent to the engine-room, my experience as a "cub" engineer rendering my services there of more importance for the time being than in the pilot house. I stood at one engine all day, while one of the firemen detailed for the purpose stood at the other, to "ship up", to back, or come ahead. There were no unnecessary bells rung. If we were going ahead and the stopping bell rang, followed by the backing bell we threw the rods on to their "hooks", and the engineer gave her full steam astern. This was usually followed by a crash forward, as the boat was thrown broadside, with almost full speed ahead, into the woods, after having struck one of the cross currents either unguardedly, or else one which was too strong in any case for the wheelsmen to meet and overcome by the rudder alone. If it chanced that the bank was overhung by trees, the forward cabin lost an additional portion of its ornamentation.

In nearly every such instance it was necessary to get the yawl overboard, and with four men at the oars and a steersman sculling astern, pull to the opposite side of the river and get a line fast to a tree. The line was then taken to the steam capstan and the boat would be hauled out of a position from which it would have been impossible to release her by the engines and wheel alone. This work was kept up from daylight until dark, and when the four men came down from the pilot house they were apt to be so exhausted that they could scarcely stand.

The boat tied up where night overtook her. In the engine-room, as soon as the day's run was ended, all hands set to work — engineers, "strikers" and firemen — to replace the lost and broken wheel-arms and buckets. This was a hard and dangerous job, for the water ran a raging torrent, six or eight miles an hour, and the nights were dark and rainy. It was precarious business, this getting out on the fantails, with only the dim light of half a dozen lanterns, unscrewing refractory nuts and bolts with a big monkey-wrench, and in the meantime holding on by one's legs only, over such a mill tail. Everybody engaged in this work understood fully that if he ever fell into the water it was the end of all things to him, for he would have been swept away in the darkness and drowned in a minute. There was no dry land for him to reach in any direction, the river sweeping across the country five or ten feet deep in every direction. It was usually far past midnight when the temporary and necessary repairs were completed, and then the engine-room force "turned in" to get three or four hours sleep before beginning another day as full of work and danger as the preceding.

All this time the army man either stood on the roof with the captain, dodging falling spars, chimneys, or limbs of trees, or at the wheel with the pilots, or paced the engine-room, and urged speed, speed, speed. "The United States will put a new cabin on your boat. Never mind that. Keep your wheel turning and your machinery in working order. We must have troops in Washington at once, or there will be no United States." It is fair to say that every man on the boat worked as though his life depended upon his exertions. Whatever may have been their political sympathies, there was nothing on the surface to indicate other than the determination to get that battery to La Crosse in the shortest possible time.

That army officer was the epitome of concentrated energy. He was a captain and quartermaster, and representing the United States, was practically supreme on board. He had his limitations as a steamboatman, but thanks to the splendid equipment which

his government had given him at West Point, coupled with the
experience he had gained during many years' service in the West in
moving troops, Indians, and supplies by steamboat, he had a pretty
good idea of what needed to be done, and could judge very clearly
whether the men in charge were competent, and were doing things
in the right way and to the best advantage.

Under ordinary circumstances such a close censorship of the
officers and crew would not have been maintained, nor would it
have been tolerated if suggested. But at this time everything
was at white heat. Fort Sumter had fallen. Men were stirred
as never before in this country, and officers of the regular army
particularly, who knew better than any others the gravity of the
impending conflict, were keyed up to the highest tension by the
responsibility placed upon them. On the other hand the officers
of our boat were likewise burdened with the responsibility of safely
taking a big vessel hundreds of miles up a narrow and crooked
river, just now covered with floating drift of every description,
with undermined trees falling at every mile. They were spurred
on by the thought that the difference of a day, or even of a few
hours, might determine the loss of the nation's capital. Under
these circumstances the insistence of the army man was passed by
as a matter of course.

Near Belle Plaine a council was called to decide whether
an attempt should be made to force a passage through the thin
strip of timber that fringed the river bank. If successful, this would
permit of sailing the boat a straight course for ten miles across
a submerged prairie, thus cutting off twenty miles of crooked and
arduous navigation. The Minnesota River pilot was sure that
we would meet with no obstacles after passing the fringe of timber — not a house, barn, or haystack, as all that somewhat unusual
class of obstructions to a steamboat had been carried away by the
great flood. After discussing the plan in all its bearings, it was
decided to try it as soon as a narrow and weak place could be
found in the timber belt.

Such a place, where the willows and cottonwoods were the
thinnest and smallest in diameter, was chosen for the attempt.
The boat, by reason of its length, could not be pointed straight
at the "hurdle", as the pilots facetiously dubbed it, but a quartering
cut was decided upon. The jack staff had long ago been carried

away; the spars and derricks were housed below, and a large portion of the forward roof was already missing. It was decided,
therefore, that a little more banging would count for nothing.
Everybody was cautioned to stand clear of the guards, and look
out for himself. A big head of steam was accumulated, and then
with two men at the wheel and everybody hanging on, the "Fanny
Harris" was pointed at the opposite shore, with its lining of woods,
and the throttle thrown wide open. She jumped across the river
in a minute and dove into the young timber, crushing trees six
inches in diameter flat on either side; the water-soaked, friable soil
affording no secure holding ground for the roots, which added
greatly to our chances of success. The boat plunged through all
right, with little damage, until the wheel came in over the bank.
Then there was music. Many of the trees were only bent out of
perpendicular, and when the hull passed clear these trees rebounded
to more or less perpendicular positions — enough so as to get into
the wheel and very nearly strip it of its buckets, together with a
dozen of the wheel-arms. The pilots heard the crash and rang
to stop. The engineers knew more about the damage than the
pilots, but would not have stopped the engine of their own accord
had the whole stern of the boat gone with it. It wasn't their
business to stop without orders, and they knew their business.

When the wheel stopped turning, the boat stopped. The
problem then was, to get the boat through the remaining hundred
feet or more. This was done by carrying the big anchor ahead,
and taking the cable to the steam capstan. The boat was dragged
"out of the woods", and all hands turned to to replace the smashed
buckets. As soon as they were in place we steamed gaily up the
current, over the prairie, clean-swept of fences, stacks, and barns,
only a few isolated houses, built on the higher knolls, having
escaped the flood. At the upper end of the prairie a weak place
was found, and with a clear start in the open water the boat was
driven through the fringe of timber, clear into the open channel, without stopping, and this time with but little injury to the
wheel.

Couriers had been sent ahead from Fort Snelling, by pony express, to the commanding officer of the fort, to have his battery
ready to embark as soon as the boat should arrive. It had taken
us four days to run the three hundred miles, and it was a dilapidat-

ed steamboat that at last made fast at the landing place at the foot of the bluff, under the shadow of Fort Ridgeley.

The fort was ideally situated for defense against Indian attacks, for which, of course, it was alone built. It would appear, however, that its builders had little idea that it would ever be put to the test — such a test as it was subjected to a little more than a year after our visit. It was located on a sort of promontory formed by the bluff on the side next the river, and a deep ravine on the other. On the third side of the triangle lay the open prairie, stretching away for miles, with only a slight sprinkling of scrub oaks to obstruct the view. The barracks, stables, and storehouse (frame structures) were built up solidly on two sides of this triangle, next the ravines, the windowless backs of the buildings forming the walls of the fort. Toward the prairie, the most vulnerable face, the buildings did not fully cover the front, there being two or three wide openings between those that formed that side of the defenses. These openings were covered by cannon of the battery which garrisoned the fort.

When the battery embarked for the East there were left only two or three small howitzers in charge of a sergeant of artillery, and it was these little pieces that saved the garrison from massacre in August, 1862, when the fort was for many days beleaguered by eight hundred Sioux Indians under the chief, Little Crow, leader of the uprising in Minnesota in that year. Undoubtedly the respect that Indians have for any sort of cannon had as much to do with their repulse as did the actual punishment inflicted by the howitzers, however well-served they may have been. I have a letter somewhere, written by a distant cousin who was a colonel in the Confederate army, relating that they had several thousand Indians in the Confederate army upon going into the battle of Prairie Grove, and from them they expected great things. When the "Yanks" opened with their artillery the sound alone brought the Indian contingent to a stand. When the gunners got the range and began to drop shells among them, the red men remembered that they had pressing business in the Indian Territory, and it is Colonel Merrick's opinion that they did not stop running until they reached their tepees. It is his opinion also that as soldiers, for use in war where Anglo-Saxons are debating grave questions of state with twelve pounders, they are not worth a red copper.

Chapter XXVII

At Fort Ridgeley

The officer in command of the battery when it left Fort Ridgeley was Captain and Brevet Major John C. Pemberton, U. S. A. He had won his brevet by gallant services in action at Monterey and Molino del Rey. He accompanied the battery as far as Washington, where he resigned (April 29, 1861), and tendered his sword to the Confederacy. He was rapidly promoted until he reached a major-generalcy in that army, and had the distinguished honor to surrender his army of thirty thousand men at Vicksburg to Major General Ulysses S. Grant, July 3, 1863. Pemberton was born in Pennsylvania, being appointed to the army from that state, so that he had not even the flimsy excuse of serving his state in thus betraying his country.

The battery was known as the Buena Vista Battery, or still better as Sherman's. But Major Sherman, although long its commander, was not with it at the time we transferred it down the river. Major Sherman rendered distinguished service during the war, and retired (December 31, 1870) with the rank of major-general. Two other officers were with the battery — First Lieutenant Romeyn Ayres, and Second Lieutenant Beekman Du Barry. The battery was known in the Army of the Potomac as **Ayres's** Battery, and under that name won a wide reputation for efficiency. Ayres himself was a major general of volunteers before the close of the war, and Lieutenant Du Barry was (May, 1865) brevetted lieutenant-colonel for distinguished services.

At the time of our visit there was a large number of Indians encamped on the prairie in front of the fort — estimated at seven or eight hundred by those best versed in their manners and customs. They had come down from the Lower Sioux Agency, sixteen miles farther up the river. They were alive to the situation, and on the alert to learn all they could of the "white man's war", which they had already heard of as being fought in some far-away place, the location of which was not clear to them, and for which they cared nothing so long as it promised to be a contest that was likely to draw away soldiers from the fort, and especially the "big guns", which they feared more than they did the "dough boys". One of the best posted of the frontiersmen, a "squaw man", who had the ear of the tribal council, told our officers that there would be trouble when the battery was withdrawn, for they felt themselves able successfully to fight and exterminate the few companies of infantry left to garrison the fort. How true this prediction was, the uprising of August, 1862, and the Indian war in Minnesota, with its massacre at New Ulm and outlying regions, abundantly verified.

As soon as we were made fast, the work was begun of loading cannon, caissons, battery wagons, ammunition, and stores, as well as horses and men. By the light of torches, lanterns, and huge bon-fires built on the bank, the work was rushed all night long, while the engineers labored to put the engines and particularly the wheel, in the best possible condition; and the carpenter, aided by artisans from the fort, put on new guards forward, and strengthened the weak places for the inevitable pounding that we knew must attend the down-stream trip. With the raging river pressing on the stern of the boat as she descended, there was ample reason for anticipating much trouble in handling the steamer.

The teamsters, with their six-mule teams, hurried the stores and ammunition down the narrow roadway cut in the side of the bluff, running perhaps half a mile along the side in making the perpendicular descent of two hundred feet. Whatever time we had from our duties on the boat was spent either in the fort, out in the Indian village, or on the side hill watching the teams come down the bluff, one after the other. Not being able to pass on the hill, they went down together, and all went back empty at the same time. The two hind wheels of the big army wagon were chained, so that they slid along the ground, instead of revolving. Then the three riders, one on each "near" mule, started the outfit down the hill, the off mules being next the bluff, while the legs of the drivers hung out over space on the other side. In places the wagons would go so fast, in spite of the drag, that the mules would have to trot to keep out of the way. This was exciting and interesting to the spectators, who were expecting to see a team go over the precipice. The drivers did not seem to care anything about the matter, and were no doubt well pleased to become the centre of attraction.

Those of the spectators who had time and patience to continue the watch were finally rewarded for their persistence, and justified in their predictions by seeing one of these teams, with its load of fixed ammunition, roll for a hundred feet down the bluff — men, mules, and ammunition in one wild mix-up, rolling and racing for the bottom. The fringe of timber alone saved the cortege from plunging into the river. Those who saw the trip made, were betting that neither a man nor a mule would come out alive. They all came out alive. Some of the mules were badly scratched and banged, but not a leg was broken among the six. The men were also badly bruised, but they also brought all their bones out whole. One mule had his neck wound around the wagon-tongue, his own tongue hanging out about the length of that of the wagon, and all hands were certain of one dead mule, at least. But when the troopers ran in and cut away the harness the mule jumped to his feet, took in a few long breaths to make good for the five minutes' strangulation, and then started up the roadway, dodging the down-coming teams by a hair's-breadth, and never stopping until he reached his corral, where he began munching hay as though nothing out of the ordinary had happened.

The next morning everything was stowed aboard. With a salute from the little howitzers in the fort, and the cheers of the "dough boys", who wanted to go but could not, the "Fanny Harris" backed into the stream, "straightened up", and began her down-stream trip. I shall not attempt to follow her down, in all her situations. With the heavy load, and the stream behind her, it was possible to check her speed in a measure at the bends, but totally impossible to stop her and back her up against the current. The result was, that she "flanked" around points that raked her whole length, and then plunged into timber, bows on, on the opposite side of the river, ripping the ginger-bread work, and even the guards, so that it would seem as though the boat were going to destruction. Some of the artillerymen were sure

of it, and all of them would sooner have risked a battle than
the chance of drowning that at times seemed so imminent. We
made good time, however, and ran the three hundred miles in two
running days of daylight, laying up nights, and repairing damages
as far as possible against the next day's run.

When we rounded to at Fort Snelling landing we had one
chimney about ten feet high above deck; the other was three feet
— just one joint left above the breeching. Both escape pipes
and the jack staff were gone — we lost the latter the first day,
going up. The stanchions on both sides of the boiler deck were
swept clean away, together with liberal portions of the roof itself.
The boat looked like a wreck, but her hull was sound. The
officers and crew were game to the last. Many of them had been
hurt more or less, and all had been working until they were scarcely able to move. It was war time, however. Fort Sumter had
fallen, and the president had called for seventy-five thousand men.
We were doing our part with a will, in hastening forward a
battery that was to give a good account of itself from Bull Run
to Appomattox.

At Fort Snelling we lost two of our firemen and a number
of our deck crew, who deserted while we were lying at that place,
taking on additional stores and men. We thought it a cowardly
thing to do, under the circumstances. A few weeks later, however, we saw the two firemen going to the front with a volunteer
company from Prescott, afterwards Company "B", 6th Wisconsin
Infantry, in which "Whiskey Jim", the Irishman, and Louis
Ludloff, the "Dutchman", distinguished themselves for valor in
battle. Richardson gave his life for his country at the Wilderness,
while Ludloff fought all the way through, rising from private
to corporal, sergeant, and first sergeant, and being wounded at
Antietam and the Wilderness.

In talking with Ludloff in later years, I learned that the
reason they deserted the steamer, leaving behind their accrued
wages and even their clothes, was because they feared that they
would not be able to get in among the seventy-five thousand if
they lost any time in formalities and details. There were others,
higher up in the world than the humble firemen, who also mis-
calculated the length of the impending war — by four years.
Distinguished editors and statesmen, and even soldiers, made this

error. And there were a good many who failed to "get in" even then.

We ran to La Crosse with our pieces of chimneys, which the artisans at the Fort had helped our engineers to piece together so that the smoke would clear the pilot house. It did not give the best of draught; but we were going downstream on a flood, and we might have drifted five miles an hour without any steam at all. We delivered the battery at La Crosse, and immediately went into dry dock, where a hundred men made short work of the repairs. The United States paid our owners, the Minnesota Packet Company, eight thousand dollars for the week's work. The officers and crew who earned the money for the company were not invited to assist in its division. It was the hardest week's work that most of us had ever known — certainly the hardest I had ever experienced up to that time. A year or so later I got into work fully as hard, and it lacked the pleasant accessories of good food and a soft bed, that accompanied the strenuous days and nights spent on the Fort Ridgeley excursion.

An incident remotely connected with this trip, offers an excellent opportunity to philosophize on the smallness of the planet we inhabit, and the impossibility of escaping from, or avoiding people whom we may once have met. At a meeting of Congregationalists held in a city far removed from the fort that stood guard on the bluffs overhanging the Minnesota River in 1861, the writer was introduced to Mr. Henry Standing Bear, secretary of the Young Men's Christian Association of Pine Ridge, South Dakota. Standing Bear is a graduate of Carlisle College, an educated and intelligent and a full-blood Sioux Indian. In conversation with him it transpired that he was one of the children who stared open-eyed at the steamboat lying at the landing place below the fort in 1861, and that he was an interested spectator of the embarkation of Sherman's Battery. He there listened to the talk of the braves who were already planning what they would do when the soldiers should all be withdrawn to fight the "white man's war" in the South. Standing Bear's own father took part in the "massacre", as we called it. Standing Bear says they themselves called it a war. Indians may go about their killings with somewhat more of ferocity and cruelty than do we whites, but it is their way of making war. In either case it is "hell", as "Old

BAD AXE (NOW GENOA), WISCONSIN. Scene of the last battle between the United States forces and the Indians under Chief Black Hawk, August 21, 1832. The Steamer "Warrior," Captain Joseph Throckmorton, with soldiers and artillery from Fort Crawford, Prairie du Chien, took an active and important part in this battle.

Tecump" said, and the distinctions that we draw after all make little difference in the results. We do not have to seek very far through the pages of history to find instances where white men have massacred helpless Indian women and children.

A talk with Henry Standing Bear, or any other educated Indian born amid surroundings such as his, will throw new light and new coloring upon the Indian situation as it existed in 1861. They saw the whites steadily encroaching upon their hunting grounds, appropriating the best to their own use, ravishing their women, killing their men, and poisoning whole tribes with their "fire-water". Against their wills they were driven from their ancient homes — "removed", was the word — after having been tricked into signing treaties that they did not understand, couched in legal terms that they could not comprehend, receiving in exchange for their lands a lot of worthless bric-a-brac that vanished in a week. [8] If they protested or resisted, they were shot down like so many wolves, and with as little mercy. What man is there among the whites who would not fight under such circumstances? Our forefathers fought under less provocation and their cause has been adjudged a righteous cause.

This is the Indian's view-point as stated by a civilized tribesman. His fathers fought, and are dead. He was adopted by the nation, educated, and started upon a higher plane of living, as he is free to confess; but it is doubtful if he can be started upon a

---

[8] This is a pretty wild statement on the part of Standing Bear, probably made through ignorance of the facts in the case rather than a wilful misrepresentation. In the treaty made with the Sioux Indians at Traverse des Sioux, July 2-3, 1851, the United States covenanted to pay $1,665,000 for such rights and title as were claimed by the Sisseton and Wahpeton tribes or bands in lands lying in Iowa and Minnesota. In another treaty, made with the M'day-wa-kon-ton and Wak-pay-koo-tay bands, also of the Sioux nation, the United States agreed to pay the further sum of $1,410,000 for the rights of these two bands in lands lying in Iowa and Minnesota. In addition the Sioux had already been paid a large sum for their rights in lands lying on the east side of the Mississippi, in Wisconsin — lands in which they really had no right of title at all, as they had gained whatever rights they claimed simply by driving back the Chippewa from the country which they had occupied for generations. The Sioux themselves did not, and could not, avail themselves of the rights so gained, and the territory was a debatable land for years — a fighting ground for the rival nations of the Sioux and Chippewa.

higher plane of thinking than that upon which his blanketed for-bears lived, in spite of the cruelties to which they were born and educated.   While I am no sentimentalist on the Indian question, when I fall into the hands of a Standing Bear I am almost per-suaded that the Indian, within his lights, is as much of a patriot as many of his bleached brethren.   As to his manhood there is no question.   In the long struggle that has taken place between him-self and the white invaders, he has always backed his convictions with his life, if need be; and such men, if white, we call "pa-triots."

Chapter XXVIII

Improving the River

It was not until commerce on the upper river was practically a thing of the past, that any effort was made to improve the channel for purposes of navigation. A number of interests united to bring about this good work when it did come — some meritorious, others purely selfish. The steamboatmen, what was left of them, entertained the fallacious idea that if the river were straightened, deepened, lighted, and freed from snags and other hindrances to navigation, there would still be some profit in running their boats, despite the railroad competition that had so nearly ruined their business. This was a mistaken supposition, and they were disabused of the idea only by experience.

The mill owners of the upper river and its tributaries, who had by this time begun to "tow through" — that is, push their rafts of logs and lumber with a steamboat from Stillwater to St. Louis, instead of drifting — were assured of quicker trips and greater safety if the river was dressed up somewhat, insuring greater profits upon their investments. Both of these parties in interest were engaged in legitimate trade, and while there was no intention of dividing the profits that might inure to them from an investment of several millions of dollars of other people's money, precedent had legitimatized the expenditure in other localities and upon other rivers. They were well within the bounds of reason, in asking that their own particular business might be made more profitable through the aid of government.

A greater influence than any arguments drawn from commercial necessities was found in the political interest involved. For years, members of congress elected from districts in which there was a harbor or a river which by any fiction might be legislated into a "navigable stream", had been drawing from the

federal treasury great sums of money for the improvement of
these streams and harbors; yet some of these never floated anything larger than the government yawls in which the engineers
who did the work reached the scene of their duties. At the same
time, country members from the interior of the great West drew
nothing. The rapid settlement of the Northwestern territories,
in the year immediately following the close of the Civil War, had
an effect that was felt in the enhanced influence exerted by members of congress representing the new commonwealths. It followed that when the biennial distribution of "pork", as it is
expressively but inelegantly called nowadays, came up, these members were in a position to demand their share, and get it, or defeat
the distribution *in toto*.

The war was over. The Union soldiers who had fought in
it were either dead, or if alive were hustling for a living. Hundreds of thousands of them were found in Iowa, Minnesota,
Kansas, and Nebraska, opening up farms and developing the
country. The contractors who had fattened on their blood were
hanging like leeches to every department of the national government, clamoring for more contracts to further inflate their already
plethoric bank accounts. The river improvement appealed strongly to this class of men. The influences that they could bring to
bear, backed by the legitimate demands of steamboatmen and mill
owners, convinced the most conscientious congressmen that their
duty lay in getting as large an appropriation as possible for the
work of river regeneration. The result was, that the river which
had given employment to three or four hundred steamboats,
manned by fifteen thousand men, without having a dollar expended in ameliorating its conditions, suddenly became the centre
of the greatest concern to congress — and to the contractors —
and all for the benefit of a dozen steamboats in regular traffic,
and perhaps a hundred boats used in towing the output of a score
of mills owned by millionaire operators.

From 1866 to 1876 there was spent on the river between the
mouth of the Missouri and St. Paul, a distance of 700 miles, the
sum of $5,200,707. That was for the ten years at the rate of
$7,429 for each mile of the river improved. It cost at that rate
$742.90 per mile per year during the decade quoted. It is doubt-
ful if the few steamboats engaged in traffic during that time were

able to show aggregate gross earnings of $742.90 per mile per annum. It seems a pity that the benefit resulting from this expenditure could not have been participated in by the great flotilla that covered the river in the preceding decade, from 1856 to 1866.

In this expenditure we find $59,098 charged to the eleven miles of river between St. Paul and St. Anthony Falls. It is doubtful if a dozen trips a year were made to St. Anthony Falls during the time noted. It was a hard trip to make against the rapid current below the falls, and a dangerous trip to make downstream. It would seem, however, that with the expenditure of $5,909 per year for ten years, over only eleven miles of river, every rock (and it is all rocks) might have been pulled ashore, and a perfect canal built up. Possibly that is the result of all this work; I haven't been over that piece of river since the work was completed — for one reason, among others, that no steamboats ever go to St. Anthony Falls, now that the river is put in order.

From St. Paul to Prescott, thirty-two miles, there was expended $638,498 in ten years. I can readily understand why so much money was planted in that stretch of river. Beginning at Prescott and going toward St. Paul, there were to be found five or six of the worst bars there are anywhere on the river; and between the accentuated bars — bars of sufficient importance to merit names of their own — the rest of the river was bad enough to merit at least some of the language expended upon it by pilots who navigated it before the improvements came. At Prescott, at the head of Puitt's Island (now Prescott Island) or Point Douglass bar, at Nininger, at Boulanger's Island, at Grey Cloud, at Pig's Eye, and at Frenchman's, were bars that were the terror of all pilots and the dread of all owners and stockholders. I will eliminate the "terror" as expressing the feelings of the pilots. "Resignation" would perhaps be the better word. They all knew pretty well where to go to find the best water on any or all of the bars named; but they also knew that when they found the best water it would be too thin to float any boat drawing over three and a half feet. With a four-foot load line it simply meant that the steamboat must be hauled through six inches of sand by main strength and awkwardness, and that meant delay, big wood bills, bigger wage-lists, wear and tear of material, and decreased earnings. A big packet not loaded below the four-foot line, was not laden to the money-making point. After the work of regeneration began, it was a constant fight on the part of the engineers to maintain a four and a half foot channel on either one of the bars named. The expenditure of the great sums of money placed in this district is therefore easily accounted for.

The work of improvement was, and still is carried on under the direction of competent engineers, detailed for the service by the chief of engineers of the United States army. No more highly trained men in their profession can be found in the world than these choice graduates of the most perfect institution of instruction in the world — West Point Military Academy. Their scientific, perhaps academic, knowledge of the laws governing the flow of water and the shifting of sands, the erosion of banks and the silting up into islands and continents, which are among the vagaries of the great river, is supplemented by the practical, if unscientific, knowledge of men who have gained their acquaintance with the river from years of service as pilots or masters of river steamboats. The government is shrewd enough to secure the services of such men to complement the science of its chosen representatives. These two classes, in pairs or by companies, have made an exhaustive study of conditions surrounding each of the more difficult and troublesome bars, as well as all others of lesser note, in order to decide what was needed, what kind of work, and how to be placed to lead, or drive the water into the most favorable channels, and there retain it under varying conditions of flood or drought, ice jams, or any and all the conditions contributing to the changes forever going on in the river.

These points determined, an estimate is made of the cost of the necessary improvements, details of construction are drawn, specifications submitted, and bids on the proposed work invited. There were, and are, plenty of contractors, provided with boats, tackle, stone quarries, and all else required in the prosecution of the work. It would not be safe, however, to assume that the government always reaped the benefit of so much competition as might be assumed from the number of men engaged in the business. It would be unsafe to assume that such competition has always been free from collusion, although possibly it has been.

On the other hand, each contractor has his "beat", from which all other bidders have religiously kept off. Not in an ostentatious manner, however, for that might invite suspicion; but in a business-like and gentlemanly manner, by putting in a bid just a few cents per cubic foot higher than the man upon whose territory the work was to be done, and whose figures have been secretly consulted before the bids were submitted. There have been suspicions that such has been the case, more than once, and that the work sometimes cost the government more than a fair estimate had provided for. The contracts have been let, however, and within the thirty years last past there have been built along the river between Prescott and St. Paul two hundred and fifty-one dikes, dams, revetments, and other works for controlling the flow of water within that short stretch of thirty-two miles.

Some of these dams are long, strong, and expensive; others are embryonic, a mere suggestion of a dam or dyke, a few feet in length, for the protection of a particular small portion of the bank, or for the diverting of the current. All these works, great and small, are intended as suggestions to the mighty river that in future it must behave itself in a seemly manner. Generally the river does take the hint, and behaves well in these particular cases. At other times it asserts itself after the old fashion, and wipes out a ten thousand dollar curb in a night, and chooses for itself a new and different channel, just as it did in the days of its savagery, fifty years earlier.

A peculiar feature attending this work for the betterment of the river was, that in its incipient stages it met with little or no encouragement from any of the men personally engaged in navigating steamboats on the river. Some deemed the proposition visionary and impracticable, while others, fearing its success, and magnifying the results to be obtained, threw every obstacle possible in the way of the engineers who had the work in charge. They even went so far as to petition Congress to abandon the work, and recall the engineers who had been detailed to prosecute it. This opposition was particularly true of work on the lower rapids, where the great ship canal now offers a ready and safe passage around rapids always difficult to navigate. Sometimes, when the water had reached an unusually low stage, they were positively impracticable for large boats. Captain Charles J. Allen, Corps of

Engineers, U. S. A., who was in charge of the preliminary work
on the lower rapids, calls attention, in his report, to this hostility,
and incidentally records his opinion of river pilots in general, and
rapids pilots in particular, in the following far from flattering
terms :

"Most of the river pilots are possessed of but little knowledge beyond
that required in turning the wheel; and their obstinacy in refusing to
recognize and take advantage of good channels cut for them has been the
experience of more than one engineer engaged in improving rivers. The
rapids pilots in particular, who may lose employment, seemed to be the
most hostile."

The last-named class were certainly sound in their conclusions that the deepening, straightening and lighting of the rapids
would take away their business. There is, therefore, little wonder
that they were not enthusiastic in their support of the proposed
improvements, which were, if successful, to deprive them of the
means of livelihood. Perhaps the gentlemen of the engineer
corps would not be enthusiastic over a proposition to disband the
United States army, and muster out all its officers. The results
justified the fears of the rapids pilots. Any pilot could take his
boat over, after the improvements were completed, and rapids
piloting, as a distinctive business, was very nearly wiped out.

The slur of the West Pointer loses its point, however, with
any one who has known many Mississippi River pilots. They
knew a great many things besides "turning the wheel." Even
had they known only that, they carried around under their hats
special knowledge not to be sneezed at, even by a West Pointer.
Later, all the men on the river came to recognize the benefits
accruing from the work of the Mississippi River Commission, and
none more heartily testified to the success of the work than the
pilots and masters of the river craft. There were, indeed, none
so well qualified to judge of results as they.

The work once begun was prosecuted with vigor. The voice
of the great Northwest was potent in Washington, and in the ten
years from 1866 to 1876 more than five millions of dollars were
expended between Minneapolis and the mouth of the Missouri. [9]

The first thought of the government engineers to whom was
entrusted the duty of improving the river, was naturally in the
direction of securing and maintaining a greater depth of water.

9 See Appendix D.

This was to be accomplished by so curbing and controlling the flow that it would follow the channel decided upon, at all times and under all conditions. The dikes and wing dams, which were built by the hundred, served this purpose in a degree, and the flow of water was controlled to a fairly satisfactory extent.

Then the menaces to navigation were considered, and measures taken for their elimination. Of the two hundred and ninety-five recorded steamboat wrecks on the Missouri River between 1842 and 1895, a hundred and ninety-three, or about two-thirds of all, were by snagging. I presume this proportion would be maintained on the upper Mississippi, if a similar compilation were at hand to decide the point. The problem was to get rid of this greatest of all dangers to steamboats. There was but one way, and that was to pull them out and carry them away, or cut them up and so dispose of them that the same snag would not have to be pulled out at each recurring rise of water, from other parts of the river.

Having no steamboats fitted for the business in that early day (1866), the contract system was resorted to. This was found to be costly and unsatisfactory. Contractors agreed to remove snags at so much per snag, within certain lengths and estimated weights, they furnishing the steamboats and machinery necessary for the work. In order to make the business pay, they had to find snags, somewhere. When they were not to be found in or near the channel, they were obtained in any place — chutes, bayous, and sloughs where no steamboat ever ran, or ever would run. After a trip or two up and down the river, there were not enough snags left to make the pulling profitable, and of course the work was given over. But the first rise brought down a new supply of snags to lodge in the channel of the falling river, and pilots set to dodging them, just as they had done before the pulling began. To be of the highest efficiency, the work must be continuous. This was deemed impossible under the contract system, and the engineers in charge recommended the purchase of two suitable steamboats for the upper river, to be fitted with improved machinery for lifting and disposing of the snags fished out of the river. These boats were to be manned and officered by the government, and placed in charge of an engineer detailed by the War Department. They were continuously to patrol the river during the season of navigation, removing every snag as soon as located, assisting steamboats in distress, cutting overhanging trees, placing guide-boards and crossing lights where needed, maintaining the same after being established, and giving their whole time and attention to the work of river improvement. This suggestion was carried into effect, and two steamboats purchased and fitted for the work.

In 1866 Colonel Dodge, of the Corps of Engineers, who had had large experience in the work of river improvement, realizing the necessity for dredging the shoalest places, in addition to directing the water by dikes and dams, invented a dredge to be attached to a steamboat, and operated by steam machinery, for the purpose of plowing out and scraping away the sand as it accumulated on the worst bars and reefs. Two or three experimental machines were built by a St. Paul mechanic upon the order of the United States officials, and under their supervision. These were attached to derricks, placed on the bows of the steamboats secured for the work, suspended by stout chains, and operated by steam. The boat, headed up river, was run to the head of the reef; the dredge was then lowered, and the boat backed downstream in the line of the channel. The dredge, twenty feet wide, stirred up the sand, and the scraper attachment drew it down to the foot of the reef, where the dredge was hoisted up and the current carried away the released sand into deep water. The boat was again run to the head of the reef and the operation repeated, each "scrape" being about the width of the dredge, the pilot so placing his boat each time as exactly to match the last preceding draft, without going over the same ground a second time.

The machine was found to work to perfection, and to be of even greater practical utility in keeping open a navigable channel than the dikes and wing dams, as there is a constant filling in of sand at the foot of every channel artificially formed by contracting the flow of water. The dredge hauls this sand away as it accumulates, and by deepening the water in the channel does much toward attracting the steady flow of water to the particular lines so dredged.

Chapter XXIX

Killing Steamboats

The upper Mississippi has always been, comparatively, a remarkably healthy stream for steamboats. A great proportion of the craft ending their days there, have died of old age, and have been decorously consigned to the scrap pile instead of meeting the tragic end usually assigned them by writers. In many cases where it is supposed or known that a steamboat of a certain name met destruction by fire or snag, the historian who attempts to verify such statement will have great difficulty in deciding just which boat bearing the name was the victim of that particular casualty. The fact is, that the same name was conferred, time after time, on boats built to take the place of those sunk, burned, or otherwise put out of commission. As early as 1840 there was the "Pike No. 8" on the lower river, indicating that there had been a procession of "Pikes." There was also, at the same time, the "Ben Franklin No. 7." Boats thus named were called simply "Pike" or "Ben Franklin", the number not appearing on the wheelhouses, save in rare cases. All the other "Pikes" having gone to the bottom, there was but one "Pike" afloat. When reference was ordinarily made to the boat by that name, the auditors knew at once that the speaker referred to the boat then in commission. But should you mention that "When the "Pike" or the "Ben Franklin" was snagged, or burned, or blew up", in order fully to be understood you must designate the particular "Pike", and add such other details, as would leave no room for doubt which boat by that name you referred to, thus: "Pike No. 6 snagged at such a towhead, or on such a bend; or burned in the year 1839 at Hannibal."

Steamboat owners and captains seem to have had no superstitious objections to thus naming or commanding a successor to the unfortunate one gone before. Before the first was comfortably

settled in the mud of the Mississippi, an order had gone on to
the shipyard, and in less than a week the keel was on the stocks
for its successor. If the first was a "Galena", or a "War Eagle",
the second also was a "Galena" or a "War Eagle". This was
before the fashion came into vogue of naming boats after persons,
instead of impersonal objects. There were not names enough to
go around, and thus it came about that the "Warriors", "Post
Boys", "Telegraphs", and "War Eagles" were worked overtime,
to the great confusion of any one attempting to localize a disaster
that had happened to one of that name in times past. It was
possible to read to-day of the total loss of the "War Eagle",
for instance; yet a month or more hence you might hear of the
arrival of the "War Eagle" at St. Paul with a full cargo and
passenger list. The boats might go to the bottom, but the names
went on forever. "Post Boy" was another favorite name handed
down from boat to boat, until seven or eight "Post Boys" had
been launched, run their appointed courses, and met their fate, all
within the span of less than forty years — an average of about
five years to the boat — which was a good average for old-time
steamers. On the upper river there were, among others, three
"Burlingtons", two "Chippewas", two "Danubes", two "Den-
marks", two "Dr. Franklins", three "Dubuques", two "Galenas",
three "St. Pauls", three "War Eagles", and many others, doublets
and triplets. All of which tends much to confuse one who is
attempting to run down and locate the history and final disposition
of boats bearing those names.

So far as I can learn, there is no reliable record of all the
losses on the upper river, giving the name of the boat, where,
when, and how lost. It is possible that the final disposition of
boats lost above St. Louis, is as fully covered in the list appended
to the end of this book, as anywhere else extant. Such a record
has been made for the Missouri River by Captain M. H. Chittenden, of the United States Engineers — a very complete and his-
torically valuable statement of the losses on that stream. Other
records are too comprehensive, attempting to give all the losses
through the entire length of the river, from New Orleans to St.
Paul. While covering so much more, territorially, they lack
in the detail that makes the compilation of real worth.

Most writers attach particular stress to boiler explosions,

probably from the fact that they are more spectacular, and the consequent loss of life usually greater. When a boat is snagged, it is generally possible to run her ashore in time to save the passengers and crew, although the vessel itself may prove a total loss. When a boiler explodes, the boat becomes immediately helpless, so that it cannot be run ashore, which occasions the considerable loss of life. In cases of explosion, also, the boat almost invariably burns in the middle of the river, and there is little chance for escape; for it is next to impossible to reach the life-boats carried on the roof, and if reached it is seldom found possible to launch them.

Before considering the reported losses on all the Western waters it will be interesting to locate, as far as possible, the casualities on the Mississippi between St. Louis and St. Paul, the division or section of the river usually denominated as "upper". In my list of upper-river boats, [10] there are noted all losses of which I have found any record. The list comprises about three hundred and sixty steamers that have made one or more trips above Rock Island. The boats plying above St. Louis, but not going above the upper rapids, have not been included in this list, thus excluding all the Alton Line vessels, and the Illinois River craft. Of the three hundred and sixty boats so listed, there are to be found records of seventy-three losses between St. Louis and St. Paul, including the port of St. Louis, which has been a veritable graveyard for steamboats. About a dozen other boats were lost after going into the Missouri River trade, but these are not included in the number stated. The record extends over the period between 1823 and 1863, inclusive. An analysis of the causes of such losses shows that thirty-two boats were snagged and sunk (total losses only are included; those raised, are not counted as losses); sixteen were burned; ten were sunk by ice; five were stove in by hitting rocks, and sank; three sank by striking bridges; three were sunk by Confederate batteries during the war; two were lost from boiler explosions; one was torn to pieces by a tornado, and one struck a wreck of another boat and sank on top of the first wreck.

What became of the other boats included in the list, I am unable to learn. The United States government appears never to have printed a report (or reports) showing the fate of the

[10] See Appendix: "Upper Mississippi River Steamboats, 1823-1863."

hundreds of steamboats over which it maintained an official watch-care while they were in active service. It would seem to have paid more attention to boiler explosions than to any other cause of disaster; for the reason, possibly, that it is supposed to have held itself, through its inspectors, more or less responsible for the condition of steam boilers. Still, as it also, through another set of inspectors, looks after the hulls of all steamboats, there would seem to be no reason why the loss of boats by snagging, or other similar causes affecting the hulls, should not also have been reported.

It will be observed that nearly one-half the known losses on the upper river between 1823 and 1863 were the result of snagging. Captain Chittenden, in his report on steamboat losses on the Missouri from 1842 to 1897, gives the snags credit for catching 193 boats out of a total loss of 295, or two-thirds of all known losses. Owing to its alluvial banks, and the consequent eating away of wooded points and islands by the ever changing current of that most erratic of rivers, the bed of the stream was literally sown with snags. The wonder of it is, that a pilot was able ever to take a boat up and back a thousand miles, without hitting a snag and losing his boat. They did it, however, although the record of losses from that cause serves to show how imminent the danger was at all times, and how many came to grief, however sharp the eyes of the pilot, or however skilled in reading the surface of the water and locating the danger.

The upper Mississippi has more miles of rock bluffs — in fact, is lined with such bluffs from Keokuk to St. Paul; thus the wear and tear of its banks is not so great as on the Missouri. Still, the great number of islands, heavily wooded, furnish many sunken trees, and one-half of the steamboat loss on this river is also directly traceable to snags.

Next to the snags, which are forever reaching out their gnarled arms to impale the unfortunate, fire is the greatest enemy of steamboat property on Western waters. Built of the lightest and most combustible pine, soaked with oil paint, the upper works are like tinder when once alight, and danger of this is ever present in a hundred different forms. A little explosion in the furnaces, throwing live coals over the deck; over-heated smokestacks, communicating a blaze to the roof; careless passengers or crew, throwing half-burned matches on deck or into inflammable merchandise in the freight; or the mass of sparks, cinders, and live coals continuously falling from the stacks, especially when burning wood in the furnaces: all these are a constant menace, and with a blaze once started the chances are a hundred to one that the boat is lost. A lighted match thrown into a haymow can scarcely bring quicker results than a little blaze in the upper works of a steamboat. It flashes up in an instant, and the draft generated by the progress of the boat instantly carries it the length of the cabin. In fifteen minutes the upper works are gone. Sixteen Mississippi boats out of seventy were burned; twenty-five of 295, on the Missouri. As in losses from ice, so also by fire, St. Louis has been the storm centre, and for the same reason namely, the great number of boats there, both summer and winter. Several visitations from this most dreaded and dreadful enemy of steamboats are recorded in the history of river navigation, in which two or more boats were lost while at the St. Louis landing. But the one which is known far and wide on Western waters was of such magnitude, and the property loss so great, as to earn for it the title of the "Great Fire".

This, the most disastrous of all calamities which ever occurred in the history of navigation in the West, commenced at about 10 o'clock in the evening of May 17, 1849, and continued until 7 o'clock the next morning. Captain Chittenden, the historian of the Missouri River, says, in describing this catastrophe:

"Fire alarms had been heard several times early in the evening, but nothing had come of them, until about the hour above-mentioned, when it was found that fire had broken out in earnest on the steamer "White Cloud", which lay at the wharf between Wash and Cherry Streets. The "Endors" lay just above her and the "Edward Bates" below. Both caught fire. At this time a well-intended but ill-considered, effort to stop the progress of the fire was made by some parties, who cut the "Edward Bates's" moorings and turned her into the stream. The boat was soon caught by the current and carried down the river; but a strong northeast wind bore it constantly in shore, and every time it touched it ignited another boat. An effort was now made to turn other boats loose before the "Edward Bates" could reach them, but a fatality seemed to attend every effort. The burning boat outsped them all, and by frequent contacts set fire to many more. These in turn ignited the rest, until in a short time the river presented the spectacle of a vast fleet of burning vessels, drifting slowly along the shore. The fire next spread to the buildings, and before it could be arrested had destroyed the main business portion of the city. It was the most appalling calamity that had ever visited St. Louis; and followed as it was by the great cholera scourge of 1849, it was a terrible disaster. At the levee there were destroyed twenty-three steam-boats, three barges, and one small boat. The total valuation of boats and cargoes was estimated at about $440,000, and the insurance was but $225,000; but this was not all paid, for the fire broke up several of the insurance companies."

Ice also plays an important part in the game of steamboat killing. The season on the upper river is short at best. An early start in the spring, before the railroads had yet reached St. Paul, brought the greatest financial returns to the daring and successful captains who, bringing their boats through all the dangers, arrived safely in harbor at the head of navigation. Great chances were taken in the fifties, in trying to get through Lake Pepin before it was clear of ice. The river above and below was usually clear two weeks before the ice was out of the lake sufficiently to enable a boat to force its way through. During the last week of such embargo, boats were constantly butting the ice at either end of the lake, trying to get up or down, or were perilously coasting along the shore, where, from the shallowness of the water and the inflow from the banks, the ice had rotted more than in the centre of the lake. A change of wind, or a sudden freshening, catching a boat thus coasting along the shore, would shove her on to the rocks or sand, and crush her hull as though it were an eggshell. The "Falls City" was thus caught and smashed. I myself saw the "Fire Canoe" crushed flat, in the middle of the lake, a little below Wacouta, Minn., she having run down a mile or more in the channel which we had broken with the "Fanny Harris". We had just backed out, for Captain Anderson had seen signs of a rising wind out of the west, that would shut the ice into our track. This result did follow after the other boat had gone in, despite the well-meant warnings of Anderson, who hailed the other boat and warned them of the rising wind and the danger to be apprehended. This caution was ignored by the "Fire Canoe's" captain, who ran his boat down into the channel that we had broken. The ice did move as predicted, slowly, so slowly as to be imperceptible unless you sighted by some stationary object. But it was as irresistible as fate, and it crushed the timbers of the "Fire Canoe" as though they were inch boards instead of five-inch planks. The rending

REED'S LANDING, MINNESOTA. At the foot of Lake Pepin. During the ice blockade in the Lake, in the spring of each year before the advent of railroads to St. Paul, all freight was unloaded at Reed's Landing, hauled by team to Wacouta, at the head of the Lake, where it was reloaded upon another steamboat for transportation to St. Paul and other ports above the Lake.

of her timbers was plainly heard two miles away. The upper
works were left on the ice, and later we ran down and picked
the crew and passengers off the wreck. When the wind changed
and blew the other way, the cabin was turned over and ground
to splinters amid the moving cakes.

In 1857 the "Galena" was the first boat through the lake
(April 30th). There were twelve other boats in sight at one
time, all butting the ice in the attempt to force a passage and be
the first to reach St. Paul. Of the boats lost on the Missouri River
between 1842 and 1897, twenty-six were lost from ice; on the
upper Mississippi, up to 1863, ten boats succumbed to the same
destroyer.

Not only in Lake Pepin, in the early spring, was this danger
to be apprehended; but in autumn also, in the closing days of
navigation, when the young "anchor ice" was forming, and drifting
with the current, before it had become attached to the banks,
and formed the winter bridge over the river. This was a most
insidious danger. The new ice, just forming under the stress
of zero weather, cut like a knife; and while the boat might feel
no jar from meeting ice fields and solitary floating cakes, all the
time the ice was eating its way through the firm oak planking,
and unless closely watched the bow of the boat would be ground
down so thin that an extra heavy ice floe, striking fairly on the
worn planking, would stave the whole bow in, and the boat would
go to the bottom in spite of all attempts to stop the leak. The
"Fanny Harris" was thus cut down by floating ice and sank in
twenty feet of water, opposite Point Douglass, being a total
loss. Ordinarily, boats intending to make a late trip to the north
were strengthened by spiking on an extra armor sheathing of
four-inch oak plank at the bow, and extending back twenty or
thirty feet.

It is a singular fact that the greatest damage from ice
was not experienced at the far north of the upper river, but at
the southern extremity of the run; although many other boats
were lost on the upper reaches, at wide intervals of time and
place. St. Louis was a veritable killing place for steamboats,
from the ice movements. This may be accounted for from the
reason that so many boats wintered at St. Louis. When a break-
up of extraordinary magnitude or unseasonableness did occur, it

had a large number of boats to work upon. Again, the season
of cold, while long and severe on the upper river, was distinctly
marked as to duration. There was no thawing and freezing
again. When the river closed in November, it stayed closed until
the latter end of March, or the early days of April. Then, when
the ice went out, that ended the embargo; there was no further
danger to be feared. Boats did not usually leave their snug-
harbors until the ice had run out; and when they did start, they
had only Lake Pepin to battle with. At St. Louis, on the contrary, the most disastrous break-ups came unseasonably and unex-
pectedly, with the result that the great fleet of boats wintering
there were caught unprepared to meet such an emergency, and
many were lost.

Two such disastrous movements of the ice were experienced
at St. Louis, the first in 1856, the other in 1876. The former
"break-up" occurred February 27, and resulted in the destruction
of a score of the finest boats in the St. Louis trade, and the
partial wrecking of as many more. It put out of commission
in a few hours nearly forty boats, a catastrophe unequalled in
magnitude, either before or since, in the annals of the river. The
disaster was not caused in the usual way, by the thawing of
the ice. In that case it would not have been so disastrous, if
indeed to be feared at all, that being the usual and normal manner
of clearing the river in the spring. The winter had been very
cold, the ice was two or three feet thick, and the water very
low. In this case the movement of the ice was caused by a
sudden rise in the river from above, which caused the ice to
move before it was much, if any, disintegrated. It was an appalling and terrible exhibition of the power of the Great River
when restrained in its course. The following account is from a
St. Louis paper, printed at the time:

"The ice at first moved very slowly and without any perceptible
shock. The boats lying above Chestnut Street were merely shoved ashore.
Messrs. Eads & Nelson's Submarine boat No. 4, which had just finished
work on the wreck of the "Parthenia", was almost immediately capsized,
and became herself a hopeless wreck. Here the destruction commenced.
The "Federal Arch" parted her fastenings and became at once a total
wreck. Lying below her were the steamers "Australia", "Adriatic",
"Brunette", "Paul Jones", "Falls City", "Altoona", "A. B. Chambers", and
the "Challenge", all of which were torn away from shore as easily as
if they had been mere skiffs, and floated down with the immense fields of

ice. The shock and the crashing of these boats can better be imagined than described. All their ample fastenings were as nothing against the enormous flood of ice, and they were carried down apparently fastened and wedged together. The first obstacles with which they came in contact were a large fleet of wood-boats, flats, and canal boats. These small fry were either broken to pieces, or were forced out on to the levee in a very damaged condition. There must have been at least fifty of these smaller water craft destroyed, pierced by the ice, or crushed by the pressure of each against the other.

"In the meantime some of the boats lying above Chestnut Street fared badly. The "F. X. Aubrey" was forced into the bank and was considerably damaged. The noble "Nebraska", which was thought to be in a most perilous position, escaped with the loss of her larboard wheel and some other small injuries. A number of the upper river boats lying above Chestnut Street, were more or less damaged. Both the Alton wharf-boats were sunk and broken in pieces. The old "Shenandoah" and the "Sam Cloon" were forced away from the shore and floated down together, lodging against the steamer "Clara", where they were soon torn to pieces and sunk by a collision with one of the ferry-boats floating down upon them. The Keokuk wharf-boat maintained its position against the flood and saved three boats, the "Polar Star", "Pringle", and "Forest Rose", none of which were injured.

"After running about an hour the character of the ice changed and it came down in a frothy, crumbled condition, with an occasional solid piece. At the end of two hours it ran very slowly, and finally stopped at half past five o'clock, P. M. Just before the ice stopped and commenced to gorge, huge piles, twenty and thirty feet in height were forced up by the current on every hand, both on the shore and at the lower dike, where so many boats had come to a halt. In fact these boats seemed to be literally buried in ice.

* * * * * * * *

"The levee on the morning after the day of the disaster presented a dreary and desolate spectacle, looking more like a scene in the polar regions than in the fertile and beautiful Mississippi Valley. The Mississippi, awakened from her long sleep, was pitching along at a wild and rapid rate of speed, as if to make up for lost time. The ice-coat of mail was torn into shreds, which lay strewn along the levee, and was in some places heaped up to a height of twenty feet above the level of the water. Where the boats had lain in crowds only a few hours before, nothing was to be seen save this high bulwark of ice, which seemed as if it had been left there purposely to complete the picture of bleak desolation. The whole business portion of the levee was clear of boats, except the two wrecked Alton wharf-boats, which were almost shattered to pieces, and cast like toys upon the shore in the midst of the ridge of ice. There was not a single boat at the levee which entirely escaped injury by the memorable breaking up of the ice on February 27, 1856."

Chapter XXX

Living It Over Again

One day in the spring of 1881, after having finished the business that had called me to St. Paul from my home in River Falls, Wisconsin (where I was a railway agent and newspaper proprietor combined), I was loafing about the Grand Central Station, killing time until my train should be ready to start. The big whistle of a big boat drew me to the adjacent wharf of the Diamond Jo Line. The craft proved to be the "Mary Morton". As soon as the lines were fast, the stages in position, and the first rush of passengers ashore, I walked aboard and up to the office. A small man, past middle life, his hair somewhat gray, was writing in a big book which I recognized as the passenger journal. By the same token I realized that I was in the presence of the chief clerk, even if I had not already seen the "mud" clerk hard at work on the levee, checking out freight. I spoke to the occupant of the office, and after a few questions and counter questions I learned that he was Charley Mathers, who had been on the river before 1860 as chief clerk, and he in turn learned my name and former standing on the river. From him I learned that the chief pilot of the steamer was Thomas Burns. It did not take a great while to get up to the pilot house. I would not have known my old chief had I not been posted in advance by Mr. Mathers. This man was grey instead of brown, and had big whiskers, which the old Tom did not have. He was sitting on the bench, smoking his pipe and reading a book. He looked up as I entered, and questioned with his eyes what the intrusion might mean, but waited until I should state my business. It took some minutes to establish my identity; but when I did I received a cordial welcome.

And then we talked of old times and new, and war times

too — for he had gone out as captain in an Illinois regiment at the same time that I went out as a Wisconsin soldier. From a pilot's view point the old times were simply marvelous as compared with the present. A hundred and fifty dollars a month, now, as against six hundred then; and a "wild" pilot, picking up seventeen hundred dollars in one month as was done by one man in 1857. Now he couldn't catch a wild boat if he waited the season through — there are none. We went over the river, the steamboats, and the men as we knew them in 1860; and then we went down below and hunted up George McDonald, the good old Scotchman, who never swore at you through the speaking tube, no matter how many bells you gave him in a minute, and who never got rattled, however fast you might send them; who never carried more steam than the license called for, and who never missed a day's duty. The same banter had to be gone through with, with the same result — he had forgotten the slim youth who "shipped up" for him twenty years ago, but whom he promptly recalled when given a clue. And then, it being train time, we all walked across to the station and Burns invited me to take a trip with him, next time, down to St. Louis and back, and work my way at the wheel.

I knew that I had not yet been weaned from the spokes, and doubted if I ever should be. I said that I would try, and I did. I filed an application for the first leave of absence I had ever asked for from the railroad company, and it was granted. I found a man to assist the "devil" in getting out my paper, he doing the editing for pure love of editing, if not from love of the editor. We set our house in order, packed our trunk and grips, and when the specified fortnight was ended, we (my wife, my daughter, and myself) were comfortably bestowed in adjoining staterooms in the ladies' cabin of the "Mary Morton", and I was fidgeting about the boat, watching men "do things" as I had been taught, or had seen others do, twenty years ago or more.

The big Irish mate bullied his crew of forty "niggers", driving them with familiar oaths, to redoubled efforts in getting in the "last" packages of freight, which never reached the last. Among the rest, in that half hour, I saw barrels of mess pork — a whole car load of it, which the "nigger" engine was striking down into the hold. Shades of Abraham! pork *out* of St. Paul! Twenty years before, I had checked out a whole barge load (three hundred barrels) through from Cincinnati, by way of Cairo. Cincinnati was the great porkopolis of the world, while Chicago was yet keeping its pigs in each back yard, and every freeholder "made" his own winter's supply of pork for himself. The steward in charge of the baggage was always in the way with a big trunk on the gangway, just as of old. The engineers were trying their steam, and slowly turning the wheel over, with the waste cocks open, to clear the cylinders of water. The firemen were coaxing the beds of coal into fiercer heats. The chief clerk compared the tickets which were presented by hurrying passengers, with the reservation sheet, and assigned rooms, all "the best", to others who had no reservations. The "mud" clerk checked his barrels and boxes, and scribbled his name fiercely and with many flourishes to last receipts. The pilot on watch, Mr. Burns, sat on the window ledge in the pilot house, and waited. The captain stood by the big bell, and listened for the "All ready, Sir!" of the mate. As the words were spoken, the great bell boomed out one stroke, the lines slacked away and were thrown off the snubbing posts. A wave of the captain's hand, a pull at one of the knobs on the wheel-frame, the jingle of a bell far below, the shiver of the boat as the great wheel began its work, and the bow of the "Mary Morton" swung to the south; a couple of pulls at the bell-ropes, and the wheel was revolving ahead; in a minute more the escape pipes told us that she was "hooked up", and with full steam ahead we were on our way to St. Louis. And I was again in the pilot house with my old chief, who bade me "show us what sort of an education you had when a youngster".

Despite my forty years I was a boy again, and Tom Burns was the critical chief, sitting back on the bench with his pipe alight, a comical smile oozing out of the corners of mouth and eyes, for all the world like the teacher of old.

The very first minute I met the swing of the gang-plank derrick (there is no jack staff on the modern steamboat, more's the pity), with two or three spokes when one would have been a plenty, yawing the boat round "like a toad in a hailstorm", as I was advised. I could feel the hot blood rushing to my cheeks, just as it did twenty years before under similar provocation, when the eye of the master was upon me. I turned around and

STEAMER "MARY MORTON," 1876; 456 tons. Lying at the levee, La Crosse, Wisconsin. (From a negative made in 1881.)

STEAMER "ARKANSAS," 1868; 549 tons. With tow of four barges, capable of transporting 18,000 sacks — 36,000 bushels of wheat per trip. The usual manner of carrying wheat in the early days, before the river traffic was destroyed by railroad competition.

found that Mr. Burns had taken it in, and we both laughed like boys — as I fancy both of us were for the time.

But I got used to it very soon, getting the "feel of it", and as the "Mary Morton" steered like a daisy I lined out a very respectable wake; although Tom tried to puzzle me a good deal with questions as to the landmarks, most of which I had forgotten save in a general way.

When eight bells struck, Mr. Link, Mr. Burns's partner, came into the pilot house; that let me out, and after an introduction by Mr. Burns, Mr. Link took the wheel. He was a young man, of perhaps thirty years of age. We lingered a few minutes to watch him skilfully run Pig's Eye, and then went down to dinner, and had introductions all around — to Captain Boland, Mr. Mathers, Mr. McDonald, and other officers.

I took the wheel again, later in the afternoon. It was easy steering, and there was no way of getting out of the channel, for a time; and later I found that some things were taking on a familiar look — that I had not forgotten all of the river, and things were shaping themselves, as each new point or bend was reached, so that very little prompting was necessary.

I had the wheel from Pine Bend to Hastings, where I was given permission to step on the end of a board lever fixed in the floor of the pilot house, on one side of the wheel, and give the signal of the Diamond Jo Line for the landing — two long blasts, followed by three short ones. Here was another innovation. In old times you had to hold your wheel with one hand while you pulled a rope to blow for a landing, which was sometimes a little awkward. This was a very little thing, but it went with the landing-stage derrick, the electric search-light, and a score of other improvements that had come aboard since I walked ashore two decades before.

A mile or two below Hastings I saw the "break" on the surface of the water which marked the resting-place of the "Fanny Harris", on which I had spent so many months of hard work, but which, looked back upon through the haze of twenty years, now seemed to have been nothing but holiday excursions.

At Prescott I looked on the familiar water front, and into the attic windows where with my brother I had so often in the night watches studied the characteristics of boats landing at

the levee. Going ashore I met many old-time friends, among
whom was Charles Barnes, agent of the Diamond Jo Line, who
had occupied the same office on the levee since 1858, and had
met every steamboat touching the landing during all those years.
He was the Nestor of the profession, and was one of the very
few agents still doing business on the water front who had begun
such work prior to 1860. Since then, within a few years past,
he also has gone, and that by an accident, while still in the
performance of duties connected with the steamboat business.

Dropping rapidly down the river, we passed Diamond Bluff
without stopping, but rounded to at Red Wing for passengers and
freight, and afterward headed into a big sea on Lake Pepin,
kicked up by the high south wind that was still blowing. We
landed under the lee of the sand-spit at Lake City, and after getting
away spent the better part of an hour in picking up a barge load
of wheat, that was anchored out in the lake.

By a wise provision of the rules for the government of pilots,
adopted since I left the river, no one is permitted in the pilot
house except the pilot on watch, or his partner, after the side-
lights have been put up. For this reason I could not occupy my
chosen place at the wheel after sunset; but I found enough to
occupy my time down below in the engine-room, watching the
great pitman walk out and in, to and from the crank-shaft,
listening to the rush of the water alongside as it broke into a
great wave on either side, and to the churning of the wheel, and
all the while discussing old times with George McDonald. As
the wind was still high and the water rough, I had an opportunity
to see Mr. McDonald answer bells, which came thick and furious
for a good while before we were well fast to the levee at Reed's
Landing. There was no excitement, however, and no rushing
from side to side as in the old days, to "ship up". He stood
amidship, his hand on the reversing bar, just as a locomotive engineer sits with his hand on the bar of his engine. When the bell
rang to set her back, he pulled his lever full back, and then opened
his throttle without moving a step. After getting started, and
under full way, he simply "hooked her back" three or four notches,
and the old-time "short link" operation had been performed without taking a step. A great advance in twenty years! But why
wasn't it thought of fifty years ago? I don't know. The same

principle had been in use on locomotives from the start. It is simple enough now, on steamboat engines. Perhaps none of the old-timers thought of it.

I turned in at an early hour, and lay in the upper berth, listening to the cinders skating over the roof a couple of feet above my face, and translating the familiar sounds that reached me from engine-room and roof — the call for the draw at the railroad bridge, below the landing; the signal for landing at Wabasha; the slow bell, the stopping-bell, the backing-bell, and a dozen or twenty unclassified bells, before the landing was fully accomplished; the engineer trying the water in the boilers; the rattle of the slice-bars on the sides of the furnace doors as the firemen trimmed their fires; and one new and unfamiliar sound from the engine-room — the rapid exhaust of the little engine driving the electric generator, the only intruder among the otherwise familiar noises, all of which came to my sleepy senses as a lullaby.

I listened for anything which might indicate the passage of the once dreaded Beef Slough bar, but beyond the labored breathing of the engines, that at times indicated shoaling water, there was nothing by which to identify our old-time enemy. So listening, I fell asleep.

"Breakfast is ready, sah", was the pleasant proclamation following a gentle rapping on the stateroom door. Very refreshing, this, compared with the sharp manifesto of the olden-days watchman: "Twelve o'clock; turn out"!

The "Morton" was ploughing along between Victory and De Soto. By the time justice had been done to the well-cooked and well-served meal, the boat had touched at the latter port and taken on a few sacks of barley (potential Budweiser), consigned to one of the big St. Louis breweries. Mr. Link was at the wheel, and as a good understanding had been reached the day before, there was no question as to who was going to do the steering. Mr. Link took the bench and talked river as only a lover could talk, while I picked out the course by the aid of diamond boards and ancient landmarks, without asking many questions. A suggestion now and then: "Let her come in a little closer". "Now you may cross over". "Look out for the snag in the next bend", and like cautions were all that was necessary.

And the pleasure of it! The beautiful morning in June, the woods alive with songbirds; the bluffs and islands a perfect green; the river dimpling under the caresses of a gentle breeze, and blushing rosy under the ardent gaze of the morning sun — a picture of loveliness not to be outdone anywhere in the wide world. And then the sense of power that comes to one who has learned to handle a steamboat with a touch of the wheel, in taking a long bend, a mile or more in length, without moving the wheel an inch, the rudders so slightly angled as to guide the boat along the arc of a circle which would be ten miles in diameter, could it be extended to completion, and leaving a wake as true as if drawn by a pair of dividers!

We did not go into Prairie du Chien, but with the glasses the old French town could be discerned across the island and the slough; it claims to be two hundred years old, and it looked its age. Time was when Prairie du Chien, the terminus of the railroad nearest to St. Paul and the upper river, gave promise of being a big city, the outlet and *entrepôt* for the trade of a great territory. Her people believed in her, and in her great future. A dozen steamboats might be seen, on many occasions, loading merchandise from the railroad, or unloading grain and produce, in sacks and packages, destined to Milwaukee and Chicago. When I was second clerk I once checked out twenty thousand sacks of wheat in something over thirty-six hours, the cargo of boat and two barges. The wheat now goes through in bulk, in box cars loaded in Iowa and Minnesota, and they do not even change engines at Prairie du Chien, the roundhouse and division terminal being located at McGregor, on the west side of the Mississippi.

At McGregor I saw Joseph Reynolds, at that time owner of five fine steamers, and manager of the Diamond Jo Line. Captain Burns pointed out a man dressed in a dark business suit, sitting on a snubbing post, lazily and apparently indifferently watching the crew handling freight, or looking over the steamer as if it were an unusual and curious sight. He did not speak to any of the officers while we were watching him, and Mr. Burns thought it very unlikely that he would. He did not come on board the boat at all, but sat and whittled the head of the post until we backed out and left him out of sight behind.   Mr. Burns allowed that "Jo" was doing a heap of thinking all the time we were watching him, and that he probably did not think of the boat, as a present object of interest, at all.

Joseph Reynolds began his river experience in 1867 with one small boat, carrying his own wheat, and towing a barge when the steamer could not carry it all.   When we saw him holding down a snubbing post at McGregor he owned and operated, under the title of the "Diamond Jo Line", the "Mary Morton", "Libbie Conger", "Diamond Jo", "Josephine", and "Josie", all well equipped and handsome steamers.   Later, he added the "Sidney", the "Pittsburg", the "St. Paul", and the "Quincy", still larger and better boats.

That night I witnessed for the first time the operation of the electric search-light as an aid to navigation.   The night came on dark and stormy, a thunder shower breaking over the river as we were running the devious and dangerous Guttenburg channel, about five or six miles below the town by that name.   Instead of straining his eyes out of his head, hunting doubtful landmarks miles away, as we used to do, Mr. Link tooted his little whistle down in the engine-room, and instantly the light was switched on to the lantern at the bow of the boat.   Lines running from the pilot house gave perfect control of the light, and it was flashed ahead until it lighted up the diamond boards and other shore-marks by which the crossings were marked and the best water indicated to the pilot.   Under a slow bell he worked his way down the ugly piece of river without touching.   He had the leads two or three times, just to assure himself, but apparently he could have made it just as well without them.

A mile and a half above the mouth of Turkey River, in the very worst place of all, we found a big log raft in trouble, hung up on the sand, with a steamboat at each end working at it.   They occupied so much of the river that it took Mr. Link over an hour to get past the obstruction, the search-light in the meantime turning night into day, and enabling him to look down on the timber and see just where the edge of the raft was.   By backing and flanking he finally squeezed past, but not without scraping the sand and taking big chances of getting hung up

himself. Coming back, we did hang up for an hour or more
in the same place, a mile above the foot of Cassville Slough.
Without the aid of the search-light it would have been impossible
to have worked the steamer past the raft until daylight came.
It is a wonderful aid to navigation, and it is as easy to run
crooked places by night as by day, with its assistance.

In St. Louis, after seeing Shaw's Garden and tasting the old
French market, the best thing you can do is to go back to the
levee and watch the river, the big Eads bridge, the boats, and
the darkies. There may be no boats other than the one you came
on and are going back upon, but you will not miss seeing the bridge,
and you must not miss seeing the darkies. They are worth studying — much better than even imported shrubbery.

There was an Anchor Line boat moored just below us the
day we were there, a big side-wheeler, in the New Orleans trade,
sixteen hundred tons. The "Mary Morton" was four hundred
and fifty, and had shrunk perceptibly since the big liner came
alongside. There were two or three other boats, little ones, ferries
and traders, sprinkled along the three miles of levee. In 1857
I have seen boats lying two deep, in places, and one deep in
every place where it was possible to stick the nose of a steamboat
into the levee — boats from New Orleans, from Pittsburg, from
the upper Mississippi, from the Missouri, from the Tennessee
and the Cumberland, the Red River and the Illinois, loaded with
every conceivable description of freight, and the levee itself piled
for miles with incoming or outgoing cargoes. Now, it was enough
to make one sick at heart. It seemed as if the city had gone
to decay. The passage of a train over the bridge every five
minutes or less, each way, reassured one on that point, however,
and indicated that there was still plenty of traffic, and that it
was only the river that was dead, and not the city.

In old times the steamboat crews were comprised principally
of white men — that is, deck hands and roustabouts (or stevedores).
The firemen may have been darkies, and the cabin crews were
more than likely to have been, but the deck crews were generally
white. Now, the deck crews are all colored men. They are a
happy-go-lucky set, given to strong drink and craps, not to mention some other forms of vice. In old times the crews were hired
by the month. The members of a modern deck crew never make

two trips consecutively on the same boat. The boat does not lay long enough in St. Louis to give them time to spend ten days' wages, and then get sober enough, or hungry enough, to reship for another trip. Therefore, as soon as the last package of freight is landed, the crew marches to the window of the clerk's office opening out onto the guards, and gets what money is coming to each individual after the barkeeper's checks have been deducted. With this wealth in hand the fellow makes a straight wake for one of the two or three score dives, rum-holes, and bagnios that line the levee. He seldom leaves his favorite inn until his money is gone and he is thrown out by the professional "bouncer" attached to each of these places of entertainment.

The boat does not remain without a crew, however. While one of the clerks is paying off the old crew, another has gone out on the levee with a handful of pasteboard tickets, one for each man he desires to ship for the next round trip to St. Paul. Mounting the tallest snubbing post at hand, he is instantly surrounded by a shouting, laughing, pushing, and sometimes fighting mass of negroes, with an occasional alleged white man. This mob of men are clothed in every conceivable style of rags and tatters, and all are trying to get near the man on the post.

After a minute's delay the clerk cries out: "All set! Stand by"! and gives his handful of tickets a whirl around his head, loosening them a few at a time, and casting them to every point of the compass so as to give all a fair chance to draw a prize. The crowd of would-be "rousters" jump, grab, wrestle, and fight for the coveted tickets, and the man who secures one and fights his way victoriously to the gang plank is at once recorded in the mate's book as one of the crew. The victorious darky comes up the gang plank showing every tooth in his head. It is the best show to be seen in St. Louis.

"Why do they not go out and pick out the best men and hire them in a business-like and Christian-like manner?" inquires the unacclimated tourist.

"Because this is a better and very much quicker way", says the mate, who knows whereof he speaks. "The nigger that can get a ticket, and keep it until he gets to the gang plank, is the nigger for me. He *is* the 'best man'; if he wasn't he wouldn't get here at all. Some of 'em don't get here — they carry 'em

off to the hospital to patch 'em up; sometimes they carry 'em off
and plant 'em. There wasn't much of a rush to-day. You ought
to see 'em in the early spring, when they are pretty hungry after
a winter's freezing and fasting, and they want to get close to a
steamboat boiler to get warm. There was not more'n three
hundred niggers out there to-day. Last April there was a thousand, and they everlastingly scrapped for a chance to get close
to the post. Some of 'em got their 'razzers', and sort of hewed
their way in. The clerk got a little shaky himself. He was
afraid they might down him and take the whole pack."

"I shouldn't think that you would care to ship the men with
'razzers' as you call them."

"Oh, I don't mind that if they can tote well. Anyway,
they all have 'em. They don't use them much on white men,
anyhow. And then we look out for them. After we back out
from here they will get enough to do to keep them busy. They
don't carry any life insurance, and they don't want to fool with
white folks, much."

Having watched the mates handling the crew on the down
trip one could form a pretty clear judgment why the "niggers"
were not solicitous to "fool with" the white men with whom
they were in contact while on the river.

That night we steamed across to East St. Louis and took
on three thousand kegs of nails for different ports on the upper
river. These were carried on the shoulders of the newly-hired
deck crew a distance of at least two hundred feet from the railroad
freight house to the boat; every one of the forty men "toting"
seventy-five kegs, each weighing a hundred and seven pounds.
At the conclusion of this exercise it is safe to say that they were
glad enough to creep under the boilers so soon as the boat pulled
out from the landing. The next morning we were well on our
way up the river. I steered most of the daylight watches for
Mr. Link all the way upstream. He had a terrible cough, and
was very weak, but had the hopefulness which always seems to
accompany that dread disease (consumption), that he "would
soon get over it". I was glad to relieve him of some hard work,
and I was also greatly pleased again to have an opportunity to
handle a big boat. Poor fellow, his hopefulness was of no avail.
He died at his home in Quincy within two years of that time.

We arrived at St. Paul on schedule time, with no mishaps to speak of, and I parted with regret from old and new friends on the boat, none of whom I have ever seen since that parting twenty-five years ago. Thomas Burns, Henry Link, George McDonald, and Captain Boland are all dead. Charles Mathers, the chief clerk, was living a few years ago at Cairo, an old man, long retired from active service.

As we started to leave the boat, we were arrested by an outcry, a pistol shot, and the shouting of the colored deck hands, followed by the rush of the mate and the fall of one of the men, whom he had struck with a club or billet. Still another colored man lay groaning on the wharf, and a white man was binding up an ugly gash in his neck made by the slash of a razor. In a few minutes the clang of the patrol wagon gong was heard, as it responded to the telephone call, and two darkies were carried off, one to the hospital and the other to the jail. The slightly-interrupted work of toting nail kegs was then resumed. Thus the last sights and sounds were fit illustrations of river life as it is to-day, and as it was a half a century ago — strenuous and rough, indeed, but possessing a wonderful fascination to one who has once fallen under the influence of its spell.

Appendix

Appendix A

List of Steamboats on the Upper Mississippi River, 1823-1863

In the following compilation I have endeavored to give as complete a history as possible of every boat making one or more trips on the upper Mississippi River — that is to say, above the upper rapids — prior to 1863, not counting boats engaged exclusively in the rafting business. Owing to the repetition of names as applied to different steamers, which were built, ran their course, and were destroyed, only to be followed by others bearing the same name, it is altogether likely that some have escaped notice. Others that may have made the trip have left no sign. In nearly every case the record is made either at St. Paul or at Galena. Whenever possible, the names of the master and clerk are given. Where boats were running regularly in the trade but one notation is made: "St. Paul, 1852; 1854; etc.", which might include twenty trips during the season. The record covers the period from 1823, when the first steamer, the "Virginia", arrived at St. Peters from St. Louis, with government stores for Fort Snelling, up to 1863, one year after the writer left the river.

ADELIA—Stern-wheel; built at California, Pa., 1853; 127 tons; St. Paul, 1855; 1856; 1857—Capt. Bates, Clerk Worsham.

ADMIRAL—Side-wheel; built at McKeesport, Pa., 1853; 245 tons; 169 feet long, 26 feet beam; in St. Paul trade 1854—Capt. John Brooks; went into Missouri River trade; was snagged and sunk October, 1856, at head of Weston Island, in shallow water; had very little cargo at time; was raised and ran for many years thereafter in Missouri River trade.

ADRIATIC—Side-wheel; built at Shousetown, Pa., 1855; 424 tons; was in great ice jam at St. Louis, February, 1856.

ADVENTURE—In Galena trade 1837—Capt. Van Houten.

A. G. MASON—Stern-wheel; built at West Brownsville, Pa., 1855; 170 tons; in St. Paul trade 1855; 1856; 1857— Captain Barry, Clerk Pearman.

ALBANY—Very small boat; in Minnesota River trade 1861.

ALEX. HAMILTON—Galena and St. Paul trade 1848—Captain W. H. Hooper.

ALHAMBRA—Stern-wheel; built at McKeesport, Pa., 1854; 187 tons; Minnesota Packet Company, St. Paul trade 1855—Captain McGuire; 1856—Captain W. H. Gabbert; 1857—Captain McGuire; same trade 1858; 1859; 1860; 1861; 1862, in Dunleith Line, Captain William Faucette.

ALICE—Stern-wheel; built at California, Pa., 1853; 72 tons; at St. Paul 1854.

ALPHIA—Galena and St. Louis trade 1837.

ALTOONA—Stern-wheel; built at Brownsville, Pa., 1853; 66 tons; was in great ice jam at St. Louis, February, 1856; at St. Paul 1857; sunk at Montgomery tow-head 1859.

AMARANTH—(First)—Galena trade 1842—Captain G. W. Atchinson; sunk at head of Amaranth Island 1842.

AMARANTH—(Second)—At Galena, from St. Louis, April 8, 1845.

AMERICA—Sunk 1852, opposite Madison, Iowa.

AMERICAN EAGLE—Cossen, master, burned at St. Louis, May 17, 1849; loss $14,000.

AMERICUS—Stern-wheel; at St. Paul 1856.

AMULET—At Galena, from St. Louis, April 9, 1846.

ANGLER—St. Paul 1859.

ANNIE—At Galena, on her way to St. Peters, April 1, 1840.

ANSON NORTHRUP—Minnesota River boat; was taken to pieces and transported to Moorhead in 1859, where she was put together again and run on the Red River of the North by Captain Edwin Bell for J. C. Burbank & Co., proprietors of the Great Northwestern stage lines.

ANTELOPE—Minnesota River packet 1857; 1858; 1860; 1861. One hundred and ninety-eight tons burden.

ANTHONY WAYNE—Side-wheel; built 1844; in Galena & St. Louis trade 1845, 1846, and 1847—Captain Morrison first, later Captain Dan Able; 1850—Captain Able; went up to the Falls of St. Anthony 1850, first boat to make the trip; made a trip up the Minnesota River into the Indian country, as far as Traverse des Sioux with a large excursion party from St. Paul in 1850; went into Missouri River trade and sank March 25, 1851, three miles above Liberty Landing, Mo., being a total loss.

ARCHER—At Galena, from St. Louis, Sept. 8, 1845; sunk by collision with steamer "Di Vernon", in chute between islands 521 and 522, five miles above mouth of Illinois River, Nov. 27, 1851; was cut in two, and sunk in three minutes, with a loss of forty-one lives.

ARCOLA—St. Croix River boat, at St. Paul 1856; sunk in Lake Pepin 1857, cut down by ice.

ARGO—Galena and St. Peters trade, 1846—Captain Kennedy Lodwick; 1847—Captain M. W. Lodwick, Clerk Russell Blakeley; regular packet between Galena and St. Paul, including Stillwater and Fort Snelling; at Galena from St. Croix Falls 1847, with 100 passengers; sunk fall of 1847 at foot of Argo Island, above Winona, Minn.

ARIEL—(First)—At Fort Snelling and St. Peters June 20, 1838; August 27, 1838; Sept. 29, 1838, from Galena; 1839—Captain Lyon, at Fort Snelling April 14; made three other trips to Fort Snelling that season. She was built by Captain Thurston.

ARIEL—(Second)—Built at Cincinnati, Ohio, 1854; 169 tons; Minnesota River packet 1861.

ARIZONA—Stern-wheel—Captain Herdman, from Pittsburg, at St. Paul, 1857.

ASIA—Stern-wheel; St. Paul trade 1853; made twelve trips between St. Louis and St. Paul during season.

ATLANTA—At St. Paul from St. Louis, Captain Woodruff, 1857; again 1858.

ATLANTIC—At St. Paul 1856—Captain Isaac M. Mason.

ATLAS—Side-wheel; new at Galena, 1846—Captain Robert A. Riley; at St. Peters, from Galena, 1846; sunk near head of Atlas Island.

AUDUBON—Stern-wheel; built at Murraysville, Pa., 1853;

191 tons; St. Paul trade 1855; Captain William Fisher made his initial trip as an independent pilot on this boat.

AUNT LETTY—Side-wheel; built at Elizabeth, Pa., 1855; 304 tons; in Northern Line, St. Louis and St. Paul, 1857— Captain C. G. Morrison; 1859, same.

BADGER STATE—Built at California, Pa., 1850; 127 tons; St. Paul trade 1855 and 1856; sunk at head of Montgomery tow-head 1856.

BALTIMORE—Sunk, 1859, at Montgomery tow-head; hit wreck of "Badger State" and stove. Wreck of "Baltimore" lies on top of wreck of "Badger State".

BANGOR—St. Paul 1857; 1859.

BANJO—Show boat—first of the kind in the river; was at St. Paul in 1856; with a "nigger show". Was seated for an audience, and stopped at all landings along the river, giving entertainments. Captain William Fisher was pilot on her part of one season.

BELFAST—At St. Paul 1857; 1859.

BELLE GOLDEN—Stern-wheel; built at Brownsville, Pa., 1854; 189 tons; at St. Paul 1855—Captain I. M. Mason.

BELMONT—At Galena, from St. Louis, April 9, 1846; again May 22, 1847.

BEN BOLT—Side-wheel; built at California, Pa., 1853; 228 tons; at St. Paul, from St. Louis, 1855—Captain Boyd; at St. Paul, 1856; 1857.

BEN CAMPBELL—Side-wheel; built at Shousetown, Pa., 1852; 267 tons; in Galena & Minnesota Packet Co., 1852— Captain M. W. Lodwick; rather slow, and too deep in water for upper river; at St. Paul 1853—Capt. M. W. Lodwick; at St. Paul 1859.

BEN COURSIN—Stern-wheel; built at Cincinnati, Ohio, 1854; 161 tons; at St. Paul 1856; 1857; sunk above mouth of Black River, near La Crosse, fall of 1857.

BEN WEST—Side-wheel; at St. Paul, from St. Louis, spring 1855; went into Missouri River trade; struck bridge and sank near Washington, Mo., August, 1855.

BERLIN—At St. Paul 1855; 1856; 1859.

BERTRAND—Rogers, master, at Galena 1846; regular St.

Louis packet; advertised for pleasure trip to St. Peters June 19, 1846.

BLACKHAWK—Captain M. W. Lodwick, 1852; bought that year by the Galena Packet Co., for a low water boat; ten trips to St. Paul 1853; Captain R. M. Spencer, opening season 1854, later O. H. Maxwell; 1855, Minnesota River packet, Capt. O. H. Maxwell; at St. Paul 1859.

BLACK ROVER—Eleventh steamboat to arrive at Fort Snelling, prior to 1827.

BON ACCORD—At Galena, from St. Louis, Captain Hiram Bersie, August 31, 1846; in Galena and upper river trade, same captain, 1847; in St. Louis and Galena trade 1848, same captain.

BRAZIL—(First)—Captain Orren Smith, at Galena April 4, 1838; at Fort Snelling June 15, 1838; advertised for pleasure excursion from Galena to Fort Snelling, July 21, 1839; advertised for pleasure excursion from Galena to Fort Snelling, 1840; sunk in upper rapids, Rock Island, 1841, and total loss.

BRAZIL—(Second)—Captain Orren Smith, new, arrived at Galena Sept. 24, 1842; 160 feet long, 23 feet beam; arrived at Galena from St. Peters, Minn., June 5, 1843.

BRAZIL—(Third)—Stern-wheel; built at McKeesport, Pa., 1854; 211 tons; at St. Paul 1856; 1857—Captain Hight, from St. Louis; at St. Paul 1858.

BRIDGEWATER—At Galena, from St. Louis, April 11, 1846.

BROWNSVILLE—Snagged and sunk in Brownsville Chute, 1849.

BURLINGTON—(First)—At Galena, from St. Peters, June 17, 1837; at Fort Snelling, Captain Joseph Throckmorton, May 25, 1838, and again June 13, 1838; third trip that season, arrived at the Fort June 28, 1836, with 146 soldiers from Prairie du Chien, for the Fort.

BURLINGTON—(Second)—Sunk at Wabasha, prior to 1871; in Northern Line; built 1860.

BURLINGTON—(Third) — Large side-wheel, in Northren Line, 1875; St. Louis and St. Paul Packet.

CALEB COPE—Galena & St. Paul Packet Company; in St. Paul 1852.

CALEDONIA—In Galena trade, 1837.

CAMBRIDGE—At St. Paul 1857.

CANADA—Side-wheel, with double rudders; Northern Line Packet Co., Captain James Ward, 1857; 1858; 1859, as St. Louis and St. Paul packet; Captain J. W. Parker, 1860, 1861, same trade; 1862, same trade.

CARRIE—Stern-wheel; 267 tons; went into Missouri River trade and was snagged two miles above Indian Mission, August 14, 1866; boat and cargo total loss; boat valued at $20,000.

CARRIER—Side-wheel; 215 feet long, 33 feet beam; 267 tons; at St. Paul 1856; snagged at head of Penn's Bend, Missouri River, Oct. 12, 1858; sank in five feet of water; boat valued at $30,000; was total loss.

CASTLE GARDEN—At St. Paul 1858.

CAVALIER—At Galena April 9, 1836, for St. Louis; in Galena trade 1837.

CAZENOVIA—At St. Paul 1858.

CECILIA—Capt. Jos. Throckmorton, at St. Peters 1845. Bought by the captain for Galena & St. Peters trade. Same trade 1846, regular.

CEYLON—Stern-wheel; at St. Paul 1858.

CHALLENGE—Built at Shousetown, Pa., 1854; 229 tons; at St. Paul 1858.

CHART—At St. Paul 1859.

CHAS. WILSON—At St. Paul 1859.

CHIPPEWA—(First)—Capt. Griffith, in Galena trade 1841; arrived at Galena from St. Peters May 2, 1843.

CHIPPEWA—(Second)—Capt. Greenlee, from Pittsburg, at St. Paul, 1857; in Northwestern Line, Capt. W. H. Crapeta, St. Louis and St. Paul trade 1858; 1859; burned fifteen miles below Poplar River, on the Missouri, in May, 1861; fire discovered at supper time on a Sunday evening; passengers put on shore and boat turned adrift, she having a large amount of powder on board; boat drifted across the river and there blew up; fire caused by deck hands going into hold with lighted candle to steal whiskey. She was a stern-wheel, 160 feet long, 30 feet beam.

CHIPPEWA FALLS—Captain L. Fulton, in Chippewa River trade, 1859; stern-wheel.

CITY BELLE—Side-wheel; built at Murraysville, Pa., 1854; 216 tons; Minnesota Packet Co., Galena & St. Paul trade 1856—Captain Kennedy Lodwick; 1857—Captain A. T. Champlin, for part of the season; 1858; burned on the Red River in 1862, while in government service; was a very short boat and very hard to steer, especially in low water.

CLARA—Stern-wheel, of St. Louis; 567 tons burden, 250 horse-power engines; at St. Paul 1858.

CLARIMA—At St. Paul 1859.

CLARION—(First)—Went to Missouri River, where she was burned, at Guyandotte, May 1, 1845.

CLARION—(Second)—Stern-wheel; built at Monongahela, Pa., 1851; 73 tons; made 25 trips up Minnesota River from St. Paul, 1853; same trade 1855; 1856—Captain Hoffman; 1857; 1858; had a very big whistle, in keeping with her name—so large that it made her top heavy.

COL. MORGAN—At St. Paul 1855; 1858.

COMMERCE—At St. Paul, from St. Louis, 1857—Captain Rowley.

CONESTOGA—St. Louis and St. Paul trade 1857—Captain James Ward, who was also the owner.

CONEWAGO—Stern-wheel; built at Brownsville, Pa., 1854; 186 tons; St. Louis and St. Paul Packet Co., 1855; 1856; 1857—Capt. James Ward; 1858; 1859.

CONFIDENCE—At Galena, from St. Louis, Nov. 7, 1845; same April 11, 1846; same March 30, 1847.

CONVOY—Stern-wheel; built at Freedom, Pa., 1854; 123 tons; at St. Paul 1857.

CORA—Side-wheel; single engine; two boilers; hull built by Captain Jos. Throckmorton at Rock Island; 140 feet long, 24 feet beam, five feet hold; engine 18 inches by 5 feet stroke, built at St. Louis. At Galena, on first trip, Sept. 30, 1846, Captain Jos. Throckmorton, in Galena and St. Peters trade; first boat at Fort Snelling 1847, Captain Throckmorton; Galena and St. Peters trade 1848, same captain, also running to St. Croix

Falls. Sold to go into Missouri River trade fall of
1848; snagged and sunk below Council Bluffs, May
5, 1850, drowning fifteen people.

CORNELIA—Sunk, 1855, in Chain of Rocks, lower rapids;
hit rock and stove.

COURIER—Built at Parkersburg, Va., 1852; 165 tons; owned
by W. E. Hunt; in St. Paul trade 1857.

CREMONA—Stern-wheel; built at New Albany, Ind., 1852;
266 tons; in Minnesota River trade 1857—Captain
Martin.

CUMBERLAND VALLEY—At Galena August 2, 1846; broke
shaft three miles above Burlington, Aug. 18, 1846.

DAISY—Small stern-wheel; St. Paul 1858.

DAMSEL—Stern-wheel; 210 tons; in St. Paul trade 1860; 1864,
Farley, clerk; chartered as a circus boat, Charles Davis,
pilot; snagged at head of Onawa Bend, Missouri River,
1876; had on board the circus company, which was taken
off by Captain Joseph La Barge, in the steamer "John
M. Chambers"; no lives lost; boat total loss.

DAN CONVERSE—Stern-wheel; built at McKeesport, Pa.,
1852; 163 tons; at St. Paul 1855, and at other times;
went into Missouri River trade and was snagged Nov.
15, 1858, ten miles above St. Joseph, Mo.; total loss.

DANIEL HILLMAN—At Galena May 25, 1847, from St.
Louis.

DANUBE—(First)—Sunk, 1852, below Campbell's Chain, Rock
Island Rapids; hit rock and stove.

DANUBE—(Second)—Stern-wheel; at St. Paul 1858.

DAVENPORT—Side-wheel; built 1860; in Northern Line; sunk
by breaking of ice gorge at St. Louis, Dec. 13, 1876, but
raised at a loss of $4,000.

DENMARK—(First)—Sunk, 1840, at head of Atlas Island,
by striking sunken log.

DENMARK—(Second)—Side-wheel, double-rudder boat; Cap-
tain R. C. Gray, in Northern Line, St. Louis & St.
Paul, 1857, 1858, 1859, 1860; 1861, same line, Captain
John Robinson; 1862, same line.

DES MOINES VALLEY—St. Paul 1856.

DEW DROP—Stern-wheel; 146 tons; at St. Paul 1857; 1858;

Capt. W. N. Parker, 1859, in Northern Line; went into Missouri River trade and was burned at mouth of Osage River, June, 1860.

DIOMED—St. Paul 1856.

DI VERNON—(Second)—Built at St. Louis, Mo., 1850; cost $49,000; at St. Paul June 19, 1851; in collision with steamer "Archer" Nov. 27, 1851, five miles above mouth of Illinois River. (See "Archer".)

DR. FRANKLIN—(First)—First boat of the Galena & Minnesota Packet Co.; bought 1848; owned by Campbell & Smith, Henry L. Corwith, H. L. Dousman, Brisbois & Rice; M. W. Lodwick, Captain, Russell Blakeley, Clerk, Wm. Meyers, Engineer; first boat to have steam whistle on upper river; Captain Lodwick 1849; 1850; in Galena and St. Paul trade; Capt. Lodwick in 1851; took a large party on pleasure excursion from Galena to the Indian treaty grounds at Traverse des Sioux, Minnesota River; 1852, Captain Russell Blakeley, Clerk Geo. R. Melville; out of commission 1853; sunk at the foot of Moquoketa Chute 1854; total loss.

DR. FRANKLIN—(Second)—Called "No. 2"; bought of Capt. John McClure, at Cincinnati, in the winter of 1848, by Harris Brothers—D. Smith, Scribe and Meeker—to run in opposition to "Dr. Franklin No. 1"; Smith Harris, Captain; Scribe Harris, Engineer; 1850 went up to St. Anthony Falls; in 1851 was the last boat to leave St. Paul, Nov. 20; the St. Croix was closed and heavy ice was running in the river; Capt. Smith Harris 1852; made 28 trips to St. Paul in 1853; Capt. Preston Lodwick, 1854.

DUBUQUE—(First)—At Galena April 9, 1836, for St. Louis, Captain Smoker; lost, 1837; exploded boiler at Muscatine Bar, eight miles below Bloomington.

DUBUQUE—(Second)—At Galena April 20, 1847, Captain Edward H. Beebe; 162 feet long, 26 feet beam, 5 feet hold; on her first trip; regular St. Louis, Galena and Dubuque trade; same 1848; at Galena July 29, 1849, Captain Edward H. Beebe, loading for Fort Snelling; sunk above Mundy's Landing 1855.

DUBUQUE—(Third)—Side-wheel, 603 tons; in Northern
    Line, St. Louis & St. Paul 1871.

EARLIA—At St. Paul 1857.

ECLIPSE—Eighth steamboat to arrive at Fort Snelling prior
    to 1827.

EDITOR—Side-wheel; built at Brownsville, Pa., 1851; 247
    tons; very fast; St. Louis & St. Paul 1854—Capt. Smith;
    same trade 1855—Capt. J. F. Smith; 1856; 1857—
    Captain Brady, Clerks R. M. Robbins and Charles
    Furman.

EFFIE AFTON—At St. Paul 1856; small stern-wheel; hit
    Rock Island Bridge and sank, 1858; total loss.

EFFIE DEANS—St. Paul 1858; Captain Joseph La Barge;
    burnt at St. Louis 1865.

ELBE—In Galena trade 1840.

ELIZA STEWART—At Galena May 26, 1848, from St. Louis,
    with 350 tons freight. Left for St. Louis, with 100
    tons freight from Galena.

EMERALD—In Galena trade 1837; sunk or burned 1837.

EMILIE—(First)—Side-wheel, Capt. Joseph La Barge, Ameri-
    can Fur Company, at St. Peters, 1841; snagged, 1842,
    in Emilie Bend, Missouri River.

ENDEAVOR—Stern-wheel; built at Freedom, Pa., 1854; 200
    tons; at St. Paul 1857.

ENTERPRISE—(First)—Small stern-wheel; twelfth boat to
    arrive at Fort Snelling, prior to 1827; again at the
    Fort June 27, 1832; sunk at head of Enterprise Island,
    1843.

ENTERPRISE—(Second)—Small side-wheel boat from Lake
    Winnebago; owned and captained by Robert C. Eden,
    son of an English baronet, on an exploring and hunting
    expedition; Geo. B. Merrick piloted for him for two
    months on the upper river and the St. Croix.

ENTERPRISE—(Third)—Built in 1858, above the Falls of
    St. Anthony, to run between St. Anthony and Sauk
    Rapids. Work superintended by Capt. Augustus R.
    Young. Before the work was completed the boat was
    sold to Thomas Moulton, and when finished she was
    run above the Falls during 1859, 1860, and 1861. She

was officered by four brothers—Augustus R. Young, Captain and Pilot; Jesse B. Young, Mate; Josiah Young, First Engineer, and Leonard Young, Second Engineer. Thomas Moulton and I. N. Moulton took turns in running as clerk. In 1863 she was sold to W. F. and P. S. Davidson, who moved her around St. Anthony Falls on skids, and launched her in the river below. She ran as freight boat in the Davidson Line between La Crosse and St. Paul for several years, and was then sold to go south. She was a stern-wheel boat, 130 feet long, and 22 feet beam. The Youngs are dead, with the exception of Leonard. Captain I. N. Moulton is living (1908) at La Crosse, where he is engaged in the coal business.

ENVOY—(First)—In Galena trade 1857.

ENVOY—(Second)—Stern-wheel; built at West Elizabeth, Pa., 1852; 197 tons; at St. Paul 1857—Capt. Martin, Clerk E. Carlton; at St. Paul 1858.

EOLIAN—Stern-wheel; built at Brownsville, Pa., 1855; 205 tons; in Minnesota River trade 1857—Captain Troy; same trade 1858; 1859.

EQUATOR—Stern-wheel; built at Beaver, Pa., 1853; 162 tons; in St. Paul trade 1855, 1856; Minnesota River 1857—Captain Sencerbox; wrecked in great storm on Lake St. Croix April 1858—Captain Asa B. Green, pilots Charles Jewell, Geo. B. Merrick; Engineer John Lay; Mate Russel Ruley.

EXCELSIOR—Side-wheel; built at Brownsville, Pa., 1849; 172 tons; St. Louis & St. Paul trade 1850; Captain James Ward, owner and captain; same 1852; arrived at St. Paul Nov. 20, 1852, with 350 tons of freight, taken at $1.00 per hundredweight for any distance; over $8,000 in the trip. In 1853 made 13 round trips from St. Louis to St. Paul; "Billy" Henderson owned the bar on this boat and sold oranges and lemons, wholesale, along the river; 1854, Captain Owen; 1855, Capt. James Ward; 1856, Capt. Kingman; 1857, Capt. Conway, in St. Paul trade.

THE UPPER MISSISSIPPI

EXPRESS—One of the first boats to reach Fort Snelling prior to 1827.

FALCON—Capt. Legrand Morehouse, St. Louis, Galena, Dubuque & Potosi regular packet 1845; same 1846; in August, in Galena and St. Peters trade, reports very low water at St. Peters; 1847, Capt. Morehouse, St. Louis and Galena regular packet.

FALLS CITY—Stern-wheel; built 1855, at Wellsville, Ohio, by St. Anthony Falls merchants, who ran her to the foot of the Falls in order to show that the river was navigable to that point; 155 feet long, 27 feet beam, 3 boilers; Captain Gilbert, 1855; in St. Louis trade 1856, and got caught in great ice jam at St. Louis that year; Capt. Jackins, 1857; wintered above the lake and was sunk by ice in Lake Pepin in April, 1857. 183 tons.

FAIRY QUEEN—At St. Paul 1856.

FANNY HARRIS—Stern-wheel; 279 tons; built at Cincinnati, and owned by Dubuque merchants; put into St. Paul trade in 1855, from Dubuque and Dunleith, Capt. Jones Worden, Clerk Charles Hargus; same 1856; 1857, Capt. Anderson, Clerk Chas. Hargus, Second Clerk Geo. B. Merrick, in Galena, Dunleith & St. Paul Packet Co.; same 1858, 1859; Capt. W. H. Gabbert 1860; wintered at Prescott; 1861, Capt. William Faucette, Clerks Hargus and Merrick, Engineers McDonald and William Hamilton, Pilots James McCoy, Harry Tripp, James Black, Thomas Burns and Thomas Cushing, Mate "Billy" Wilson; went up Minnesota River in April, three hundred miles to bring down Sherman's Battery; Thos. Burns raised a company for the 45th Illinois in 1861; Capt. Faucette in command 1862; Merrick left her for the war in August, 1862; she was sunk by the ice at Point Douglass in 1863; Charles Hargus died at Dubuque, August 10, 1878.

FANNY LEWIS—Of St. Louis, at St. Paul.

FAVORITE—Side-wheel; Minnesota River packet 1859; same 1860, Capt. P. S. Davidson; transferred to La Crosse trade in 1860; Capt. P. S. Davidson, 1861, in La Crosse trade; Minnesota River trade 1862; 252 tons burden.

FAYETTE—At Fort Snelling May 11, 1839; reported at St. Croix Falls May 12, 1839.

FIRE CANOE—Stern-wheel; built at Lawrence, Ohio, 1854; 166 tons; at St. Paul May, 1855—Captain Baldwin; 1856; 1857—Captain Spencer; in Minnesota River trade 1858; sunk by ice in Lake Pepin, three miles below Wacouta, April, 1861; passengers and crew were taken off by "Fanny Harris", which was near her when she sank.

FLEETWOOD—At St. Paul June 26, 1851.

FLORA—Stern-wheel; built at California, Pa., 1855; 160 tons; St. Paul trade 1855; Dubuque and St. Paul 1856, in Dubuque and St. Paul Packet Co.

FOREST ROSE—Built at California, Pa., 1852; 205 tons; at St. Paul 1856.

FORTUNE—Bought by Captain Pierce Atchison in April, 1845, at Cincinnati at a cost of $6,000, for St. Louis & Galena trade; same trade 1846; same 1847; sunk, Sept., 1847, on upper rapids.

FRANK STEELE—Small side-wheel; length 175 feet; beam 28 feet; Capt. W. F. Davidson, in Minnesota River trade 1857; same 1858; same trade, Capt. J. R. Hatcher, 1859, and spring of 1860; transferred to La Crosse & St. Paul trade 1860, in Davidson's Line; same 1861; Minnesota River 1862.

FRED LORENZ—Stern-wheel; built at Belle Vernon, Pa., 1855; 236 tons; Capt. Parker, St. Louis & St. Paul Line, 1857, 1858, 1859; in Northern Line Packet Co., St. Louis & St. Paul, Captain I. N. Mason, 1860, 1861.

FREIGHTER—In Minnesota River trade 1857, 1858; Captain John Farmer, 1859. She was sold, 1859, to Captain John B. Davis, who took a cargo for the Red River of the North, and attempted to run her via Lake Traverse and Big Stone Lake, and over the portage to Red River. His attempt was made too late in the season, on a falling river, with the result that the "Freighter" was caught about ten miles from Big Stone Lake and was a total loss. Her timbers remained for many years a witness to Captain Davis's lack of caution.

FRONTIER—New 1836; built by D. S. and R. S. Harris, of Galena; Captain D. Smith Harris, Engineer R. Scribe Harris, arrived at Fort Snelling May 29, 1836.

FULTON—Tenth steamboat to arrive at Fort Snelling prior to 1827; at Galena, advertised for St. Peters, June, 1827.

G. B. KNAPP—Small stern-wheel; 105 tons, built and commanded by Geo. B. Knapp, of Osceola, Wisconsin; ran in the St. Croix River trade most of the time.

G. H. WILSON—Small stern-wheel; built for tow-boat, and powerfully engined; 159 tons; at St. Paul first 1857; afterward in Northern Line as low water boat; sunk opposite Dakota, Minnesota, 1862.

G. W. SPARHAWK—Side-wheel; built at Wheeling, Va., 1851; 243 tons; in St. Paul trade 1855; sunk one mile below Nininger, Minnesota.

GALENA—(First)—Built at Cincinnati for Captain David G. Bates; Scribe Harris went from Galena to Cincinnati and brought her out as engineer, David G. Bates, Captain; at Galena 1829, 1835, 1836, 1837.

GALENA—(Second)—Captain P. Connolly, at Galena, in Galena & St. Peters trade; nearly wrecked in great wind storm on Lake Pepin in June, 1845; J. W. Dinan, clerk, August 12, 1845; at Dubuque Nov. 28, 1845, at which time she reports upper river clear of ice, although Fever River is frozen so that boats cannot make that port; 1846, Captain Goll, Clerk John Stephens.

GALENA—(Third)—Side-wheel; 296 tons; built 1854 at Cincinnati for Galena & Minnesota Packet Company; in St. Paul trade, D. B. Morehouse, 1854; Captain Russell Blakeley 1855; Captain Kennedy Lodwick, 1856; Captain W. H. Laughton, 1857; first boat through lake 1857, arriving at St. Paul at 2 A. M., May 1; passed "Golden State" and "War Eagle" under way between Lake Pepin and St. Paul; there were twelve boats in sight when she got through; burned and sunk at Red Wing in 1857, the result of carelessness, a deck passenger having dropped a lighted match into some combustible freight; several lives lost; had 46 staterooms.

GALENIAN—At Galena March 30, 1846.

GENERAL BROOKE—Side-wheel; built 1842; Captain Joseph Throckmorton, at Galena, from St. Peters, May 26, 1842; seven trips Galena to St. Peters, 1843; at Galena 1845; sold to Captain Joseph La Barge, of St. Louis, in 1845, for $12,000, to run on the Missouri; continued in that trade until 1849, when she was burned at St. Louis levee.

GENERAL PIKE—Side-wheel; built at Cincinnati, Ohio, 1852; 245 tons; at St. Paul 1857; 1859.

GIPSEY—(First)—In Galena trade, 1837; at Galena, for St. Peters, 1838; at Fort Snelling with treaty goods for Chippewa Indians, Oct. 21, 1838; Captain Gray, at Fort Snelling, May 2, 1839.

GIPSEY—(Second)—Stern-wheel; built at California, Pa., 1855; 132 tons; at St. Paul, 1855; 1856.

GLAUCUS—Captain G. W. Atchison, in Galena trade, 1839; at Fort Snelling, May 21, 1839, and again June 5, 1839.

GLENWOOD—At St. Paul 1857.

GLOBE—Captain Haycock, in Minnesota River trade, 1854, 1855, 1856.

GOLDEN EAGLE—At St. Paul 1856.

GOLDEN ERA—Side-wheel; built at Wheeling, Va., 1852; 249 tons; in Minnesota Packet Company; Captain Hiram Bersie, 1852; Captain Pierce Atchison, at St. Paul, from Galena, May, 1855; later in season Captain J. W. Parker, Dawley, clerk; Captain Parker, 1856; Captain Sam Harlow and Captain Scott in 1857, in Galena, Dunleith & St. Paul Line; same line 1858; Captain Laughton, in La Crosse & St. Paul Line 1859; Captain Laughton, in Dunleith Line 1860; Captain W. H. Gabbert, in Dunleith Line 1861.

GOLDEN STATE—Side-wheel; built at McKeesport, Pa., 1852; 298 tons; 1856—Captain N. F. Webb, Chas. Hargus, clerk; 1857, Captain Scott, Clerk Frank Ward, in Galena, Dunleith & St. Paul Line; at St. Paul 1859.

GOODY FRIENDS—At St. Paul 1859.

GOSSAMER—At St. Paul 1856.

GOV. BRIGGS—At Galena July 23, 25, and 28, 1846, in Galena & Potosi run.

GOV. RAMSEY—Built by Captain John Rawlins, above the
Falls of St. Anthony, to run between St. Anthony and
Sauk Rapids; machinery built in Bangor, Maine, and
brought by way of New Orleans and up the Mississippi
River.

GRACE DARLING—At St. Paul 1856.

GRAND PRAIRIE—Side-wheel; built at Gallipolis, Ohio, 1852;
261 tons; made three trips from St. Louis to St. Paul
1853; in St. Paul trade 1856.

GRANITE STATE—Side-wheel; built at West Elizabeth, Pa.,
1852; 295 tons; in Minnesota Packet Company, 1856—
Captain J. Y. Hurd; 1857—Captain W. H. Gabbert,
Galena, Dunleith & St. Paul Line.

GREEK SLAVE—Side-wheel; Captain Louis Robert, 1852;
made 18 trips Rock Island to St. Paul in 1853; St. Paul
trade 1854; Captain Wood 1855; St. Paul trade 1856.

GREY CLOUD—Side-wheel; built at Elizabeth, Ky., 1854;
246 tons; St. Louis & St. Paul trade 1854; 1855.

GREY EAGLE—Large side-wheel; built at Cincinnati, Ohio,
by Captain D. Smith Harris, for the Minnesota Packet
Company; cost $63,000; length 250 feet; beam 35 feet;
hold 5 feet; four boilers, 42 inches diameter, 16 feet
long; cylinders 22 inches diameter, 7 feet stroke; wheels
30 feet diameter, 10 feet buckets, 3 feet dip; 673 tons
burden; launched spring of 1857; Captain D. Smith
Harris, Clerks John S. Pim and F. M. Gleim; Engineers Hiram Hunt and William Briggs; in Galena, Dunleith & St. Paul trade 1857, 1858 and 1859; in St.
Louis and St. Paul trade 1860, 1861; sunk by striking
Rock Island Bridge, May 9, 1861, at 5 o'clock in the
evening going downstream. Captain Harris was in
the pilot house with the rapids pilot when a sudden gust
of wind veered her from her course and threw her
against the abutment; she sank in less than five minutes,
with the loss of seven lives. Captain Harris sold out
all his interest in the Packet Company and retired from
the river, broken-hearted over the loss of his beautiful
steamer, which was the fastest boat ever in the upper
river. She had made the run from Galena to St. Paul

at an average speed of 16½ miles per hour, delivering her mail at all landings during the run.

H. S. ALLEN—Small stern-wheel; Minnesota River boat 1856, 1857, 1858, 1859; after 1860 went into St. Croix River trade as regular packet between Prescott and St. Croix Falls, Captain William Gray, Pilots Chas. Jewell, Geo. B. Merrick.

H. T. YEATMAN—Stern-wheel; built at Freedom, Pa., 1852; 165 tons; wintered above lake, at Point Douglass, 1856-7; left St. Paul for head of Lake, April 10, 1857, and was sunk at Hastings by heading into rocks at levee, staving hole in bow; drifted down and lodged on bar one-half mile below landing; in Minnesota River trade 1855, 1856.

H. M. RICE—Minnesota River packet 1855.

HAMBURG—Large side-wheel; Captain J. B. Estes, Clerk Frederick K. Stanton, Dubuque and St. Paul packet, 1855; Captain Rowe, St. Louis & St. Paul trade 1856, 1857; at St. Paul 1858.

HANNIBAL CITY—Sunk, 1855, at foot of Broken Chute.

HARMONIA—Stern-wheel; Captain Allen, at St. Paul, from Fulton City, Iowa, 1857.

HASTINGS—At St. Paul 1859.

HAWKEYE STATE—Large side-wheel; in Northern Line; at St. Paul 1859; same trade, Captain R. C. Gray, 1860, 1861, St. Louis & St. Paul; same line 1862; 523 tons; made 14 trips St. Louis to St. Paul 1866.

HAZEL DELL—At St. Paul 1858.

HEILMAN—Sunk 1856, half way between Missouri Point and second ravine below Grafton, Mo.

HELEN—At Galena April 11, 1846, from St. Louis.

HENRIETTA—Stern-wheel; built at California, Pa., 1853; 179 tons; 2 trips to St. Paul, 1853; 1854—Captain C. B. Goll; St. Paul trade 1855, 1856, 1858, 1859.

HENRY CLAY—New 1857; in Northern Line; Captain Campbell 1857; Captain Chas. Stephenson 1858; at St. Paul 1859; Captain Chas. Stephenson 1860; Captain C. B. Goll 1861; sunk by Confederate batteries at Vicksburg 1863.

HENRY GRAFF—Stern-wheel; built at Belle Vernon, Pa., 1855; 250 tons; St. Paul 1856; 1857—Captain McClintock, Clerk Stewart, at St. Paul from St. Louis.

HERALD—At Galena July 11, 1845, from St. Louis.

HERMIONE—Captain D. Smith Harris, at Galena, prior to 1852.

HEROINE—In Galena trade 1837; sunk or burned same year.

HIBERNIAN—At Galena, for St. Peters, 1844; same 1845, Captain Miller, Clerk Hopkins.

HIGHLANDER—In upper river trade, burnt at the levee, at St. Louis, May 1, 1849; valued at $14,000.

HIGHLAND MARY—(First)—Sunk, 1842, at foot of Thomas Chute.

HIGHLAND MARY—(Second)—Galena & St. Paul trade 1848, Captain Joseph Atchison; arrived at St. Paul April 19, 1850, together with the "Nominee", first arrivals of the season, Captain Atchison in command; she was sold to Captain Joseph La Barge to run on the Missouri in 1852; was greatly damaged by fire at St. Louis July 27, 1853. (Captain Jos. Atchison died of cholera, which was very prevalent on the river in 1850, and his boat was temporarily withdrawn from service.)

HINDOO—Two trips to St. Paul, from St. Louis, in 1853.

HUDSON—(First)—Upper River trade about 1830, at which time she was at Fort Snelling; sunk one mile below Guttenburg Landing, Iowa.

HUDSON—(Second)—Stern-wheel; 176 tons; still running, 1868.

HUMBOLDT—Eleven trips to St. Paul 1853; in St. Paul trade 1854.

HUNTRESS—In Galena trade 1846.

HUNTSVILLE—At Galena May 6 and May 17, 1846, from St. Louis; Clerk Hopkins.

IDA MAY—St. Paul 1859.

ILLINOIS—Captain McAllister, in Galena trade 1841.

IMPERIAL—Large side-wheel; burned at the levee at St. Louis in 1861 by rebel emissary, as is supposed.

INDIANA—Fifth steamboat at Fort Snelling prior to 1827; Captain Fay, at Galena, 1828.

INDIAN QUEEN—Captain Saltmarsh, at Galena 1840.

IOLA—Made five trips to St. Paul 1853; in St. Paul trade 1854, 1855.

IONE—In Galena trade 1840; made pleasure trip Galena to St. Peters, 1840; Captain LeRoy Dodge, in Galena trade 1842, also 1845. (Captain James Ward, afterward one of the most successful steamboatmen from St. Louis, was carpenter on this boat.)

IOWA—Captain Legrand Morehouse, Clerk Hopkins, in Galena trade 1842; same captain, in Galena and St. Peters trade 1844, 1845. She was a side-wheel steamboat of 249 tons burden, and cost her captain $22,000 to build. Snagged and sunk at Iowa Island Sept. 10, 1845, in her third year; total loss.

IRENE—At Galena, for St. Peters, June, 1837.

IRON CITY—At Galena Nov. 7, 1844, from Pittsburg; at Galena Oct. 24, 1845; last boat out of Galena Nov. 28, 1845, at which date Fevre River closed; at Galena April 11, 1846, from St. Louis, Captain J. C. Ainsworth; same trade and same captain 1847, 1848; crushed and sunk by ice at St. Louis, Dec. 31, 1849, killing the cook and steward.

ISAAC SHELBY—At St. Paul Nov. 14, 1857; in Minnesota River trade 1858, 1859.

ITASCA—Side-wheel; new 1857; sister boat to "Key City"; 230 feet long, 35 feet beam; 560 tons; cylinders 22-inch, seven feet stroke; wheels 28 feet diameter, 10 feet buckets; Captain David Whitten, Clerks Chas. Horton and W. S. Lewis, 1857; Prairie du Chien and St. Paul 1857, 1858, 1859, Captain Whitten; St. Louis & St. Paul, Captain Whitten, 1860; Dunleith & St. Paul 1861, 1862, Captain J. Y. Hurd; burned at La Crosse Nov. 25, 1878.

J. BISSEL—Captain Bissel, from Pittsburg, 1857; in Minnesota River trade 1857, 1858.

J. B. GORDON—Minnesota River boat 1855.

J. M. MASON—Stern-wheel; sunk 1852, above Duck Creek Chain, Rock Island Rapids; hit rock and stove.

JACOB POE—St. Paul 1857.

JACOB TRABER—Large stern-wheel; had double wheels, operated by independent engines; very slow; at St. Paul 1856, 1857, 1858.

JAMES LYON—Stern-wheel; built at Belle Vernon, Pa., 1853; 190 tons; at St. Paul, from St. Louis, 1855, 1856; 1857 —Captain Blake; 1858; went into Missouri River trade, and was snagged and sunk at Miami Bend, Missouri River, 1858; total loss.

JASPER—Made seven trips Galena to St. Peters, Minn., 1843.

JAMES RAYMOND—Stern-wheel; built at Cincinnati, Ohio, 1853; 294 tons; show boat; at St. Paul 1858; William Fisher piloted her for one season.

JEANETTE ROBERTS—Small stern-wheel; Captain Louis Robert 1857, 1858, in Minnesota River trade; Captain F. Aymond 1859, same trade; same trade 1860, 1861, 1862; 146 tons.

JENNIE WHIPPLE—Small stern-wheel boat, built for Chippewa River trade; at St. Paul 1857.

JENNY LIND—Stern-wheel; built at Zanesville, Ohio, 1852; 107 tons; one trip to St. Paul 1853; at St. Paul 1859.

JO DAVIESS—Captain D. Smith Harris, in Galena and St. Peters trade prior to 1850.

JOHN HARDIN—Built at Pittsburg 1845, for St. Louis, Galena and upper river trade.

JOHN P. LUCE—At St. Paul 1856.

JOHN RUMSEY—Stern-wheel; Captain Nathaniel Harris, Chippewa River boat 1859.

JOSEPHINE—(First)—Ninth steamboat to reach Fort Snelling; arrived there 1827; at Galena 1828, Capt. J. Clark; in Galena & St. Louis trade 1829, Captain J. Clark.

JOSEPHINE—(Second)—Stern-wheel; St. Paul trade 1856, 1857, 1858.

JULIA—(First)—Side-wheel; snagged in Bellefontaine Bend, Missouri River, about 1849.

JULIA—(Second)—In Upper River trade 1862.

JULIA DEAN—Small stern-wheel, at St. Paul 1855, 1856.

KATE CASSELL—Stern-wheel; built at California, Pa., 1854; 167 tons; at St. Paul 1855; wintered above the lake; 1856—Captain Sam. Harlow, Clerk Chas. Hargus; Geo. B. Merrick and Sam. Fifield made their first appearance on the river as pantry boys on this boat this season; Russell Ruley mate, Nat. Blaisdell, engineer; at St. Paul 1859.

KATE FRENCH—Captain French, at St. Paul 1857, from St. Louis.

KENTUCKY—Side-wheel; Captain W. H. Atchison, at Galena April 3, 1847, from St. Louis; in Sept. same year, Captain Montgomery, running from Galena to the Rapids, and connecting there with the "Anthony Wayne" and "Lucy Bertram" for St. Louis, not being able to run the rapids on account of low water.

KENTUCKY NO. 2—Side-wheel; built at Evansville, Ind., 1851; 149 tons; at St. Paul 1855; owned by Captain Rissue, of Prescott; at St. Paul 1857; sunk on bar at foot of Puitt's Island, one mile below Prescott, 1858.

KEOKUK—Side-wheel; St. Paul trade 1858, 1859; Captain E. V. Holcomb, in Minnesota Packet Company, La Crosse & St. Paul, 1860, 1861; Davidson's Line, La Crosse & St. Paul, 1861; first boat at Winona, April 2, 1862, Captain J. R. Hatcher; 300 tons.

KEY CITY—Side-wheel; new 1857; built for the Minnesota Packet Co.; sister boat to "Itasca"; length 230 feet, beam 35 feet, 560 tons burden; very fast; Captain Jones Worden, Clerk George S. Pierce, 1857, Galena, Dunleith & St. Paul run; same 1858, 1859; same captain, in St. Louis & St. Paul run, 1860, 1861; same captain, in Dunleith & St. Paul run, 1862. "Ned" West was pilot of the "Key City" every season, I think, from 1857 to 1862. He was one of the very best pilots on the upper river. He died at St. Paul in 1904.

KEY STONE—Side-wheel; built at Brownsville, Pa., 1853; 307 tons.

KEY WEST—At St. Paul 1857.

KNICKERBOCKER—At Fort Snelling June 25, 1839.

LACLEDE—(First)—Built at St. Louis in 1844, for the Keokuk Packet Co.; burned at St. Louis August 9, 1848.

LACLEDE—(Second)—Stern-wheel; built at California, Pa., 1855; 197 tons; at St. Paul 1855, 1856, 1857—Captain Vorhies at St. Paul from St. Louis; St. Paul 1858.

LA CROSSE—At St. Paul, from Pittsburg, 1857—Captain Brickle; again 1861.

LADY FRANKLIN—Side-wheel; built at Wheeling, Va., 1850; 206 tons; at St. Paul June 19, 1851, for first time; in Minnesota Packet Company; at St. Paul, from St. Louis, May 5, 1855, with 800 passengers—Captain J. W. Malin, Clerks Ed. W. Halliday, Orren Smith; 1856—Captain M. E. Lucas, at St. Paul; sunk at foot of Coon Slough fall of 1856—snagged.

LADY MARSHALL—In St. Louis & Galena trade 1837.

LADY WASHINGTON—Captain Shellcross, at Galena, loading for Fort Snelling, 1829.

LAKE CITY—Stern-wheel; built at Pittsburg 1857; Captain Sloan, at St. Paul 1857; in St. Paul trade 1858, 1859; burned by guerrillas at Carson's Landing, Mo., 1862.

LAKE OF THE WOODS—At Galena, from St. Louis, June 5, 1847.

LAMARTINE—First trip to St. Paul 1850; went up to Falls of St. Anthony 1850; at St. Paul June 19, 1851.

LASALLE—At Galena from St. Louis, April 19, 1845.

LATROBE—Stern-wheel; built at Brownsville, Pa., 1853; 159 tons; at St. Paul from St. Louis, 1855.

LAWRENCE—Sixth steamboat to reach Fort Snelling; arrived there in 1826.

LEWIS F. LYNN—Captain S. M. Kennett, at St. Peters, from Galena, 1844.

LIGHT FOOT—In company with "Time and Tide" took excursion from St. Louis to Fort Snelling in 1845; Captain M. K. Harris, first boat at Galena from St. Louis April 20, 1847; at Galena Sept. 25, 1846.

LINN—At Galena, for St. Anthony Falls, May, 1846. (Possibly intended for "Lewis F. Lynn".)

LITTLE DOVE—Captain H. Hoskins, regular Galena & St. Peters packet, season 1846.

LLOYD HANNA—Advertised for a pleasure excursion from Galena to St. Peters, summer of 1840.

LUCIE MAY—Stern-wheel; built at West Brownsville, Pa., 1855; 172 tons; in St. Louis & St. Paul trade 1856, 1857; 1858—Captain J. B. Rhodes, same trade; 1859,

Northwestern Line, St. Louis & St. Paul; sunk five miles below Lagrange, Mo., 1860.

LUCY BERTRAM—Running from St. Louis to the foot of rapids, summer of 1847, in connection with "Kentucky", running above rapids, forming a low water line from St. Louis to Galena.

LUELLA—Stern-wheel; built at Nashville, Tenn., 1851; 162 tons; first trip to St. Paul fall of 1852—Captain D. Smith Harris; seven trips to St. Paul 1853, 1854, 1855 —Captain Sam. Harlow, Galena & St. Paul run; 1856; had boilers and engines of a much larger boat which had been sunk, and was consequently very fast; dismantled at Dunleith.

LYNX—At Galena from St. Louis, 1844, Captain W. H. Hooper; Captain John Atchison, Galena & St. Peters trade 1845, Mr. Barger, clerk; Captain Atchison, in Galena & St. Peters trade 1846, 1847; sunk at head of Atlas Island 1849; first through lake 1846.

MAID OF IOWA—At Galena June 15, 1845; running to Fort Winnebago (now Portage, Wis.) on Wisconsin River, in connection with steamer "Enterprise" on Fox River, the two forming a line from Green Bay to Galena; Captain Peter Hotelling master and owner.

MALTA—Side-wheel; Captain Joseph Throckmorton, at Fort Snelling July 22, 1839; advertised at Galena in summer of 1840 for pleasure trip to St. Peters; went into Missouri River trade, where she was snagged in Malta Bend, August, 1841, and sank in 15 feet of water, in little more than a minute after striking a snag; boat and cargo total loss; no lives lost; Captain Throckmorton was in command at the time and owned nearly all or quite all of the boat.

MANDAN—Side-wheel; fourth boat to arrive at Fort Snelling prior to 1827; snagged at mouth of Gasconade River, on the Missouri, sometime in the forties; Captain Phil Hanna, master at the time.

MANSFIELD—Stern-wheel; built at Belle Vernon, Pa., 1854; 166 tons; St. Paul 1856, 1857—Captain Owens; Clerk Bryant.

MARTHA NO. 2—Built at Shousetown, Pa., 1849; 180 tons;
at St. Paul April 24, 1851, from St. Louis; 1852.

MARY BLANE—Captain J. C. Smith, regular St. Louis and
Galena Packet, 1848.

MARY C—At St. Paul 1853.

MATTIE WAYNE—Side-wheel; built at Cincinnati, Ohio,
1852; 335 tons; at St. Paul 1856; greatly damaged by
fire at St. Louis 1855.

MEDORA—Owned in St. Paul by William Constans, 1857;
Captain Ed. McLagan, in Minnesota River trade 1858.

MENDOTA—Captain Robert A. Reilly, at St. Peters, from
Galena, 1844; same captain, in St. Louis & Galena trade
1845; Captain Starnes, in St. Louis & Galena trade
1846; snagged opposite Cat Island October, 1847, but
raised.

MERMAID—Side-wheel; in collision with Steamer "St. Croix",
near Quincy, April 11, 1845; larboard wheel and cook's
galley knocked off.

MESSENGER—Large stern-wheel; built at Pittsburg, Pa.,
1855; 406 tons; very fast, in St. Paul trade in opposition to Minnesota Packet Company, 1857, from St.
Louis; raced with "Key City" for championship of
Upper River and was defeated.

METROPOLITAN—Very large side-wheel; St. Louis & St.
Paul trade 1856; Captain Thos. B. Rhodes, same trade
1857; Northwestern Line, same captain, 1858, 1859;
Captain J. B. Jenks 1860; Captain Thos. B. Buford
1861; sunk at St. Louis by breaking of ice jams, Dec.
16, 1865; valued at $18,000.

MILWAUKEE—Large side-wheel; one of the crack boats of the
Minnesota Packet Company, built at Cincinnati winter
of 1856; 240 feet long, 33 feet beam; 550 tons burden;
Captain Stephen Hewitt, in Prairie du Chien & St. Paul
run 1857, 1858, 1859; Captain John Cochrane, in
Dunleith & St. Paul run 1860, 1861; Captain E. V.
Holcombe, in Dunleith run 1862.

MINNESOTA—(First)—Stern-wheel; built at Elizabethtown,
Ky., 1849; at St. Paul, from Galena, 1849—Captain

R. A. Riley; at St. Paul June 25, 1851; 1857, 1858, Captain Hay, in Minnesota River trade.

MINNESOTA BELLE—Side-wheel; built at Belle Vernon, Pa., 1854; 226 tons; 1854, 1855, 1856—Captain Humbertson, in St. Louis & St. Paul trade; 1857—Captain Thos. B. Hill, same trade; 1859, in Northern Line, St. Louis & St. Paul, Captain Hill.

MINNESOTA VALLEY—At St. Paul 1856.

MISSOURI FULTON—Captain Culver, first part 1828; at Galena for St. Peters, Captain Clark later in 1828; arrived at Fort Snelling May 8, 1836, Captain Orren Smith; same captain, in Galena & St. Peters trade 1837.

MOHAWK—Sunk 1859, at head of Clarkesville Island.

MONDIANA—At Galena, from St. Louis, June 6, 1847.

MONITOR—Small stern-wheel, 99 tons, from Pittsburg, at St. Paul, 1857.

MONONA—At Galena from St. Louis March 10, 1845, Captain Nick Wall; sunk opposite Little Washington, Missouri River, Oct. 30, 1846; raised; in Galena & St. Peters trade, Captain E. H. Gleim, 1846; at Galena, from St. Louis, April 3, 1847, Captain Ludlow Chambers.

MONTAUK—(First)—At Galena Oct. 18, 1847, from St. Louis; at Galena, from St. Louis 1848, Captain John Lee; regular packet.

MONTAUK—(Second)—Stern-wheel; built at California, Pa., 1853; 237 tons; at St. Paul from St. Louis, 1855; 1856 —Captain Parker, from St. Louis; 1857—Captain Burke, Clerks Mullen and Ditto, from St. Louis.

MONTELLO—Small stern-wheel from Fox River, Wis., in Minnesota River trade 1855; built over hull of barge —no boiler deck.

MOSES McLELLAN—Side-wheel; built at Cincinnati, Ohio, 1855; 400 tons; Captain Martin, in Davidson Line, La Crosse & St. Paul, 1862.

MOUNT DEMING—At St. Paul 1857.

MUNGO PARK—At Galena from St. Louis April 16, 1845; regular packet.

MUSCODA—Captain J. H. Lusk, in Galena trade 1841.

NAVIGATOR—Large stern-wheel; Captain A. T. Champlin, in St. Louis & St. Paul trade 1854; same trade 1855; 300 tons; built at Pittsburg, by William Dean.

NEIVILLE—Second steamboat to arrive at Fort Snelling prior to 1827.

NELLIE KENT—Small stern-wheel, built at Osceola, Wis., by Captain Kent, to run between Prescott and St. Croix Falls.

NEW HAVEN—At Galena, for St. Louis, Nov. 5, 1844; regular St. Louis, Galena, Dubuque & Potosi Packet, 1845, Captain Geo. L. King; at Galena June 12, 1846.

NEW ST. PAUL—Side-wheel; built at New Albany, Ind., 1852; 225 tons; Captain James Bissell; went into Missouri River trade, and was snagged and sunk at St. Albert's Island, Aug. 19, 1857; boat and cargo total loss; boat cost $25,000.

NEW YORK—At St. Paul 1856.

NIMROD—At Galena from St. Louis, June 14, 1845; American Fur Company boat; went into Missouri River trade.

NOMINEE—Side-wheel; built at Shousetown, Pa., 1848; 213 tons; Captain D. Smith Harris, arrived at St. Paul, April 19, 1850, in company with "Highland Mary", first boats through lake; in Minnesota Packet Co.; Captain Orren Smith, at St. Paul April 16, 1852, 8 P. M., first boat through lake; Captain Russell Blakeley, 29 trips Galena to St. Paul, 1853; Captain Russell Blakeley, first boat at St. Paul April 8, 1854; sunk below Britt's Landing, 1854; Mr. Maitland was clerk in 1852.

NORTHERNER—Side-wheel; built at Cincinnati, Ohio, 1853; 400 tons; very fast; contested with "Key City" for championship of Upper River, but was beaten; in Northern Line, St. Louis & St. Paul; Captain Pliny A. Alford, commanded her 1858, 1859, 1860, 1861, 1862; burned at St. Louis prior to 1871.

NORTHERN BELLE—Side-wheel; 498 tons; built at Cincinnati, under supervision of Captain Preston Lodwick in 1856, for Minnesota Packet Co.; 226 feet long, 29 feet beam, light draft and very handsomely finished, outside and in; Galena & St. Paul Line 1856, Captain Preston Lodwick; Captain J. Y. Hurd, Dunleith Line, 1858; same captain, in La Crosse Line 1859; same captain, in Dunleith Line, 1860; in La Crosse Line, Captain W. H. Laughton, 1861; took five companies of the First Minnesota Infantry Volunteers from St. Paul to La Crosse, June 22, 1861; Captain W. H. Laughton, in Davidson's La Crosse Line, 1862.

NORTHERN LIGHT—Large side-wheel; built at Cincinnati for Minnesota Packet Co., winter of 1856; length 240 feet, beam 40 feet, hold 5 feet; 740 tons; cylinders 22 inches, seven feet stroke; 8 boilers, 46 inches diameter, 17 feet long; wheels 31 feet diameter, 9 feet buckets, 30 inches dip; came out in the spring of 1857 with Captain Preston Lodwick, Clerks J. D. DuBois and K. C. Cooley; Engineers James Kinestone and Geo. Radebaugh; Mate James Morrison; had oil paintings of St. Anthony Falls, Dayton Bluffs and Maiden Rock in panels in the cabin; paddle boxes had paintings of *aurora borealis*; Captain P. Lodwick, in Galena, Dunleith & St. Paul Line 1857, 1858, 1859; same captain, in St. Louis & St. Paul Line 1860; Captain John B. Davis, St. Louis Line 1861; Captain Gabbert, in Dunleith Line 1862; sunk in first bend below head of Coon Slough, by Jackson Harris, pilot, who swung stern of boat into solid shore ice in making fast turn of the bend, tearing out the stern of the boat and sinking her in 30 feet of water in a few minutes.

NORTH STAR—Built above the Falls of St. Anthony by Captain John Rawlins in 1855; running from St. Anthony to Sauk Rapids until 1857.

NUGGET—Stern-wheel; snagged April 22, 1866, abreast Dacota City, Nebr., on Missouri River; boat and cargo total loss; boat valued at $20,000.

OAKLAND—Stern-wheel; built at California, Pa., 1853; 142 tons; Captain C. S. Morrison, at St. Paul, 1855; at St. Paul from St. Louis 1856, 1857, 1858.

OCEAN WAVE—Side-wheel; built at Elizabeth, Ky., 1854; 235 tons; very short boat and very hard to steer; cost

$17,000; in Minnesota Packet Company, Captain E. H. Gleim 1856; 1857, Captain Andrews in spring, and Captain James in fall, in Galena & St. Paul Line; 1858, 1859—Captain Scott, in Prairie du Chien Line; 1860, Captain N. F. Webb, in Dunleith Line; 1861, Captain Webb, in La Crosse Line.

ODD FELLOW—Cline, master, at Galena 1848.

OHIO—Captain Mark Atchison, in Galena trade 1842; at Galena for St. Louis, Nov. 5, 1844.

OLIVE BRANCH—Captain Strother, at Galena, for St. Louis, April 9, 1836.

OMEGA—At Galena for St. Peters, Minnesota, spring of 1840, Captain Joseph Sire, Pilot Joseph La Barge; owned by American Fur Co.; went into the Missouri River trade.

ORB—Stern-wheel; built at Wheeling, Va., 1854; 226 tons; at St. Paul from St. Louis, 1857, Captain Spencer.

OSCEOLA—Small stern-wheel boat, built for St. Croix River trade; at St. Paul 1855.

OSPREY—In St. Louis & Galena trade 1842, Captain N. W. Parker; same trade 1845, 1846.

OSWEGO—At St. Paul Nov. 13, 1851.

OTTER—Built and owned by Harris Brothers; D. Smith Harris, captain; R. Scribe Harris, engineer; in Galena and St. Peters trade 1841, 1842; 7 trips to St. Peters in 1843; Captain Scribe Harris, in same trade 1844, 1845; arrived at Galena from St. Peters, April 8, 1845, having passed through lake on up trip; in same trade 1846, 1847; Harris Bros. sold her in 1848; her engines were taken out and placed in the "Tiger" prior to 1852.

PALMYRA—Captain Cole, arrived at Fort Snelling June 1, 1836, with a pleasure excursion consisting of some 30 ladies and gentlemen from Galena; in Galena & St. Peters trade 1837, Captain Middleton; arrived at Fort Snelling July 14, 1838, bringing the official notice of the Sioux treaty, opening of St. Croix Valley to settlers; also brought machinery for sawmill to be built on St. Croix, and Mr. Calvin Tuttle, millwright, with a number of workers to erect the mill.

PANOLA—At St. Paul 1858.

PARTHENIA—Stern-wheel; built at California, Pa., 1854; 154 tons; in St. Paul trade 1856, 1857.

PAVILION—Captain Lafferty, at Galena for St. Peters, June 1, 1837.

PEARL—At Galena for St. Louis, March 16, 1845; same October, 1847, Montgomery, master; regular Galena & St. Peters trade 1848; also for St. Croix Falls.

PEMBINA—Side-wheel; in Northwestern Line and Northern Line; Captain Thos. H. Griffith, St. Louis & St. Paul 1857, 1858, 1859; Captain John B. Hill, same trade 1860, 1861.

PENNSYLVANIA—Captain Stone, at St. Paul June 1, 1839.

PIKE—At Galena, on her way up the river, Sept. 3, 1839; arrived at Fort Snelling with troops Sept. 9, 1839; arrived again Sept. 17, 1839; in same trade 1840.

PILOT—At Galena from St. Louis, Sept. 6, 1846.

PIZARRO—At Galena, new 1838; built by Captain R. Scribe Harris; 133 feet long, 20 feet beam, 144 tons burden; in Galena trade 1840.

PLANET—At Galena from St. Louis May 21, 1847.

PLOW BOY—Side-wheel; 275 tons; snagged above Providence, Mo., on Missouri River, 1853.

POMEROY—Minnesota River boat, Captain Bell 1861.

POTOSI—Collapsed flue at Quincy, Ill., October 4, 1844, killing two passengers; at Galena, Ill., from St. Louis, April 11, 1846.

PRAIRIE BIRD—Captain Nick Wall, in Galena, St. Louis & St. Peters trade 1846; at Galena April 11, 1846; at Galena, April 3, 1847, Captain Nick Wall, same trade; 213 tons burden; cost $17,000; sunk above Keithsburg, Iowa, 1852.

PRAIRIE ROSE—Stern-wheel; built at Brownsville, Pa., 1854; 248 tons; in St. Louis and St. Paul trade, 1855, Captain Maratta.

PRAIRIE STATE—(First)—One of the early boats on the Upper River; exploded boilers at Pekin, Ill., April 25, 1852, killing 20 of the deck passengers and crew.

PRAIRIE STATE—(Second)—Stern-wheel; 281 tons; 59 horse power; Captain Truett, St. Louis & St. Paul Packet, 1855.

PRE-EMPTION—Built by Harris Bros., of Galena; Captain D. Smith Harris, some time prior to 1852.

PROGRESS—Stern-wheel; built at Shousetown, Pa., 1854; 217 tons; Captain Goodell, at St. Paul, loading for St. Louis, 1857.

QUINCY—In Galena trade 1840.

RARITAN—Captain Rogers, at Galena 1846.

REBUS—St. Paul trade 1854.

RED ROVER—Captain Throckmorton, in Galena trade 1828, 1829, 1830.

RED WING—(First)—Side-wheel; 24 feet beam; new 1846; Captain Berger, in St. Louis & St. Peters regular trade, 1846; at Galena April, 1846; Clerk Green; Captain Berger, St. Louis & St. Peters, 1847, 1848.

RED WING—(Second)—Side-wheel; at St. Paul 1855; Captain Woodburn, at St. Paul 1857; Captain Ward, latter part 1857; Captain Ward, at St. Paul 1858.

RED WING—(Third)—In Northwestern Line, 1879-1880; side-wheel, 670 tons burden.

REGULATOR—Stern-wheel; built at Shousetown, Pa., 1851; 156 tons; in St. Louis & St. Paul trade 1855.

RELIEF—Captain D. Smith Harris, prior to 1852.

RESCUE—Stern-wheel; built at Shousetown, Pa., 1853; 169 tons; built for towboat; very fast; Captain Irvine, at St. Paul from Pittsburg, 1857.

RESERVE—At St. Paul 1857.

RESOLUTE—Stern-wheel (towboat); very powerful engines; 316 tons; owned by Capt. R. C. Gray, of Pittsburg Tow-boat Line.

REVEILLE—Small stern-wheel; wintered above the lake 1855; St. Paul trade 1855, 1856, 1857.

REVEILLE—At Galena, from St. Louis, April 18, 1846; regular packet in that trade; (do not know whether it is the same as above).

REVENUE—Captain Turner, in Galena trade 1847; burned on Illinois River, May 24, 1847.

REVENUE CUTTER—Captain McMahan and Oliver Harris,

owners, McMahan, master, at Galena, from St. Louis, May 9, 1847; in Galena & St. Peters trade; bought to take place of steamer "Cora" sold to go into Missouri River trade.

ROBERT FULTON—At St. Paul July 3, 1851.

ROCHESTER—Built at Belle Vernon, Pa., 1855; 199 tons; at St. Paul 1856.

ROCKET—At St. Paul from St. Louis, 1857.

ROCK RIVER—Small boat, owned and commanded by Augustin Havaszthy, Count de Castro, an Hungarian exile; in Galena and upper river trade 1841; made trips between Galena & St. Peters once in two weeks during season of 1842; in same trade 1843, 1844; laid up for winter at Wacouta, head of lake, in fall of 1844, her cook and several others of the crew walking on the ice to La Crosse; the captain and two or three others remained on board all winter, and in the spring, as soon as the ice was out of the lake, went south with the boat, which ran on some lower river tributary, and the Count was lost sight of.

ROLLA—At Galena for St. Peters, June 18, 1837; had on board Major Tallaferro, U. S. A., with a party of Indians; arrived at Fort Snelling Nov. 10, 1837, bringing delegations of chiefs who had been to Washington to make a treaty whereby the St. Croix Valley was opened to settlers; collapsed a flue and burned near Rock Island, Ill., November, 1837, killing one fireman and severely scalding the engineer on watch.

ROSALIE—(First)—In Galena and St. Louis trade 1839.

ROSALIE—(Second)—Stern-wheel; built at Brownsville, Pa., 1854; 158 tons; Captain Rounds, from Pittsburg, with stoves and hardware, sunk below St. Paul 1857; was raised and continued in St. Paul trade, 1858, 1859.

ROYAL ARCH—Side-wheel; built at West Elizabeth, Pa., 1852; 213 tons; Captain E. H. Gleim, in Minnesota Packet Co., 1854; 1855; 1856, same line; sunk opposite Nine Mile Island 1858.

RUFUS PUTNAM—Third steamboat to reach Fort Snelling; arrived there in 1825.

RUMSEY—Small Minnesota River boat; sunk on mud flat opposite levee at St. Paul.

SAM GATY—Large side-wheel; built at St. Louis, Mo., 1853; 367 tons, 288 horse-power engines; Captain Vickers, at St. Paul 1855; went into Missouri River trade; struck a bluff bank at point opposite Arrow Rock, Mo., knocked her boilers down and set fire to boat, burned and sank, June 27, 1867. She had been a money-maker for many years, both on the Mississippi and on the Missouri.

SAM KIRKMAN—At St. Paul 1858.

SAM. YOUNG—Built at Shousetown, Pa., 1855; 155 tons; at St. Paul 1856; Captain Reno, from Pittsburg, at St. Paul 1857.

SANGAMON—Stern-wheel; built at New Albany, Ind., 1853; 86 tons; Captain R. M. Spencer, at St. Paul 1854.

SARACEN—New 1856; built at New Albany, Ind., Captain H. B. Stran, Clerk Casey, at St. Paul 1857.

SARAH ANN—Captain Lafferty, in Galena trade 1841; sunk, 1841, at head of Island 500; raised; regular St. Louis & Galena packet.

SAXON—At St. Paul 1859.

SCIENCE—Running between St. Louis and Fort Winnebago, on the Wisconsin (now Portage); made three trips to the Fort in 1837 with troops and government supplies.

SCIOTA—Seventeenth steamboat to arrive at Fort Snelling prior to 1827.

SENATOR—At Galena, from St. Louis, April 20, 1847, first; Captain E. M. McCoy; in Galena and upper river trade 1847; bought by Harris Brothers 1848; Captain D. Smith Harris, in Galena & St. Peters trade 1848; arrived at Galena, from St. Peters April 13, reporting heavy ice in Lake Pepin, but was able to get through; Captain Orren Smith, 1849, 1850, in Galena & St. Paul trade. She was the second boat owned by the Minnesota Packet Company, the "Dr. Franklin" being the first.

SHENANDOAH—Made five trips to St. Paul, from St. Louis, in 1853; same trade 1855; was in great ice gorge at St. Louis, February, 1856.

SILVER WAVE—Stern-wheel; built at Glasgow, Ohio, 1855; 245 tons; in upper river trade 1856.

SKIPPER—At St. Paul 1857.

SMELTER—Captain D. Smith Harris, Engineer Scribe Harris, Galena & St. Peters trade 1837; was one of the first boats on the upper river to be built with a cabin answering to the "boiler deck" of modern steamboats.

SNOW DROP—At St. Paul 1859.

STATESMAN—Built at Brownsville, Pa., 1851; 250 tons; at St. Paul 1855.

STELLA WHIPPLE—Stern-wheel; Captain Haycock, Minnesota River trade, 1861; built for the Chippewa River.

ST. ANTHONY—Side-wheel; 157 feet long, 24 feet beam, 5 feet hold; 30 staterooms; small boat, but highly finished and furnished for that time; hull built by S. Speer, of Belle Vernon, Pa., engines by Stackhouse & Nelson, of Pittsburg, modeled by Mr. King; Captain A. G. Montford, in Galena & St. Peters trade 1846, regularly.

ST. CROIX—Side-wheel; built by Hiram Bersie, William Cupps, James Ryan and James Ward; Captain Hiram Bersie, Mate James Ward, 1844, in St. Louis, Galena & St. Peters trade; in collision with "Mermaid", near Quincy, April 11, 1845, losing her barge; damaged by fire May 13, 1845; in upper river trade 1845, 1846, 1847, Captain Bersie, master.

ST. LOUIS—Stern-wheel; built at Brownsville, Pa., 1855; 192 tons; at St. Paul 1856, 1859.

ST. LOUIS OAK—Side-wheel; Captain Coones, St. Louis, Galena & Dubuque trade 1845; snagged and lost at head of Howard's Bend, Missouri River, 1847, Captain Dozier in command.

ST. PAUL—Side-wheel; built at Wheeling, Va., 1852, for Harris Bros., Galena, Ill.; 1852, Captain M. K. Harris, in Galena & St. Paul trade; was very slow, and drew too much water for upper river trade; 1854, Captain Bissell, at St. Paul for St. Louis; at St. Paul 1855.

ST. PETERS—(First)—Captain Joseph Throckmorton, at St. Peters and Fort Snelling July 2, 1836; brought as one of her passengers Nicollet, who came to explore the Northwest Territory.

ST. PETERS—(Second)—Built and owned by Captain James Ward (formerly mate of the "St. Croix"), who commanded her; burned at St. Louis May 17, 1849; valued at $2,000.

SUCKER STATE—Side-wheel; in Northern Line; Captain Thos. B. Rhodes, in St. Louis & St. Paul Line, 1859, 1860, 1861; Captain James Ward, in same line, 1862; was burned at Alton Slough, together with three or four other boats, while lying in winter quarters.

SUTLER—Captain D. Smith Harris, prior to 1850.

TEMPEST—(First)—Regular St. Louis, Galena, Dubuque & Potosi packet; at Galena April 11, 1846, Captain John Smith.

TEMPEST—(Second)—Side-wheel; went into Missouri River trade and was snagged and lost about 1865, at Upper Bonhomme Island.

THOS. SCOTT—Large side-wheel; at St. Paul, from St. Louis, 1856.

TIGER—Had engines of old "Otter"; Captain Maxwell, in St. Paul trade 1850; same captain, in Minnesota River trade 1851, 1852; 104 tons, 52 horse power; very slow.

TIGRESS—Large stern-wheel; 356 tons; Ohio River towboat; powerful engines and very fast; at St. Paul 1858; sunk by Confederate batteries at Vicksburg 1863.

TIME—At Galena May 15, 1845; regular St. Louis & Galena packet; at Galena April 11, 1846, from St. Louis, Captain Wm. H. Hooker, in regular trade; snagged and sunk one-half mile below Pontoosuc, Ia., August, 1846.

TIME AND TIDE—(First)—Captain D. Smith Harris, Keeler Harris, engineer, brought excursion party to Fort Snelling, in company with steamer "Light Foot", in 1845; at Galena April 13, 1847, E. W. Gould, master, in regular St. Louis, Galena & St. Peters trade.

TIME AND TIDE—(Second)—Stern-wheel; built at Freedom, Pa., 1853; 131 tons; Captain Louis Robert, at St. Paul 1855, 1856; same captain, in Minnesota River trade 1857, 1858; Captain Nelson Robert, same trade 1859.

TISHOMINGO—Side-wheel; built at New Albany, Ind., 1852; 188 tons; very fast boat; bought by one Johnson, of Winona, Minn., from lower river parties, to run in opposition to Minesota Packet Company; was in St. Paul trade 1856, but lost money and was sold for debt at Galena in winter of 1856; bought for $25,000 by Captain Sargent; reported as having left St. Louis April 14, 1857, Jenks, master, for St. Paul with 465 cabin passengers and 93 deck passengers, besides a full cargo of freight, worth to the boat about $14,000.

TUNIS—At St. Paul 1857.

TWIN CITY—Side-wheel; built at California, Pa., 1853; 170 tons; in St. Paul trade 1855; burned at St. Louis Dec. 7, 1855.

UNCLE TOBY—Captain Geo. B. Cole, at St. Peters, from St. Louis, 1845; at Galena April 9, 1846, from St. Louis Captain Geo. B. Cole; regular St. Louis, Galena & Dubuque packet for season; 1847, Captain Henry R. Day, regular St. Louis & St. Peters packet; in same trade 1851; arrived at Point Douglass, Minn., Nov. 20, 1851, and there unloaded and had freight hauled by team to St. Paul on account of floating ice; put back from Point Douglass to St. Louis.

U. S. MAIL—At St. Paul 1855.

VALLEY FORGE—Advertised a pleasure trip from Galena to St. Peters, 1840.

VERSAILLES—Arrived at Fort Snelling May 12, 1832, from Galena.

VIENNA—Stern-wheel; built at Monongahela, Pa., 1853; 170 tons; in St. Louis & St. Paul trade 1855, 1856.

VIOLET—At St. Paul 1856.

VIRGINIA—At St. Louis April, 1823, with government stores for Fort Snelling, John Shellcross, master; arrived at Fort May 10, 1823; built at Pittsburg; 118 feet long, 22 feet beam, 160 tons.

VIXEN—Stern-wheel; built at St. Paul; from Pittsburg, 1857, 1858, 1859.

VOLANT—Thirteenth steamboat to arrive at Fort Snelling, prior to 1827.

W. G. WOODSIDE—Built at Moundsville, Va., 1855; 197 tons; at St. Paul 1856.

W. H. DENNY—Side-wheel; built at California, Pa., 1855; 276 tons; Captain Lyons, at St. Paul from St. Louis, 1857; sunk opposite head of Fabius Island 1857.

WM. L. EWING—Large side-wheel; Captain Smith, St. Louis & St. Paul, 1857; in Northwestern Line, Captain Green, 1858; same 1859; Northern Line 1860, 1861, Captain J. H. Rhodes, St. Louis & St. Paul.

W. S. NELSON—Captain Jameson, at St. Paul 1857; at St. Paul 1859.

WAR EAGLE—(First)—Built by Harris Brothers for Galena & St. Peters trade in 1845; 156 tons burden; commanded by Captain D. Smith Harris, Scribe Harris, engineer; in Galena & St. Peters trade 1845, 1846, 1847; St. Louis & St. Peters 1848; in 1848 Harris Bros. sold her and bought the "Senator", in order to get a faster boat.

WAR EAGLE—(Second)—Built at Cincinnati, winter of 1853-4; side-wheel; 219 feet long, 29 feet beam, 296 tons; had 46 staterooms; 3 boilers, 14 feet long; in Minnesota Packet Company, Captain D. Smith Harris, Galena & St. Paul, 1854, 1855, 1856; made the run from Galena to St. Paul, 1855, in 44 hours, handling all way freight; 1857, Captain Kingman, Clerks Coffin and Ball, in Dunleith & St. Paul Line; Captain W. H. Gabbert, 1858, same line; La Crosse Line 1859; Captain J. B. Davis, 1860, in La Crosse Line; spring of 1861 started out from La Crosse with following roster of officers: Captain A. Mitchell, Clerk Sam Cook, Second Clerk E. A. Johnson, Pilots Jackson Harris, and William Fisher; Engineers Troxell and Wright; Steward Frank Norris; later in the season Captain Mitchell was succeeded by Captain Chas. L. Stephenson and ran in Dunleith Line; June 22, 1861, left St. Paul with five companies of the First Minnesota Infantry Volunteers, the "Northern Belle" having the other five companies, which were landed at La Crosse and transferred to the railroad for transportation to Washington; 1862, in Dunleith Line, Captain N. F. Webb; in St. Paul trade 1862,

1863; Thomas Cushing, master in latter year; burnt, La Crosse (year not learned).

WARRIOR—Built in 1832 by Captain Joseph Throckmorton, for upper river trade; took part in the battle of Bad Axe, where the Indians under Blackhawk were defeated and dispersed, Captain Throckmorton in command of boat, E. H. Gleim, clerk, William White, pilot; arrived at Fort Snelling on first trip of the season, June 24, 1835, having among her passengers General Geo. W. Jones, U. S. A., Captain Day and Lieut. Beech, U. S. A., and Catlin, the artist, on his way to study the Indians of the northwest; at Fort again July 16, 1835; at Galena advertised for Pittsburg, Nov. 7, 1835; in Galena & St. Peters trade 1836.

WAVE—Small stern-wheel; Captain Maxwell, in Minnesota River trade, 1857, 1858. At Galena, from St. Louis, 1845. (Possibly another boat.)

WENONA—Stern-wheel; built at Belle Vernon, Pa., 1855; 171 tons; Captain L. Brown, in Minnesota River trade; also in St. Croix River trade for a time; at St. Paul 1859.

WEST NEWTON—Captain D. Smith Harris, 1852, in Galena & St. Paul trade; first boat at St. Paul 1853, Captain Harris; made 27 trips between Galena and St. Paul 1853; sunk at foot of West Newton Chute, below Alma, in Sept., 1853.

WHITE BLUFF—At St. Paul 1856.

WHITE CLOUD—(First)—Burnt at St. Louis May 17, 1849.

WHITE CLOUD—(Second)—Side-wheel; very fast; had double rudders; Captain Alford, from St. Louis at St. Paul, 1857; sunk at St. Louis, Feb. 13, 1867, by ice; total loss.

WINNEBAGO—Built 1830, by Captain George W. Atchison and Captain Joseph Throckmorton; in Galena & St. Louis trade, Jos. Throckmorton, master; also visited Fort Snelling with government stores.

WINONA—Side-wheel; Captain J. R. Hatcher, Davidson Line, La Crosse & St. Paul, 1861.

WIOTA—New 1845; built and owned by Captain R. A. Reilly, Corwith Bros., and Wm. Hempstead, of Galena; side-wheel, 180 feet long, 24 feet beam, 5 feet hold; double engines, 18 inch diameter, 7 feet stroke, 3 boilers, wheels 22 feet diameter, 10 feet buckets; gangway to boiler deck in front, instead of on the side as had been customary; in St. Louis & Galena trade, R. A. Reilly, master.

WISCONSIN—Captain Flaherty, at Galena, for St. Louis, April 9, 1836.

WYANDOTTE—Captain Pierce, Dubuque & St. Paul Line, 1856.

WYOMING—In Galena & St. Louis trade 1837.

YANKEE—Stern-wheel, 145 feet long, 200 tons burden, at St. Paul Sept. 27, 1849; August 1, 1850, started on trip of 300 miles up the Minnesota River with a party of ladies and gentlemen, on an exploring expedition; Captain M. K. Harris, Clerk G. R. Girdon, Pilot J. S. Armstrong, Engineers G. W. Scott and G. L. Sargent; reached a point many miles further up the river than had heretofore been reached by steamboats; at St. Paul June 26, 1851, Captain Orren Smith.

YORK STATE—Side-wheel; built at Brownsville, Pa., 1852; 247 tons; Captain Griffiths, in St. Louis & St. Paul trade 1855; at St. Paul 1856—Captain James Ward, who also owned her.

Appendix B

Opening of Navigation at St. Paul, 1844-1862

Year	First Boat	Date	River Closed	Length of Season (No. of Days)	No. of Boats	Total No. of Arrivals
1844	Otter	April 6	November 23	231	6	41
1845	Otter	April 6	November 23	234	7	48
1846	Lynx	March 31	December 5	245	9	24
1847	Cora	April 7	November 29	236	7	47
1848	Senator	April 7	December 4	241	6	63
1849	Highland Mary	April 9	December 7	242	8	85
1850	Highland Mary	April 19	December 4	229	9	104
1851	Nominee	April 4	November 8	218	10	119
1852	Nominee	April 16	November 18	216	6	171
1853	West Newton	April 11	November 30	233	17	235
1854	Nominee	April 8	November 27	223	23	310
1855	War Eagle	April 17	November 20	217	68	536
1856	Lady Franklin	April 18	November 10	212	79	759
1857	Galena	May 1	November 14	198	99	965
1858	Grey Eagle	March 25	November 15	236	62	1090
1859	Key City	March 19	November 27	222	54	802
1860	Milwaukee	March 28	November 23	240	45	776
1861	Ocean Wave	March 8	November 26	203	32	977
1862	Keokuk	March 18	November 15	212	18	846

Appendix C

Table of Distances from St. Louis

LANDING	ESTIMATED, 1858	DISTANCE BETWEEN PORTS	GOVERN-MENT SUR-VEY, 1880
Alton, Ill.	25	—	23
Grafton, Ill.	—	16	39
Cap au Gris, Mo. . . .	65	27	66
Hamburg, Ill.	—	22	88
Clarkesville, Mo. . . .	102	14	102
Louisiana, Mo. . . .	114	10	112
Hannibal, Mo.	144	29	141
Quincy, Ill.	164	20	161
La Grange, Mo. . . .	176	10	171
Canton, Mo.	184	7	178
Alexandria, Mo. . . .	204	19	197
Warsaw, Ill.	204	—	197
Keokuk, Iowa	208	5	202
Montrose, Iowa	220	12	214
Nauvoo, Ill.	223	3	217
Fort Madison, Iowa . .	232	8	225
Pontoosuc, Ill. . . .	238	7	232
Dallas, Ill.	240	2	234
Burlington, Iowa . . .	255	14	248
Oquawaka, Ill	270	13	261
Keithsburg, Ill. . . .	282	12	273
New Boston, Ill. . . .	289	6	279
Port Louisa, Iowa . . .	294	9	288
Muscatine, Iowa . . .	317	14	302
Buffalo, Iowa	—	19	321
Rock Island, Ill. . . .	347	10	331
Davenport, Iowa . . .	348	1	332
Hampton, Ill.	—	10	342

LANDING	ESTIMATED, 1858	DISTANCE BETWEEN PORTS	GOVERNMENT SURVEY, 1880
Le Claire, Iowa . . .	365	6	348
Port Byron, Ill. . . .	365	—	348
Princeton, Iowa . . .	371	6	354
Cordova, Ill.	372	1	355
Camanche, Iowa . . .	381	9	364
Albany, Ill.	384	2	366
Clinton, Iowa	390	5	371
Fulton, Ill.	392	2	373
Lyons, Iowa	393	1	374
Sabula, Ill.	412	17	391
Savanna, Ill.	415	2	393
Bellevue, Iowa . . .	438	21	414
Galena, Ill.	450	12	426
Dubuque, Iowa	470	12	438
Dunleith, Ill.	471	1	439
Wells' Landing, Iowa .	485	13	452
Cassville, Wis.	500	16	468
Guttenberg, Iowa . . .	510	10	478
Glen Haven, Wis. . .	—	1	479
Clayton, Iowa	522	7	486
Wisconsin River, Wis. .	—	7	493
McGregor, Iowa . . .	533	4	497
Prairie du Chien, Wis. .	536	3	500
Lynxville, Wis.	553	17	517
Lansing, Iowa	566	12	529
De Soto, Wis.	577	5	534
Victory, Wis.	582	7	541
Bad Axe, Wis.	589	8	549
Warner's Landing, Wis.	—	5	554
Brownsville, Minn. . .	591	8	562
La Crosse, Wis. . . .	617	10	572
Dresbach, Minn. . . .	627	8	580
Trempealeau, Wis. . .	632	11	591
Winona, Minn.	645	13	604
Fountain City, Wis. . .	655	7	611
Mount Vernon, Minn. .	666	9	620
Minneiska, Minn. . . .	669	3	623
Buffalo City, Wis. . .	676	—	—
Alma, Wis.	684	10	633

LANDING	ESTIMATED, 1858	DISTANCE BETWEEN PORTS	GOVERNMENT SURVEY, 1880
Wabasha, Minn. . . .	693	9	642
Reed's Landing, Minn. .	696	3	645
North Pepin, Wis. . .	701	4	649
Lake City, Minn. . . .	708	6	655
Florence, Minn. . . .	713	—	—
Frontenac, Minn. . . .	719	—	—
Maiden Rock, Wis. . .	—	10	665
Wacouta, Minn. . . .	723	—	—
Stockholm, Wis. . . .	—	3	668
Red Wing, Minn. . .	726	8	676
Trenton, Wis.	—	4	680
Diamond Bluff, Wis. .	741	6	686
Prescott, Wis.	756	13	699
Point Douglass, Minn. .	757	1	700
Hastings, Minn. . . .	759	2	702
Nininger, Minn. . . .	764	5	707
Pine Bend, Minn. . .	775	—	—
Newport, Minn. . . .	782	13	720
St. Paul, Minn. . . .	791	9	729
St. Anthony Falls, Minn.	805	12	741

Appendix D

Improvement of the Upper Mississippi, 1866-1876

The following table gives in detail the different divisions into which the river was divided for convenience in letting contracts, and prosecuting the work of improvement, the number of miles covered in each division, and the amount expended in each in the ten years from 1866 to 1876:

DIVISION	MILES	AMT. EXPENDED
St. Anthony Falls to St. Paul	11	$ 59,098.70
St. Paul to Prescott	32	638,498.56
Prescott to Head Lake Pepin	29	111,409.17
Harbor at Lake City	—	16,091.62
Foot Lake Pepin to Alma	12	341,439.26
Alma to Winona	29	365,394.25
Winona to La Crosse	31	236,239.39
La Crosse to McGregor	72	308,311.07
McGregor to Dubuque	59	137,236.65
Dubuque to Clinton	67	131,905.29
Clinton to Rock Island	40	228,298.99
Rock Island to Keithsburg	58	70,071.85
Keithsburg to Des Moines Rapids	60	515,971.20
Keokuk to Quincy	40	355,263.71
Quincy to Clarksville	60	552,051.47
Clarksville to Cap au Gris	43	389,959.31
Cap au Gris to Illinois River	27	137,116.97
Illinois River to Mouth of Missouri River	25	70,688.77
Miscellaneous, maintenance of Snag-Boats, Dredges, wages, provisions, etc.		549,760.92
	695	$5,200,707.25

Appendix E

Indian Nomenclature and Legends

The name Mississippi is an amelioration of the harsher syllables of the Indian tongue from which it sprang. Dr. Lafayette H. Bunnell, late of Winona, Minnesota, a personal friend and old army comrade, is my authority for the names and spelling given below, as gleaned by him during many years' residence among the Chippewa of Wisconsin and the Sioux (or Dakota) of Minnesota. Dr. Bunnell spoke both languages fluently, and in addition made a scholarly study of Indian tongues for literary purposes. His evidence is conclusive, that so far as the northern tribes were concerned the Mississippi was in the Chippewa language, from which the name is derived: *Mee-zee* (great), *see'-bee* (river) — Great River. The Dakota called it *Wat-pah-tah'-ka* (big river). The Sauk, Foxes, and Potawatomi, related tribes, all called it: *Mee-chaw-see'-poo* (big river). The Winnebago called it: *Ne-scas-hut'-ta-ra* (the bluff-walled river). Thus six out of seven tribes peopling its banks united in terming it the "Great River".

Dr. Bunnell disposes of the romantic fiction that the Indians called it the "Great Father of Waters", by saying that in Chippewa this would be: *Miche-nu-say'-be-gong* — a term that he never heard used in speaking of the stream; and old Wah-pa-sha, chief of the Dakota living at Winona, assured the Doctor that he had never heard an Indian use it. The Chippewa did, however, have a superlative form of the name: *Miche-gah'-see-bee* (great, endless river), descriptive of its (to them) illimitable length.

Dr. Bunnell suggests the derivation of the name Michigan, as applied to the lake and state. The Chippewa term for any great body of water, like Lakes Michigan, Superior, or Huron, is: *Miche-gah'-be-gong* (great, boundless waters). It was very easy for the white men who first heard this general term as applied to the lake, to accept it as a proper name, and to translate the Indian term into Michigan, as we have it to-day.

It is a source of gratification that the names applied to the Great River by the Jesuit fathers who first plied their birch-bark canoes upon its surface, did not stick. They were wonderful men, those old missionaries, devoted and self-sacrificing beyond belief; but when it came to naming the new-found lands and rivers, there was a monotony of religious nomenclature. Rivière St. Louis and Rivière de la Conception are neither of them particularly descriptive of the Great River. In this connection it must be said, however, that there was something providential in the zeal of the good missionaries in christening as they did, the ports at either end of the upper river run. The mention of St. Louis and St. Paul lent the only devotional tinge to steamboat conversation in the fifties. Without this there would have been nothing religious about that eight hundred miles of Western water. Even as it was, skepticism crept in with its doubts and questionings. We all know who St. Paul was, and his manner of life; but it is difficult to recall just what particular lines of holiness were followed by Louis XIV to entitle him to canonization.

Trempealeau Mountain, as it is called, situated two miles above Trempealeau Landing, Wisconsin, is another marvel of nature that attracted the attention of the Indians. It is an island of limestone, capped with sandstone, rising four hundred feet above the level of the river. Between the island and the mainland is a slough several hundred feet wide, which heads some five or six miles above. The Winnebago gave it a descriptive name: *Hay-me-ah'-shan* (Soaking Mountain). In Dakota it was *Min-nay-chon'-ka-hah* (pronounced Minneshon'ka), meaning Bluff in the Water. This was translated by the early French voyageurs into: *Trempe a l'eau* — the Mountain that bathes its feet in the water. There is no other island of rock in the Mississippi above the upper rapids; none rising more than a few feet above the water.

It is but natural that the Indians who for centuries have peopled the banks of the Mississippi, should have many legends attaching to prominent or unusual features of the river scenery. Where the Indians may have failed, imaginative palefaces have abundantly supplied such deficiencies.

There is one legend, however, that seems to have had its foundation in fact — that of the tragedy at Maiden Rock, or Lover's Leap, the bold headland jutting out into Lake Pepin on the Wisconsin side, some six or eight miles below the head of the lake. Dr. Bunnell devoted much study to this legend, and his conclusion is that it is an historic fact. Divested of the multiplicity of words and metaphor with which the Indian story-teller, the historian of his tribe, clothes his narrative, the incident was this:

In the days of Wah-pa-sha the first, chief of the Dakota band of that name, there was, in the village of Keoxa, near the site of the present Minnesota city of Winona, in the latter part of the eighteenth century, a maiden whose name was Winona (*Wi-no-na*: first-born daughter). She had formed an attachment for a young hunter of the tribe, which was fully reciprocated by the young man. They had met often, and agreed to a union, on which all their hopes of happiness centered. But on applying to her family, the young suitor was curtly dismissed with the information that the girl had been promised to a warrior of distinction who had sued for her hand. Winona, however, persisted in her preference for the hunter; whereupon the father took measures to drive him out of the village, and the family began to use harsh measures to coerce the maiden into a union with the warrior whom they had chosen for her husband. She was finally assured that she was, with or without her consent, to be the bride of the man of their choice.

About this time a party was formed to go to Lake Pepin to lay in a store of blue clay, which they used as a pigment. Winona, with her family, was of the party. Arriving at their destination the question of her marriage with the warrior again came up, and she was told that she would be given to him that very day. Upon hearing this final and irrevocable decree the girl withdrew, and while the family were preparing for the wedding festival she sought the top of the bluff now known as Maiden Rock. From this eminence she called down to her family and friends, telling them that she preferred death to a union with one she did not love, and began singing her death song. Many of the swiftest runners of the tribe, with the warrior to whom she had been sold, immediately ran for the summit of the cliff in order to restrain her; but before they reached her she jumped headlong from the height, and was dashed to pieces on the jagged rocks a hundred and fifty feet below.

This story was in 1817 related to Major Long, of the United States Army, by a member of Wahpasha's tribe, Wa-ze-co-to, who claimed to have been an eyewitness of the tragedy. Wazecoto was an old man at the time, and his evident feeling as he related the tale went far toward convincing Major Long that the narrator was reciting the tale of an actual occurrence.

Maiden Rock itself is a bluff about four hundred feet in height. One hundred and fifty feet of it is a sheer precipice; the other two hundred and fifty is a steep bluff covered with loose rocks, and grown up to straggling scrub oaks. Some versions of the legend state that Winona in her grief leaped from the bluff into the waters of the lake and was drowned. On my only visit to the top of the Leap, in company with Mr. Wilson, the mate, we found it somewhat difficult to throw a stone into the water from the top of the bluff. If Winona made it in one jump she must have been pretty lithe, even for an Indian.

I hope that I may not be dubbed an iconoclast, in calling attention to the fact that Indian stories similar to this have been localized all over our country. Lovers' Leaps can be counted by the score, being a part of the stock in trade of most summer resorts. Another difficulty with the tale is, that the action of the young pair does not comport with the known marriage customs of Indians.

MAP OF THE MISSISSIPPI BETWEEN ST. LOUIS AND ST. PAUL.

Index

Index

GEORGE BYRON MERRICK (1841–1931) was born in Niles, Michigan, on the St. Joseph River, where he developed an early fascination with steamboats. After his family moved to Prescott, Wisconsin, in 1854, he began his lifelong love of the Mississippi River. He worked on steamboats on the Upper Mississippi as a cabin boy, cub engineer, second clerk, and cub pilot during the 1856 to 1862 seasons; in 1862 he left the river to enlist in the Thirteenth Wisconsin Infantry. He gathered the memories in *Old Times on the Upper Mississippi* following a career as a newspaper editor and publisher.